The Wealth and Poverty of Cities

The Wealth and Poverty of Cities

Why Nations Matter

MARIO POLÈSE

OXFORD

UNIVERSITY PRESS

Oxford University Press is a department of the University of Oxford. It furthers
the University's objective of excellence in research, scholarship, and education
by publishing worldwide. Oxford is a registered trade mark of Oxford University
Press in the UK and certain other countries.

Published in the United States of America by Oxford University Press
198 Madison Avenue, New York, NY 10016, United States of America.

CIP data is on file at the Library of Congress
ISBN 978–0–19–005371–0

1 3 5 7 9 8 6 4 2

Printed by Integrated Books International, United States of America

Contents

Acknowledgments

Throughout the writing of this book, I have had the good fortune of being able to draw on the insights and advice of friends and colleagues around the world. This book is as much theirs as mine. As this is a book on cities, I shall take the liberty of listing the numerous persons to whom I am intellectually indebted by city (in alphabetical order), with my apologies beforehand to those I may have inadvertently overlooked.

In Montreal: my longtime friend, Claude Chapdelaine, former head of the provincial housing board; Sébastien Breau and Sarah Moser, respectively, Professor and Director of the Urban Studies Program, Department of Geography, McGill University; Richard Shearmur, Chair of the School of Urban Planning, McGill University; Martin Wexler, former head of the residential policy division, City of Montreal. *In Paris*: Anne Laferrère, formerly of INSEE (French Statistical Office); Jean-Claude Prager, Director, Economic Studies, *Société du Grand Paris*. *In Puebla*: Enrique Bueno and Salvador Perez, respectively Professor and Chair, Department of Economics, *Universidad Autónoma de Puebla*. *In Toronto*: Enid Slack, Director, Institute for Municipal Finance and Governance, University of Toronto; Richard Stren, Professor Emeritus and former Director of the Cities Centre, University of Toronto. *In Vienna*: Professors Harvey Goldstein and Egon Smeral, both of MODUL University, Vienna; Peter Mayerhofer, WIFO (Austrian Institute for Economic Research). I also owe a special note of thanks to Jacques Thisse, Professor Emeritus, University of Louvain-la-Neuve (Belgium), for his invaluable insights on various aspects of this book.

It is difficult to thank an entire institution, but I cannot fail to thank INRS (*Institut National de la Recherche Scientifique*),[1] specifically *Centre-Urbanisation Culture Société* in Montreal, my home now for almost fifty years, whose members at all levels (staff, faculty, and administration) have unfailingly supported me over the years. My heartfelt thanks to all of you. It's been a wonderful journey.

I would also be remiss if I did not thank the Social Sciences and Humanities Research Council of Canada (SSHRC) which has generously funded my research over the years, notably during my years as titleholder of the Senior Canada Research Chair in Urban and Regional Studies (2001–2015).

No person has contributed more to the making of this book than David Pervin, senior editor at Oxford University Press (OUP), who believed in me (a second time). After receiving the initial manuscript, David encouraged me to rewrite entire sections. He was right. The book is far better for it. By the same token, I am indebted to three anonymous reviewers whose comments greatly contributed to making this a better book. A special word of thanks to Betty Pessagno, my copy editor, whose meticulous corrections and useful comments did much to improve the final manuscript. My thanks also to Macey Fairchild and the entire OUP team for their terrific logistical support. It's been a joy working with you.

Last but certainly not least, this book could not have been written without the infinite patience of my wonderful wife, Céline, who never complained (well, rarely) while I squirreled myself away in my upstairs office working on my manuscript. À toi, un grand merci.

The Wealth and Poverty of Cities

Introduction

In Search of the Foundations of Urban (Economic) Success and Failure

A recurring question winds itself throughout this book: why have some cities succeeded in providing a good quality of life and decent standard of living for most (if not all) of their citizens, while others have visibly failed to do so? Why have the great cities of the Third World not produced greater wealth? Why does New York generate four times the wealth (per capita) of Mexico City? What's missing in Mexico City? Why have many great American cities—Cleveland, Detroit, St. Louis, and others—descended into seemingly irreversible cycles of decline. What went wrong? Why is Vienna continually rated as one the world's most livable cities? What is its secret?

In search of an answer, we shall visit different cities around the world—called city stories—viewed through the lens of what I have dubbed *The Ten Pillars of Urban Success* (see Table I.1 later in this chapter). The first message of the present volume is simple: the prerequisites for a successful city are manifold. There are ten pillars for a reason: many stars need to be favorably aligned. The second message is that the success (or failure) of cities is never just a city story.

Why Nations Matter

This book proposes a different way of looking at cities from that commonly found in the literature on the economy cities. The subtitle of this book reads *Why Nations Matter* for a reason.

For readers familiar with the literature, this book challenges the oft-heard proposition (whose most prominent exponent is Jane Jacobs) that cities are the primary drivers of the wealth of nations.[1] This book turns that proposition around. Nations come first as the depositories of the values and institutions that make economic development possible. In this book, the term *nation* is used broadly: a population with a defined territory, shared history, and distinct institutions. More will be said later on *institutions*, a key concept in this volume.

When examining urban success or failure, the normal inclination is to focus on *city* attributes. Surely, if a particular city has problems, it is because something is not right *in* the city, putting aside outside events and techno- logical change.[2] In short, something needs to be fixed *in* the city. To under- stand what went wrong in Detroit, one obviously needs to understand what happened *in* Detroit, not least the errors made by local civic and business leaders. Knowing a city's history is always an essential step in understanding failure (or success). Atlanta, whose successful rise as an international air hub is recounted in Chapter 7, is an example of how local leaders—a vi- sionary mayor and dynamic entrepreneurs—made a difference. However, local leadership—or the lack thereof—is always only part of the story.

Nations matter because successful economic endeavors require a functioning "national" state. The values, norms, and institutions that shape social relationships are national attributes. The preconditions for the cre- ation of wealth—the rule of law, public education, and sound macroeco- nomic management among the most fundamental—are the responsibility of the state. It is "national" (senior) government—which can also mean states, provinces, Länder, and so on in federations such as the United States, Canada, or Germany—that defines how lower levels of government (cities, municipalities, communes, etc., depending on national nomenclatures) are structured and what they can or cannot do in matters such as taxation (who and what they can tax) and their power to regulate construction and land use.

The manner in which the fruits of wealth are taxed, spent, and redistributed across political jurisdictions and individuals is necessarily a senior government prerogative, as are the laws that establish which public services are financed locally and which are shared across jurisdictions. The task of building reasonably socially cohesive societies[3] (a concept to which I shall return later), an essential pillar of development, must ultimately fall to "national" governments. As we shall discover, the absence of institutions to ensure an acceptable level of social cohesion is often a major factor be- hind urban failure.

Nations vary in size, shape, and geography. The conditions governing competition between cities—who wins and who loses—will not be the same in large geographically diverse nations as in small nations. Nor will the playing field in which cities compete (for resources and markets) be the same in federations as in unitary states.

My view of cities as mirrors of the societies that spawned them owes much to my personal journey, which begins as an immigrant in the New York of the 1950s and is recounted in Chapter 1. Early on, I looked at cities through a particular lens. New York was not Eindhoven (the city I had left), nor was it Vienna, the city of my parents. My later academic career[4] as a student and lover of cities spanning some fifty years would allow me to visit cities around the world, reinforcing my view of cities as unique products of distinct cultures. In this book, we shall visit cities as different as Puebla (Mexico), Buffalo (New York), Montreal (Canada), Paris (France), and Port au Prince (Haiti), some of them happier places than others.

All of this begs the question of why culture and institutions are largely absent from the urban economics literature. The omission is entirely understandable. One would not expect national laws, mores, and regulations to vary significantly between cities *of the same nation*. As such, institutions cannot logically be invoked as meaningful variables for explaining differences in city performance *within* nations. National institutions were thus largely absent in my earlier book, *The Wealth and Poverty of Regions— Why Cities Matter*,[5] in which I sought to explain regional development differences *within* nations. The title of that book might lead the reader to conclude that I have changed my mind; I have not. Cities do matter, especially their size and industrial heritage, for regions in competition within the same nation. Much of the challenge of regional development hangs on the need to build a strong urban base. In this book, I take a step back to ask how wealth is created in the first place and to explain the role cities play in the creation (or not) of wealth.

Institutions, culture, and mores are as a rule taken as givens in the urban economics literature, organic parts of the national landscape so to speak. One of the unintended consequences of this perspective is to attribute wealth-creating virtues to cities whose roots, once one digs deeper, are in fact embedded in national attributes and cultures. As we shall discover in Chapter 2, this unintentional omission is at the heart of Jane Jacobs's overly sanguine view of the regenerating powers of cities, a view that continues to permeate much of the urban economics literature.

The majority of empirical work in the scholarly literature, often using advanced econometric techniques, examines the performance of cities in a *national* context, if only because of the availability of statistics.[6] Such studies understandably focus on city-specific attributes and ask why *within* the United States, France, or Canada some cities have witnessed greater population, job, or per capita income growth than others.[7] It is a useful question. I have done a number of such studies myself for Canadian cities, generally with the help of colleagues who are better versed in econometrics than I am.[8] The answer, as documented by numerous studies, is no longer a matter of controversy—at least for American cities. In the simplest terms, cities with highly educated populations, great universities, and a pleasant climate (plus a few beaches and mountains) stand a better chance of growing and creating wealth than cold Rustbelt cities.[9]

This answer is not wrong, but it also states the obvious. As such, looking at the United States, we should not be surprised by the contrasting destinies of its great cities; think of Detroit and San Francisco as extremes along a continuum of possible outcomes. Such contrasting destinies are, I shall argue, not separate facts but predictable (at least in part) outcomes of an interdependent national system of cities in a distinct institutional setting.

Looking Across National Borders

Perhaps no contrast better illustrates that *nations matter* than the comparison between U.S. and Canadian cities. I moved to Canada from the United States more than forty years ago.[10] As I became increasingly familiar with my new homeland, nothing surprised me more than Canada's radically different approach to urban governance.[11] Cities on both sides of the border look pretty much the same and share similar lifestyles. Toronto, Vancouver, and Montreal at first blush look and feel like American cities. But appearances are deceiving. Behind this façade of North American sameness lurks a profound difference in political culture with far-ranging consequences, as we shall discover, for the social and economic dynamics of cities. The absence in Canada of Detroit-type urban failures cannot simply be explained away by geography (i.e., the absence of plantation crops and the legacy of slavery) or by industry mix. Understanding why is one of the motivations for this book.

In search of an answer, I shall recount the history of Buffalo, which I use in this book as a metaphor for all ailing U.S. Rustbelt cities, a once great metropolis that has sunk into a seemingly irreversible spiral of economic decline. I shall compare Buffalo with Toronto, a metropolis of equivalent size not so long ago and also located on the Great Lakes. Toronto today is six times Buffalo's size. It is impossible to underhand such diverging destinies without considering, as we shall discover, institutional differences between the two nations and the actions of senior government, respectively, the province of Ontario and the state of New York.

In Europe, by comparing two great imperial cities—Vienna and Paris—we shall discover that national policies with respect to regional governance and housing have produced very different outcomes. Paris's social fractures are no accident, being the result in part of what can only be called a flawed model of metropolitan governance. Vienna's consistently good performance on livability are in part founded, as we shall see, on the Austrian state's unique approach to housing whose roots go back to the 1920s.

Moving Beyond Big Cities

Focusing on the national roots of wealth allows us to correct an implicit bias in much of the urban economics literature. The vast literature on the creative power of cities focuses almost exclusively on big cities.[12] The message is clear: these are the wellsprings of wealth and economic progress. The picture changes once we accept the notion that the creation of wealth involves *more* than what economists call "agglomeration economies."[13] Agglomeration economies matter but primarily *within* nations as predictors of wealth. Seen from above, cities are part of national urban systems. At any given moment, goods and services more subject to agglomeration economies will be advantageously produced in big cities, others in smaller places; but all are needed for the creation of the national economic pie. In more technical language, the impact of agglomeration economies is, as I shall explain in Chapter 2, primarily allocational or "static" in the vocabulary of economics.

Looking at cities from a national perspective allows us to resolve an apparent paradox in urban economics: the seeming contradiction between the pull of big cities generating high incomes—a traditional indicator of the power of agglomeration economies—and the absence of a statistical link with growth. Bigger cities do not as a rule grow faster than smaller cities. The regularity *within nations* of city size distributions remains one of the more surprising facts of economic geography, "confronting the mystery of urban hierarchy," to quote the title of a recent article by Nobel Prize economist Paul Krugman.[14] Vernon Henderson, a leading urban economist, notes the "remarkable stability" over time of the size distribution of cities in the United States.[15] This regularity, verified for nation after nation, is sometimes referred to as Zipf's rank-size rule or Gibrat's law.[16] This regularity should not really surprise us: if the largest cities consistently attracted more people, the entire national population would end up living in a single supermetropolis, an unlikely outcome. As we shall discover, size also produces a counterreaction, one of the reasons why small cities exist.

Untying Creating and Capturing Wealth

Looking at cities through a national lens allows us to merge two research strands that rarely meet: development economics and urban economics. In simplified terms, the first strand asks how wealth is created, while the second asks how the spatial concentration of people (in cities) creates wealth. Starting from the nation allows us to disentangle the two; that is: (a) the mechanics of wealth creation and (b) the mechanics of agglomeration and the wealth thus created. Human capital provides an example of the distinction between the two. Education contributes, we may reasonably assume, to the creation of wealth, as do high concentrations of educated individuals. These are two distinct processes: the first (a), for lack of a better term, is a social process, and the second (b) is a spatial process, in the language of human geographers. The question then becomes: how important is (b) relative to (a), where (b) is a subset of (a)?

For an attempt at an answer, let us consider the contrasting destinies of Detroit and the Francisco Bay Area, the latter including Silicon Valley. Both processes are at play. The Bay Area's success combines *creating* and *capturing* wealth or, rather, the actors of wealth creation, which may sound like a woolly academic distinction, but it is not once we realize that two distinct processes are at work. Asking why in a nation like the United States some cities capture (or alternatively lose) wealth is not the same as asking how wealth is being created in the first place. The unrivaled concentration of human capital in the Bay Area manifestly contributes to the national economic pie. But might that same human capital have been equally (or more) productively employed elsewhere and at a lower social cost, given different national institutions? Was Detroit's failure a necessary complement of the

Bay Area's success? A clear answer to either question is impossible. But it is difficult to totally eliminate the possibility that the two are in part linked.

* * *

As the reader will have surmised by now, the United States looms large in this book. I have never ceased to be fascinated (and troubled) by America's urban failures, starting with my early years in New York. This book is part of my quest for a better understanding of those failures.

I would be derelict if I did not admit that the election of Donald J. Trump to the presidency of the United States did not influence the direction this book has taken. Trump's election was unforeseen, indeed unimaginable, when I began writing. That event reawakened me—I should never have forgotten—to the fragile nature of the social and political bonds that underpin the well-being and peace of our cities, not just in America. Where nations go, cities will inevitably follow.

A Word on Definitions and Style

A word is in order regarding my use of certain terms. Throughout the book, I use *wealth* as a generic term for various measures of well-being, income, or product per capita, among the most common statistical indicators. However, my use of the term *wealth* goes beyond purely material wealth. Successful cities are not only places that provide decent jobs and income, but also are generally pleasant places where all can safely walk the streets and share in the wonders that well-run cities have to offer. Such things are difficult to measure, a reason I have chosen to tell city stories in which personal impressions matter as much as cold statistics.

City: An Elusive Concept, the Root of Much Confusion

The word *city* is more problematic. *City* has at least two meanings. It can refer to a *city* (*municipality* in North America) with a defined boundary and government. The City of New York with its five boroughs is such a city. Jersey City across the Hudson River is *not* part of this *city*; it is a separate *city* with its own mayor. But *city* used as a generic term can also refer to the greater urban region. Jersey City *is* part of this *city*, as are other municipalities whose residents commute daily into New York City. When we say that New York is America's biggest city, home to some twenty million people, *city* implicitly means the greater urban region. Various synonyms exist for urban region—metropolis, urban area, agglomeration, metropolitan area—but the inclination in popular usage is to fall back on the generic term *city*.

The ambiguity between the two meanings of *city* bedevils much of the literature on cities. Take the title of almost any book on cities; it is rarely clear which meaning is intended.[17] This matters only little where the intention is to reason on a largely academic plane, applying technical concepts such as "agglomeration economies" or "knowledge spillovers," as is the case for much of the scholarly literature. But if we are to make statements useful for public policy, a more precise definition is required.

The object of this book is the *urban region*, even though I shall also often fall back on the generic term *city*. This is of some importance since on few aspects do nations differ more than on the institutions that shape metropolitan areas. The Viennese model of regional governance, for example, is almost the polar opposite of the typical U.S. model (or rather absence of one).

In more technical language, the term *cities* as used here refers to urban *agglomerations* or *metropolitan areas,* the terms preferred by most statistical agencies—integrated labor markets where the majority of the workforce is not engaged in agriculture. Different national statistical agencies can have different criteria, but the core idea is everywhere the same. Metropolitan areas are, as a rule, geographically delimited by their commuting sheds, and thus in constant flux, generally expanding. This is one reason why durable metropolitan governance structures are, as we shall discover, so devilishly difficult to put in place.

Finally, a word on style. There is no reason why urban economics should be dull. Cities are real places with real people. Jane Jacobs was not dull, which is undoubtedly why her work lives on. With notable exceptions such as Edward Glaeser's marvelous 2011 book on the economy of cities and Sir Peter Hall's now classic opus on cities in history,[18] most books on cities and economics have rarely sought to go beyond an academic audience. I have tried, as best I can, to make this book fun to read. I hope I have succeeded. I've had fun writing it.

Table I.1 The Ten Pillars of Urban Success (or Failure)

Institutions

---

1. **Wise Parents—*National/State Policies Conducive to the Creation of Wealth.***
Sound macroeconomic management. The rule of law, independent judiciary. Efficient
and (reasonably) equitable fiscal regimes (both across individuals and jurisdictions).
Appropriate laws defining the status and powers of local governments.

2. **Cooperative/*Social Cohesion*.** Metropolitan governance regimes that limit spatial
differences by income, race, or ethnicity. Central/shared financing, at least in part, of
people services (daycare, education, health, etc.). Efficient and accessible public transit.

3. **Conscientious/*Integrity*.** Reasonably honest local governments. Adequate
provision of basic urban services (sanitation, power, roads, traffic control, policing,
lighting, etc.). Safeguards against corruption, collusion, and other examples of
malpractice.

4. **Competitive/*Costs*.** Affordable housing. Efficient urban land markets. Reasonable
local taxes. Competitive wages, the latter being especially important for smaller cities
lacking the advantages of agglomeration economies.

People

---

5. **Brains/*Human Capital*.** Educated, literate population. Quality national/state
educational system at all levels (from primary school to university).

6. **The Right Skills/*Enterprising*.** Industry mix and work cultures conducive to
business start-ups, innovation, and entrepreneurship.

7. **Endurance/*Glue*.** Strong identity, civic pride, and other (noneconomic) attributes
that motivate populations to stay and persevere in the face of adversity.

Centrality

---

8. **Reach/*Connectivity*.** A central place: service center and transport hub for a wider
community, especially important for larger cities (for smaller cities: access/proximity
to markets).

9. **Healthy Heart/*Strong Center*.** Dense downtowns and central neighborhoods,
diversified employment nodes, conducive to face-to-face meetings, again especially
important for larger cities.

Chance

---

10. **Lucky/*Chance*.** Location. The right parents (back to Pillar 1). Outside events.
Leadership: the right individual at the right moment.

The Ten Pillars of Urban Success (or Failure): From Nation to Neighborhood

Once we turn Jane Jacobs's perspectives upside down, the view of what
causes cities to succeed (or to fail) takes on a different color. Cities are

no longer the starting point but rather are actors in a continuum that starts with the nation and the rules, mores, and regulations that define social and economic relations. Moving down from nation to neighborhood, Table I.1 summarizes what I have dubbed the Ten Pillars of Urban Success.

The Ten Pillars distill in a few key words the desirable attributes cities need to generate wealth and provide decent standards of living and livable environments, at least for the majority. The labels of the Ten Pillars, with a little poetic license, are admittedly anthropomorphic—in part to make them snappier—but they are also a way of communicating the idea that city stories, like personal stories, are full of unexpected twists. And like individuals, it helps to be born in the right place and, stating the obvious, to be born to wise and preferably wealthy parents (Pillar 1).

The purpose of the Ten Pillars is not to rank cities, but rather to invite the reader to look at cities differently: to explore areas of public policy that he or she might not otherwise have entertained and to make connections that might not seem self-evident at first glance. New York's lively central neighborhoods and strong financial district (Pillar 9), to take but one example, are contingent on "wise" central government management of the economy (Pillar 1), not least on maintaining a stable currency, liberal trade policies, and an open door to human capital. The health of the Manhattan economy depends on the actions not only of city officials but also of the Federal Reserve Bank, the Department of Commerce, and ICE (Immigration and Customs Enforcement).

As we move down the Ten Pillars, we are confronted at each stage by the tension between what a sole actor—mayor, city council—can achieve and the actions of higher levels of government. Each pillar implies policy choices for which the answer will not necessarily be the same in all societies: Who should finance primary education? Should local governments have the power to borrow? Similarly, the various pillars will almost always imply policy trade-offs, which again different societies will view differently—the trade-off, to take an example to which we shall return at some length in Chapter 3, between the a priori laudable goal of local democracy (the right of locals to decide what should be built nearby) and the no less laudable goal of limiting the emergence of racially or socially exclusive neighborhoods.

The Ten Pillars will not have the same relative importance for big and small cities. Relative labor costs (Pillar 4) will, for example, matter more for small cities. The Ten Pillars are grouped under three headings.

Institutions

Pillar 1, as its place on top suggests, is the overriding institutional pillar, identifying explicitly "national" domains (currency, immigration, and defense are examples), but also the values, mores, and cultural attributes that make a "nation" a distinct society, language among the most common attributes.

I shall not elaborate here on Pillar 2. The concept of social cohesion is discussed at length in chapter 3. Pillar 3 (Conscientious/*Integrity*) provides a useful illustration of *institutions* and their necessary national foundations. The efficient and honest provision of urban services is obviously a local responsibility. But attitudes toward corruption and political misbehavior are among the best examples of what cultural anthropologists call "values," which are at the heart of the differences that define societies and nations. Within federal nations like the United States and Canada, political cultures can also vary across states and provinces. Even in federations, however, the national state will remain the ultimate arbitrator of what is socially acceptable. In the United States, final responsibility for enforcement of the law and prosecution of corrupt state or local officials falls on the federal Department of Justice. Federal courts are also the ultimate arbitrators, to take a hypothetical example from Pillar 2 (Cooperative/*Social Cohesion*), of the constitutionality of exclusionary zoning ordinances adopted by city x or (to take the opposite case) of bylaws obligating developers to include targeted populations.

People

People are mobile, which is why these three pillars—Brains/*Human Capital*; The Right Skills/*Enterprising*; and Endurance/*Glue*—are grouped together. Pillars 5 and 6 are not terribly original, being recurrent themes in the scholarly literature on urban growth. As such, some readers will undoubtedly be surprised to find human capital in fifth place. As noted earlier, human capital consistently shows up, together with good weather, as a predictor of urban growth, notably for American cities.[19] No scholar has done more to document this relationship than Edward Glaeser, one of my favorite authors[20] whom we shall frequently meet in this book. I am tempted to call the three People pillars the Glaeser pillars, for he truly is their godfather. Where I diverge from Glaeser is in the importance I accord human capital (measured by education, skills, or entrepreneurial flair) as the primary force driving the growth of cities. Human capital is indisputably a necessary condition; but it is not a sufficient condition, applicable to all places. All this will, hopefully, become clearer in Chapter 5 when I discuss education. I do not wish to divulge all my arguments just yet. Thinking separately about institutions and human capital helps us understand why some places have underperformed despite high concentrations of educated individuals, while others, alternatively, have succeeded without being top centers of learning.

Centrality

The third heading in the table will come as no surprise to economic geographers. That the strength of a city's economy is in part a function of the size and wealth of its commercial *hinterland*—its catchment area as a service center—is a basic tenet of economic geography. A *central place*, the term economic geographers use to denote strong service centers, will also normally have a strong urban core where financial institutions, the media, corporate head offices, and ancillary service industries concentrate, denoted by the acronym CBD (central business district), which is why Pillar 9 (Healthy Heart/*Strong Center*) is grouped with Pillar 8 (Reach/ *Connectivity*). The latter is admittedly the most geographically determined pillar. There is a priori little governments can do about location. However, national policies with respect to transportation and travel—on landing rights to take an example from air travel—can directly impact a city's position as a transportation hub. Montreal is a prize example, as we shall discover in Chapter 6. Pillar 9 is near the bottom of Table I.1 for a reason: the material, neighborhood, anchor of the pillars that preceded it. As we shall discover in the telling of less happy city stories, a physically (and economically) deteriorating center is almost always the signal that many things are going wrong and need to be fixed, sending us from neighborhoods back to the nation.

Finally, Pillar 10 (Lucky/*Chance*) is largely self-explanatory and so needs no commentary. What can one usefully say about chance? A former British prime minister, Harold Macmillan, scion of an old Conservative family, when asked by a reporter what he dreaded most, is reputed to have answered: "Events, my dear boy, events." Count on the English to find the right words.

1

Urban (Economic) Success Is Never a Straight Line

New York, Vienna, and Other Urban Journeys

"You get old and you realize there are no answers, just stories."
—Garrison Keillor[1]

I now invite the reader on four urban journeys: to New York, Vienna, Port au Prince, and Buenos Aires. The journeys have a strong autobiographical component for which I hope the reader will forgive me: places that helped shape my view of cities as places of economic opportunity, but also all too often as places of poverty and exclusion.

New York—Where I First Learned That Great Cities Are the Mirrors of a Nation, Bringing Out the Best and the Worst

My New York journey began like a Hollywood "coming-to-America" movie on a sunny April morning in 1953: There I was, a nine-year-old boy looking out awestruck at the Statue of Liberty and the approaching skyline, standing on the deck of the passenger liner *Nieuw Amsterdam*, six days out of Rotterdam, as it sailed into New York harbor. Immigrants still arrived by boat in those days. The liner continued up the mouth of the Hudson River to dock in Hoboken, New Jersey, across from Manhattan, the majestic midtown skyline now coming into full view. For the nine-year-old boy, the significance of the display unfolding before his eyes was clear. He was about to land in the greatest city of the greatest and richest nation in world.

My parents and I were met at the dock by my aunt Silvia and her current husband (exchanging spouses was a favorite Silvia pastime[2]) in their new Cadillac convertible. One did not see cars that size in Europe in the 1950s.

Did all Americans drive big cars? My wonder grew as we drove through the Holland Tunnel exiting in midtown Manhattan into the heart of the throbbing metropolis. Around me were the tallest buildings in the world, of that I was sure. You couldn't even see to the top. Shops of every kind, people of all races and color, smells and noises, very different from the ordered Dutch town I called home only a week ago. We finally arrived at my aunt's Upper West Side apartment where we would spend the first weeks before moving into our own apartment, a five-story brownstone walk-up on 90th Street West, corner of Columbus Avenue.

A City in Decline

This is where the scenario changes. The Upper West Side was changing. Initially, a mixed white working-class neighborhood with strong Irish, Italian, and Jewish roots, the area underwent a complete transformation during the 1950s as mainly poor, often rural, Puerto Rican (mainly) migrants moved in. From a basically safe neighborhood, it soon became one of the most violent. Gang wars were frequent; they were often between rival Puerto Rican bands, but also between other race-based gangs. In this city, I soon learned, race mattered. Race mattered a lot. I well remember, during our first days in our new apartment, going to Central Park, a block away, to play with my toys, only to be assaulted by I do not know which gang who promptly made off with my precious toys but not before beating me up. I never told my mother, making up a cockamamie story about falling from a tree to explain my bruises. I doubt she believed me. But I had learned a lesson.

I rapidly learned the codes of the inner-city ghetto, which would serve me well many years later in my wanderings through the less wholesome neighborhoods of African and Latin American cities. Rule number one: never twaddle; instead, walk with a resolute step demonstrating that you know where you are going, even though you may be totally lost. Rule number two: avoid eye contact at all times; look straight ahead (earnestly) as you walk no matter how much you might like to like to give a little smile to the cute chick sitting on a stoop. That smile might be suicidal if the cute chick turns out to be the gang leader's girl. Rule number three: shut your mouth; do not under any circumstance answer taunts no matter how insulting or hurtful. Allusions to one's dubious maternal origins or sexual prowess were particularly popular in my neighborhood, and they were also my first lessons in colloquial Spanish. The last rule: learn how to read street maps; identify useful locations (grocery stores, subway entrances, etc.) and visually commit itineraries to memory, which was especially helpful in applying rule 1. Going to and coming from school, I methodically observed a carefully laid-out itinerary, avoiding the most dangerous streets.

New York in the 1950s and 1960s—unless one lived on the cherished Upper East Side or in the outer suburbs—was descending into a spiral of neighborhood crime and neglect, fueled by a history of municipal misman-agement which was to culminate in the City's near bankruptcy in 1975. The subway was not safe. Only a suicidal maniac would venture into Central Park after dark. Those years were also marked by blackouts and police, sani-tation worker, and teacher's strikes, plus mounting racial tensions with spo-radic riots and looting, all adding up to a generally shared sentiment that the city was heading downhill, and nowhere more so than in my neighborhood. The media at one point awarded West 88th Street the dubious distinction of being the most dangerous street in New York. The police refused to enter the area, and taxis, understandably, refused calls. The neighborhood continued to deteriorate. Buildings were poorly maintained, if at all. Cockroaches and other assorted tiny beasties were a fact of life. I soon became adept at setting mousetraps. Fires were a constant, together with blaring sirens. Our apart-ment was broken into four times. Insurance companies would no longer insure us, whether for theft or for fire. We learned not to keep anything of value in the apartment. I stopped going out at night, and on the rare occa-sion I did my parents' understandable worrying only made me feel worse. This fortress-like existence did little for my social life, turning me into the bookworm that I have remained. On a lighter note, I was devastated when the Brooklyn Dodgers—my team—left New York for Los Angeles in 1957, another sign that the city's glory period was past. I could never bring myself to root for those uppity New York Yankees, no way.

The family eventually moved out of the neighborhood to semi-suburban Jackson Heights in Queens where I spent my remaining New York years. My view of the city had, however, been formed. I saw a dysfunctional city torn by racial strife, with no obvious end in sight. My dismal view of urban America was subsequently reinforced by my three years in Philadelphia (1966–1969) as a graduate student at the University of Pennsylvania. Philadelphia was an even more racially divided city, with no-go zones covering large swathes of the central city; that is, if your skin color was white (for African Americans

the no-go zones were the mirror opposite). I quickly learned the racial geography of Philadelphia, where to go and not to go. I will spare the reader
my adventures on the few occasions I unwisely wandered into the wrong
streets. Perhaps because of my European origins, I had difficulty accepting
the idea of living in a city where neighborhoods were closed to me because
of my skin color. The University of Pennsylvania has a superb campus, but
it is almost completely surrounded by black ghettos. My years on campus
were among the best of my life, but they did not lessen my sense of unease.
I well remember, seated along one of the beautifully landscaped campus
walkways, looking at my fellow students, conscious of my good fortune
but acutely aware of the disparity between the many white (and sometimes
Asian) faces and the racial makeup of the surrounding city of Philadelphia.

My verdict was in: time to get out before matters got worse. In 1969,
I moved to Montreal. New York was manifestly going downhill, representing
simply the most dramatic example of the cancer afflicting all of urban
America.

Renaissance

We now know that my verdict was wrong.[3] New York rebounded. New York
today truly is the great metropolis that a nine-year-old boy imagined some
six decades earlier. The turnaround was not only economic—the statistics
did not lie—but also visible in the city's urban landscape, a city reinvented.
My old neighborhood is no more, and my five-story brownstone has
long since been gutted (no great loss), replaced by condominiums. The
area is now predictably gentrified with the inevitable natural food stores,
overpriced restaurants, and European-style cafés.

The most significant transformation took place several blocks south.
Midtown Manhattan was being reborn, once again becoming a true "center"
where people of all walks of life and origins came not only to work but also
to meet, shop, eat, and play or to simply behold the ever-changing spectacle
of big-city life. The 42nd Street and Times Square of the 1960s I knew were
bounded by sex shops and other establishments of ill repute. Bryant Square,
behind the New York Public Library, was a favorite haunt for drug addicts.
Bryant Park today is one of chicest venues in the city, with the mandatory
café-terrace overlooking landscaped gardens comparable to the best Paris

and London have to offer, packed at lunchtime with patrons from the surrounding office towers.

I could go on and list the alphabet soup of neighborhoods in Mid- and Lower Manhattan (TriBeCa, SoHo, NoHo . . .) that have since been reborn. New York's *heart* (I cannot think of a better term) had regained its health, and its heart was beating strongly. And the heart was no longer limited to Manhattan below 86th Street, overflowing into Harlem and parts of Brooklyn and Queens, with equally pricey real estate. It is in New York that I first came to grasp the significance of a strong center and its ability to generate agglomeration economies and the economic rents they engender, well before I became familiar with those academic concepts. Manifestly, people and firms *wanted* to be in New York, not just in New York but in the center where the potential for meeting the right people, moving up the career ladder, and making money was greatest. Why else would people and firms be willing to pay such high rents?

Few transformations are more indicative of central New York's newfound strength than the emerging ecosystem of information technology (IT) start-ups appropriately dubbed "Silicon Alley," which now, by some accounts, is the nation's second IT cluster, rivaling California's Silicon Valley. The emergence of an IT cluster in this part of Manhattan, wedged between the downtown financial district and the midtown entertainment district, is no accident. A hallmark of start-up ecosystems is the need for constant face-to-face meetings with financial backers and creative types. Meetings are the economic rationale for dense centers, and that precisely was (and remains) New York's strength.

Should I not have seen New York's rebound coming? Indeed I should have. My earlier account of my early New York years was almost entirely negative, but the story was not all black. The seeds of New York's resurgence were no less real. I simply needed to look further. True, the streets of my neighborhood were dangerous, but another New York existed. The New York Museum of Natural History, probably the finest of its kind in the world, was a mere four blocks away, where I spent many an hour learning about the geography, fauna, and flora of distant places. Across Central Park was the Metropolitan Museum of Art, where I never ceased to wonder at the artifacts of ancient Greece and Rome. Further south was the New York Public Library, which with its wood-paneled reading rooms became a second home. New York's innumerable bookstores were among my favorite haunts; I spent hours in the secondhand book stores on 4th Avenue rummaging through old manuscripts.

I think I've made my point. New York, despite its travails, provided an unparalleled window for learning and self-improvement. New York allowed me to get an education I'm not sure I would have been able to obtain elsewhere. From public school to City College, I had the good fortune of being exposed to first-class teachers, many of whom were refugees from war-torn Europe—and all this at the taxpayers' expense, the flip side of New York's then impending fiscal crisis. New York continued to invest in human capital, arguably beyond its means.

No less important but not sufficiently understood at the time was the economic restructuring all industrialized nations were undergoing, as they shifted from manufacturing to knowledge-rich service industries, spearheaded by finance, consultancies of all stripes, and so-called creative industries (entertainment, broadcasting, etc.), all heavily reliant on face-to-face meetings. New York was uniquely positioned to capture these rapidly growing industries.

As I would later come to understand, other forces were at work buttressing the city's resurgence. New York also stands out among U.S. metropolitan areas in the weight of its central city,[4] the City of New York, which has allowed it to largely escape the city/suburban social divide that plagues so many American cities (a subject I shall return to when we consider the plight of Buffalo). New York City had the good fortune of annexing large swathes of territory before the arrival of the automobile changed the dynamics of urban growth (Brooklyn was annexed in 1896), facilitating among other things the development early-on of a dense subway-based public transit system and subsequent creation of the New York and New Jersey Port Authority in 1921. The Port Authority acted (and continues to act) much like a quasi-regional government.

Finally, New York was the premier central place for a vast hinterland,[5] the nation's financial, cultural, and corporate capital. This allowed the city to capture the markets and brains of a continent (and beyond), in turn enabling the concentration of human capital in a single grand metropolis. New York, as such, provides a forceful demonstration of the umbilical relationship between metropolitan and national economies. Had the young American Republic remained within its initial borders (not consummating the Louisiana Purchase in 1803 or engaging in the Mexican War in 1848 and expanding to the Pacific), New York would still have prospered, but it would not be the metropolis it is today.

Access to a vast, rich hinterland is only part of the story. This vast space would be governed according to the principles of a free market economy, freer than most I'm tempted to say, and with generally sound institutions and reasonably competent senior governments, sending us back into arms of Pillar 1. New York was able to concentrate human capital because it could; that human capital in turn was able to blossom because it could.

Local actors also mattered, of course. Much of the credit for New York's rebound after 1980 must go to the city's administration. The clean-up and subsequent rebirth of Times Square required attention to the details of street life, considering everything from designing urban furniture (street benches, flower pots, pocket park, etc.) to community policing and the enforcement of drug laws. But the lesson from New York is clear: city and neighborhood-based actions bore fruit because other pillars were in place as well.

Vienna—An Urban Journey into Darkness and Back

My parents were born in Vienna. They fled Vienna for Holland after Nazi Germany annexed Austria—the *Anschluss*—in March 1938 and were witnesses to Hitler's triumphal entry into Vienna. His coming to Vienna was true delirium, my mother said, as if the Savior Himself had arrived. They spent the war years in Holland in Vught, where I was born in November 1943a village liberated by the British Eighth Army in October 1944. After the war, as soon as travel was again possible, my parents returned to Vienna to learn what had happened to friends, family, and the few belongings left behind. My grandmother, Adrienne, who had also fled to Holland, moved back to Vienna.

I do not recall the exact year of my first visit to Vienna; it was sometime between 1947 and 1950. What I do remember is my first impression of Vienna as our train rolled into the city's western railway station: Soviet soldiers goose stepping, fully armed, and in full regalia. A young boy, I was duly impressed and more than a little bit frightened too. Vienna was an occupied city, divided into four zones (French, British, American, and Soviet), with the Soviet the visibly dominant partner. Vienna, like Berlin, was an enclave within the larger Soviet zone of occupation in Austria. An enormous statue to the glory of the Red Army continues to adorn one of Vienna's main squares, a constant reminder of the geopolitics of this part of old Europe.

Vienna's dominant color was gray. Buildings were gray, often pockmarked by bullet and shell holes left over from combat during the closing days of the war as the Red Army fought its way into the city; the tiled roof of the *Stephansdom's*, Vienna's glorious cathedral was now a gaping hole. The people themselves were gray, dressed more often than not in hand-me-downs. I would often return to Vienna, both before and after our departure for New York.

The Vienna of the early 1950s was not a place for optimism; it was seemingly trapped in a downhill spiral that had seen the city lose a quarter of its population. Metropolitan Vienna's population was now 1.6 million, compared to 2.1 million in 1911, when the last census, conducted before the collapse of the Austro-Hungarian Empire, was taken. Cities (municipalities) can lose population as residents move to suburbs, though a declining metropolitan population is a rare occurrence. To understand the scale of the calamities that struck Vienna, we need to go back to the years preceding World War I, before Europe blindly plunged itself into three decades of inexplicable folly.

A Cultural Magnet

Vienna before World War I was the capital and the largest city of an empire of some fifty million people. Like New York, it was the central place of the nation, *the* place where the talented and the ambitious wanted to be, its fashions providing markers for the rest of the nation and, often, other nations as well. The language of business, political, and cultural elites across the Empire, including Vienna, was German. For the elites of Prague, today in the Czech Republic, Krakow, today in Poland, or Zagreb, today in Croatia (all part of Austria-Hungary at the time), *the* cultural reference was Vienna, and German was their natural second language. In the eastern provinces of Galicia and Bukovina, the home language of many households, often Jewish, was German. Today, both provinces lie in Ukraine, with Jewish life and the German language all but extinguished. Jews were among the chief *Kulturträger* (carriers of culture) of German culture—in one of history's bitter ironies, a culture that would later endeavor to annihilate them and almost succeeded.

Vienna's status as central place and political capital for a vast cultural space had major economic implications. Its industries, producing culture-sensitive goods and services (printing and publishing, fashion and apparel, etc.), could count on a protected market. The clothing and leather industries supplied the imperial army. The Empire also had to be administered. On the revenue side, the central imperial government could draw on the tax revenues of a nation of fifty million inhabitants and thousands of firms and farms spread across the Empire.[6] On the expenditure side, like Washington, D.C., today, the result was mammoth ministries with thousands of public-sector jobs. Vienna's famed *Ringstrasse,* the tree-lined boulevard that circles the inner city, is even today bounded by colossal Greek-columned government ministries, reminders of an empire lost. And as in Washington, D.C., big government attracts lobbyists and hangers-on of every stripe. Whereas Washington has lawyers, Vienna had princes, counts, and lesser aristocrats currying favor at the imperial court. Any self-respecting aristocrat from Prague, Krakow, or Budapest with even a modicum of ambition needed to keep a residence in Vienna, if only to stay *au courant* of the latest political gossip.

Imperial Vienna was growing at a precipitous rate, doubling its population every thirty years as migrants poured into the city from across the Empire. In the streets of Vienna, one heard as many Slavic and Magyar voices as German, a melting pot of cultures, religions, and peoples. City planners foresaw a metropolis of six million inhabitants, an entirely reasonable prediction at the time, laying out appropriate infrastructures with admirable foresight.

The Fall: A Hinterland Lost and Human Capital Destroyed

All this came to an abrupt end in 1918 when, as one of the defeated nations of World War I, Austria-Hungary imploded and the Empire was summarily dismantled by the victorious Entente powers (Great Britain, France, and Italy[7]). Had the noble principle of national self-determination, cherished by President Woodrow Wilson, been truly respected by the victorious powers, the name "Austria" would undoubtedly have disappeared from the map of Europe. As the Empire disintegrated, each nationality went its own way—the Poles of Galicia to the newly reborn Poland; the Czechs to the newly minted Republic of Czechoslovakia; the Italians of Istria to Italy; and so on. Left to their own devices, the German-speaking parts of the old Empire with Vienna at its heart would almost certainly have chosen to join Germany. Few believed that a truncated German-Austrian state could survive. Most historians agree that a plebiscite would have returned an overwhelming majority in favor of integration into Germany. This outcome, however, the victorious powers could not allow. It would have meant that a defeated Germany would come out of the war larger than when it went in. Thus, the treaty signed on September 10, 1919, between the Entente powers and the newly created Republic of German-Austria, as it was first called, brought into being the Austria we know today (the adjective "German" was eventually dropped). The forced creation of Austria, in essence against the wishes of its own people, was but one of the many hurdles the young republic would have to overcome, not least the management of what was now a grossly oversized capital city.

Vienna in 1920 with its more than two million inhabitants now found itself stranded in a small republic of six million people. Everything was out of scale; among the more comic examples was the impressive Ministry of the Navy for a nation that had no seacoast. Thousands of civil servants became redundant overnight but had to be paid nonetheless. Businesses lost their markets. New York taught us that the size of cities (central places) is a function of the size of their hinterland, a basic rule of urban economics. Big markets produce big cities. Imagine if the Hudson River were suddenly to become an international border cutting New York off from all lands to the west. Jobs would inevitably disappear, and New York's population would shrink. This is exactly what happened to Vienna. The town of Pressburg (now Bratislava), a mere tram ride away, was now in another country. Vienna was too big for its new country. Its population would continue to fall over the next six decades.

Other calamities were to follow. Vienna during the 1920s and 1930s experienced, in that order, hyperinflation, civil war, and the Great Depression. In the years immediately following the war, the Austrian Treasury (like Germany's) tried to print its way out of its accumulated war debt. Money soon became worthless as the Treasury printed more *Kroner* (the Austrian currency). As my mother tells it, by the end of 1922 all the family's savings was worth merely the price of an ice cream cone. The war bonds that my grandfather had patriotically bought were not worth the paper they were printed on. The second calamity—civil war—was not far behind.

The Austrian Republic's unnatural birth did not provide a solid foundation on which to build a functioning democracy. Political movements of all stripes—nostalgic monarchists, protofascists, communists, socialists—vied for power. Add in thousands of demobilized soldiers and the result was a predictably volatile mix, political parties on the left and the right forming their private militias. Two civil conflicts ensued, with fighting in the streets, first in 1927 and then in 1934, both of which were eventually suppressed by the government of the time.

The third calamity—the Great Depression—was not unique to Vienna, though Vienna did play a pivotal role in its propagation. The collapse of Wall Street in October 1929 is generally seen as the opening event of the Great Depression. The second great collapse occurred in May 1931 with the failure of the Viennese *Kreditanstalt*, the largest bank at the time in Central Europe and part of the Rothschild financial empire. This event produced a ripple effect among German banks, thus exacerbating the Depression in Germany and contributing to the rise of Hitler and the Nazi regime's ascension to power in 1933.

Thus, the wheels were set in motion for the unmentionable horror to come: the destruction of Vienna's Jewish population and with it a good part of its intellectual and business elite. During the 1930s, the fragile Austrian republic morphed into a clerical-authoritarian state, which brought a semblance of normality but was continually destabilized by local Nazis with the connivance of a now powerful Nazi neighbor. When the *Anschluss*—Germany's annexation of Austria—occurred in 1938, it should have surprised no one.[8] After all, the republic was an artificial creation, a temporary solution, until German-Austria could finally "come home to the Fatherland" (*Heim ins Reich*). Hitler was Austrian and no less German for it. Vienna now became simply another German city like Hamburg or Munich, and the conduct of Austrians was no different from that of other Germans. Some were fervent Nazis, some were "good" Germans, and most were somewhere in between. In the end, the majority, as in the rest of the Reich, stood by as the Nazi regime plunged Europe into its bloodiest war and slaughtered six million Jews.

The war over and the Nazis defeated, let us now return to the Vienna I first saw. Vienna in the early 1950s was not only gray but also deeply uneasy about its past and its place in the world. A latent sense of shame, but also of disbelief, hung over the city like a stubborn mist. How could such unspeakable things have taken place in Vienna, the city of Mozart, waltzes, chocolate cakes, and schnitzel? It was all a bad dream; it never really happened. Denial would be the term a psychologist would use. Yet, reminders of the past were everywhere. The ugly concrete flack towers hovering over several of Vienna's parks, eyesores impossible to remove, were unmistakable, as were the old Jewish homes and neighborhoods, now without Jews.

Let me leave the realm of sentiment and perception, although they matter, and return to the economic consequences of Vienna's descent into hell. Simply put, Vienna lost two fundamental pillars of a successful metropolis: *reach* and *brains*. For *reach*, matters were about to get worse. An Iron Curtain was descending upon Europe that would divide the continent into two antagonistic halves: in the West, liberal democracies with market economies aligned with the United States; in the East, communist command economies chained to the Soviet Union. In 1950, it was not yet clear whether the Iron Curtain would fall to the west or to the east of Vienna. If the Soviets chose to deal with Austria as it had with Germany, culminating in forming two states, Vienna would find itself on the eastern side of the divide within the Soviet sphere. The Soviet Union instead chose to allow the creation of a unified neutral Austria.[9] The State Treaty recognizing the re-created Austrian Republic was signed in May 1955. Vienna would lie on the western side of the Iron Curtain.

The treaty proved to be an unalloyed piece of good fortune for Vienna, for which Austrian politicians at the time deserve a good share of credit. Thanks in no small part to the negotiating skills of Austria's chancellor Leopold Figl,[10] reference to Austria's war guilt was struck from the treaty document, a matter of some consequence. Austrian politicians deftly played the card of little Austria, the first victim of Nazism. The re-created republic shrewdly distanced itself from its Teutonic past; being German no longer carried any advantage. Whatever one may think of this ethical sleight-of-hand and identity change, it worked, laying the groundwork for Vienna's rebirth. Vienna could now market itself as a politically untainted meeting place (*Kongressstadt,* that is, Congress City) between East and West, located in a small, neutral, nonmenacing republic. Later, we shall see how Austria skillfully harnessed the city's remade image to its advantage. But for the moment let us return to postwar Vienna.

The Iron Curtain meant that Vienna was now cut off from its old trading area to the East. The Iron Curtain, a mere forty-five-minute car ride from Vienna, was more than a national border: it was a heavily guarded, fortified wall. A trip to Budapest or Prague, Vienna's age-old sister cities, required a visa as well as a considerable outlay of funds in the form of obligatory purchases of worthless communist currencies. The link with its old neighborhood (hinterland) was now irretrievably cut. Vienna's population continued to decline.

Vienna's loss of human capital was arguably even more damaging. What happened during those tragic years is beyond belief—and also beyond this book's purview. The loss was not limited to the destruction of Vienna's Jews (via emigration or death camps), who had been disproportionately present in the city's intellectual life and formed the majority among doctors, lawyers, and bankers.[11] Although many non-Jewish professionals, artists, and others also fled Vienna, Jews constituted the bulk of Vienna's loss. A comparison with New York today illustrates the scale of the calamity. In the 1920s, Vienna was home to some 200,000 Jews, or 11 percent of Vienna's population, which is about the same share as Jews in New York today. I ask the reader to imagine a New York without Jews and to contemplate the consequences for its cultural and economic life. The Nazis succeeded in putting the final lid on Vienna as an intellectual beacon, once arguably the most intellectually creative city in Europe.

Nothing better illustrates Vienna's catastrophic brain drain than the fate that befell the Faculty of Medicine of the University of Vienna, the alma mater of Sigmund Freud and seven Nobel laureates and among the top medical schools in the world prior to the *Anschluss*. All that changed on March 13, 1938. Over half of the University's medical instructors, most of whom were Jewish, as well as affiliated physicians, were dismissed. Those who did not succumb in death camps fled, never to return. The effects of the Nazi poison did not end there. After the war, some 75 percent of the remaining medical instructors had to be dismissed because of their affiliation with the Nazi regime.[12] The road back would be difficult. The Faculty has since been renamed the Medical University of Vienna; although it has attained a good reputation, it is no longer ranked as a top world medical school.

Rebirth

Let us now fast forward to Vienna today. According to various current indicators, Vienna today is unquestionably a successful city. The Economist Intelligence Unit ranks Vienna as the world's most livable city. For nine consecutive years, Mercer (a consultancy) has ranked Vienna first in its quality-of-life survey. Vienna's unemployment rate systematically registers among the lowest in Europe, and the city has one of the highest standards of living.[13] Today Vienna's GDP per capita is comparable to that of New York,[14] which is no mean achievement. Vienna's population has started to grow again and is expected to return to its 1911 level in the near future. Vienna has come full circle: after a troubled journey of almost a century, it is again a prosperous and growing city.

What was the basis for this remarkable resurgence? Few would argue that Vienna has suddenly become a magnet for the young and ambitious. Vienna is not a terribly "cool" or entrepreneurial city.[15] The image the city projects, its wealth notwithstanding, is that of a city immersed in its past. Its trick was to turn an ostensibly negative attribute into an asset, successfully marketing the glories of its past. The empty palaces proved perfect venues for international organizations and events in search of a little grandeur and class and available at a more reasonable price than in Paris or London. Lower real estate costs were in part the outcome of its stagnant growth, but also its unique housing heritage (see Chapter 3). Vienna systematically ranks below comparable western European cities on cost-of-living indexes.[16]

Vienna's resurgence is all the more remarkable when one considers its relatively humdrum performance on human capital, which is the predictable result of its sad past. Vienna's population is fairly well educated, as befits a nation at Austria's level of development; but it does not stand out in Europe. The share of tertiary (university) degree holders is on the same level as that of similar-sized German cities but only half that of London and below that of similar-sized European metropolitan areas such as Brussels or Amsterdam.[17] The University of Vienna is outclassed by twelve German universities, eight Dutch universities, and six Swiss universities.[18] Vienna's strength is in secondary education, producing a technically competent and reliable labor pool.[19] Vienna has not emerged as a major high-tech hub.

The Viennese Coffee House

Vienna has something else. If brains and entrepreneurial buzz are not it, then what? Beautiful palaces are nice; but they cannot be the sole explanation. Or is it Austria's skillful marketing of Vienna as a neutral meeting ground between East and West? But the Cold War is over.

Few institutions better epitomize the city's unique urban culture than the Viennese coffee house (*Wiener Kaffeehaus*), which has miraculously survived over the decades. The rhythm and mores of the *Kaffeehaus* are the polar opposites of Manhattan. Where New York is fast-paced and hyperactive, the *Kaffeehaus* is slow and unhurried, providing an oasis of tranquil sophistication more in tune with the world of diplomacy and royalty. In short, it is an ideal setting for discreet negotiations. The white-aproned waiter will bring the customer's coffee (or glass of wine), meticulously served on a silver tray with a complementary glass of water, leaving him or her unbothered for the rest the day if so desired. In the old days, patrons would receive their mail and entertain their mistresses or lovers there (and perhaps still do). Today, one is likely to observe a Russian oligarch quietly discussing business with his Viennese banker. It is not entirely a coincidence that Austria's bank secrecy laws are no less restrictive than Switzerland's, but Vienna does it more discreetly. Some businesses find Vienna's particular ambiance—a unique mix of Germanic efficiency, discretion, and relaxed sophistication—conducive to their affairs.

When the Iron Curtain fell, Vienna's location again became an asset, later reinforced by Austria's entry into the European Union, followed in 2004 by the successor states of the Habsburg Empire (the Czech Republic, Hungary, Slovakia, Slovenia, and Poland), Romania and Bulgaria in 2007, and finally Croatia in 2013. The old economic space of the Empire was again unified, though no longer connected by a common lingua franca. Ironically, the now dismantled Iron Curtain became an advantage. The East's pre-1989 misery— planned communist economies where the art of managing a market economy was lost—gave Viennese business service providers a competitive advantage once the borders opened, laying the groundwork for a range of consultancies that now constitute one of the foundations of the Viennese economy.[20] Vienna's specific advantage—call it the *Kaffeehaus* advantage—is illustrated in the number of German firms (e.g., Siemens) that have chosen to locate their regional head offices and marketing facilities for Eastern Europe in Vienna. But why locate in Vienna when German cities such as Munich and Berlin are no less well situated to serve eastern markets? The simple reason is that history allowed Vienna to develop a distinct advantage for dealing with Europe's East. For the average Russian or Romanian businessman, Vienna is simply easier to navigate than Lutheran Berlin or Calvinist Zurich.

In short, Vienna reinvented itself building on its past skill advantage, transforming from an imperial city to a mediator/consultancy city by providing a tailored environment for business transactions in Central and Eastern Europe. On a more paradoxical note, Vienna's past misfortunes now became advantages. The city's disproportionate size became a political plus, its weight within (small) Austria ensuring that the city's concerns were difficult to ignore by the national government, a big fish in a small lake. Its past lethargic growth also produced a totally accidental but fortunate outcome. Vienna's stable (even declining) population meant that its urbanized area remained largely contained within its historical municipal boundaries, thus avoiding the social divides that plague many metropolitan areas (see also Chapter 3).

* * *

Vienna's story holds a number of lessons, especially when set against New York's earlier story. Nation size and national borders matter; when Austria's borders shrank, so did the population of Vienna. But it was more than that: Vienna changed nations so to speak, demonstrating the cultural bonds that bind nations and cities. Vienna's lack of "coolness" today is not accidental. The nation that spawned the creative, cosmopolitan Vienna of Mozart and Freud is dead, today replaced by a small, culturally homogeneous republic. Not only did Vienna shrink literally but also culturally. The contrast with New York is telling. The Big Apple continues to attract talent from a vast empire and beyond and hopefully will continue to do so.

The New York story confirmed a basic tenet of urban economics: dense concentrations of human capital will as a rule generate agglomeration economies and concomitant wealth—that is, given sound national institutional foundations. But, Vienna's newfound success also teaches us that urban size and concentrations of highly educated human capital are not indispensable preconditions for wealth creation. A city need not equal New York's size and buzz to generate a comparable standard of living—that is, if it offers something else.

Port au Prince—Trust and the Devastating Consequences of Its Absence

A lesson the reader should avoid drawing from the New York and Vienna stories is that cities are naturally resilient. True, both cities rebounded.

There ae many examples of cities bouncing back from the abyss. Hiroshima and Berlin, for example, have come back from what can only be described as urban hell. Shanghai, after decades of communist mismanagement, is poised to become one of the world's richest cities. A degree of resilience is built into cities. Yet, to have faith in the natural healing powers of urban life would be an error. My first encounter with what can only be called a failed city occurred shortly after I left New York. For that, we shall now leave the rich world and travel south.

I arrived in Port au Prince, capital of Haiti, in February 1972 as part of a Canadian university delegation hoping to establish bilateral relations with Haitian educational institutions. The delegation was headed by a Haitian-Canadian professor, Georges Anglade, who some forty years later would perish with his wife, Mireille, in the devastating earthquake that struck Port au Prince on January 12, 2010. It is estimated that some three hundred thousand persons perished in that earthquake, or an astounding seventh of the city's population. I am aware that this does not make for a very joyous opening, but then, this story does not have a happy ending.

My initiation to a Third World city began at the airport: what greeted me was total chaos, as I was immediately besieged by porters and assorted hawkers. Were it not for Georges's guiding hand, I would most probably have panicked. The drive to our hotel did little to dispel my fears. Driving in Port au Prince was visibly a blood sport in which accidents were part of the ritual and pedestrians fair game. Our hotel, an old colonial mansion, was situated off the *Champs-de-Mars,* the city's main square, across from the presidential palace. Today, visitors (consultants, occasional tourists, and other luminaries) tend to stay in gated luxury hotels far from the city center. But in 1972 Port au Prince's old town was still reasonably welcoming and walkable.

To say that Port au Prince at the time was a poor city would be a euphemism. Was it possible for a city to be any poorer? The main shopping street was appropriately called *Rue pavée* (Paved Street). The city had no traffic lights and no real sidewalks; sewage floated in open gutters. Rare were the stores with glass windows. Electric power was an occasional affair, if available at all; power shortages were the rule. Yet, the city did not lack a certain grandeur. Reminders of Port au Prince's proud colonial past, once one of the richest cities in the Caribbean, were visible everywhere. Handsome balconied buildings and stately homes that had seen better times lined the streets of the old town. And, remarkably, the city was essentially safe. From my center-city hotel I wandered the streets of the old town, unaccompanied. True, the occasional peddler or overeager bystander would badger me—my skin color naturally gave me away—but I never felt physically threatened. My ghetto past helped. Remember rule 1: don't twaddle and don't look lost. Moreover, people on the street were generally friendly and not immune to a little gratuitous banter. Speaking French also helped.

More to the point, people did not seem to lack hope. Despite the glaring poverty, a feeling of optimism floated in the air. The old dictator, François Duvalier (President for Life), popularly referred to as *Papa Doc*, had finally done the right thing and died. He was succeeded by his son. Jean-Claude (Baby Doc), who with a band of young technocrats promised to enact much-need reforms. Our delegation was one of many now that the international community was returning to Haiti. Had its moment finally come after so many decades of flagrant misrule? Thus, when two weeks later I boarded my plane for the return flight to Montreal, I was confident that Haiti was at the beginning of an era of progress, although I had no illusion as to the scale of its challenges. How could things get worse? It was simply inconceivable that Port au Prince, already the capital of the poorest nation in the Americas, could sink any lower. Lamentably, I was so wrong.

Two decades would pass until I visited Port au Prince again, this time as coordinator of a Canadian-financed university-linkage program. I would return to Port au Prince often. My first return visit in 1990 immediately told me how wrong I had been. Little had improved since 1972 except perhaps the new Canadian-built airport. True, there were more cars on the streets, but those streets were as chaotic and dangerous as ever. The built-up environment had visibly deteriorated. Our old colonial hotel was crumbling, unmaintained, progressively consumed by tropical foliage. Crime had increased. There were to be no more unaccompanied wanderings through the old town. On each successive visit to Port au Prince, my impression was that conditions had worsened. Power blackouts were increasingly frequent. Alas, these were more than mere impressions, for they were confirmed by published statistics. The United Nations and World Bank published statistics showed that Haiti's GDP per capita had actually declined between 1970 and 2000, an "achievement" only equaled by the poorest African nations. The decline would continue, with the terrible 2010 earthquake the final punishment, as if God had it in for Haiti.

I have been back to Port au Prince since the earthquake. The presidential place lies in ruins, waiting to be repaired, and the *Champs-de-Mars* central square is covered with squatter tents. Little has been rebuilt. Public services remain sporadic and unreliable, if provided at all. For all practical purposes, Port au Prince lacks a functioning state.

Cities as Social Contacts

Port au Prince today is a sprawling urban monster of some three million inhabitants, larger than Vienna, but its citizens are fifty times poorer.[21] Such poverty begs an explanation. Port au Prince taught me that cities do not magically manage themselves. Going back to Table I.1, there is nothing automatic about the first three Pillars, the basic foundations for a functioning city. I shall focus on Pillar 2 (Collaborative/Social Cohesion). It is in Port au Prince that I fully came to recognize the importance of cooperation, compromise, and trust for a city to work, traits that do not come naturally to the human species. Cities are demanding beasts, requiring patterns of social organization that have to be learned, patterns that are the outcome of decades—even centuries—of adaptation. Economists and other social scientists all too often take these as givens, as did I before landing in Port au Prince.

Conflicts in cities, unlike those in the countryside, must constantly be arbitrated on a daily basis, if only in such small activities as crossing a street. Arbitrating who has the right to cross, where and when—and enforcing the requisite rules—demands an advanced level of social organization and social consensus. The maintenance of sidewalks, lighting, and city streets is contingent on the existence of a tacit social contract that we call government, where such infrastructures are collectively paid for through taxation. These are among the simpler examples, but they can be extrapolated to the hundreds of "little" things that make a city work: sewage systems; policing; power grids; cadasters; land titles; refuse collection—I invite the reader to reflect on the array of public services, often hidden, that make his or her city work properly.

These are what economists call *public goods*, which, if not provided collectively, will not be provided at all, or at best only partially. Individuals or families will not provide them. At best, a home owner can pave the sidewalk or street in front of his house, but this effort is of little use—as well as being terribly inefficient—if his or her neighbors do not do likewise. Such public goods are less prevalent in the countryside. A substance farmer—and many remain in Haiti—needs little in the way of public services. The city is different. Urbanization is more than a move from the farm to the city. It is a move to a new social contract, one that requires a high level of interpersonal trust.[22] That precisely is what is lacking in Haiti. The people of Port au Prince are marvelously resourceful—they have to be in order to survive—but Haitian society is among the least consensual I have come across in my travels. The lack of social glue manifests itself not only in the inability to get things done once they involve more than one actor, but more fundamentally—and sadly—in a generalized climate of mistrust between individuals and disregard for the fate of others, especially those down the social ladder.

Let me recount three anecdotes that range from the tragic to the comic. *Anecdote 1*: Returning from the north of the city, I found myself in a chauffeured car next to a high-ranking Haitian official. The chauffeur was driving too fast for my taste. We were on the main road linking Port au Prince to northern Haiti, and the roadside was, as always, crowded with locals. (Walking was and still is the principal means of locomotion for the vast majority of Haitians.) The car struck a little girl who had inadvertently wandered onto the road, but shockingly, the chauffeur did not slow down. He simply continued at the same speed, acting as if he had merely hit a road bump and not a child. Looking through the back window, I could make out the little girl lying on the road, locals running to her side. I have no idea what was the extent of the injuries, nor do I know whether she succumbed. "Should we not stop," I almost screamed. My companion's answer was short and to the point: "There is nothing we can do, and anyway we would probably be mobbed if we did." I was aghast. I did not sleep well that night.

Anecdote 2: I was invited to speak at a local branch of the chamber of commerce. The discussion eventually moved to the subject of the innumerable informal settlements (*Bidonvilles*: shantytowns) that cover most of the city. After admitting that I had no easy solution, I turned to my hosts, mostly well-to-do Haitian businessmen, and asked what they would propose. The answer was immediate and unanimous: "tear them down and expel the buggers." I did not sleep well that night either.

Anecdote 3 (on a lighter note): Before flying down to Port au Prince to give a class, I would call ahead (providing the phone worked) to remind school authorities to reserve an overhead projector. Sophisticated computer setups for PowerPoint presentations and the like were out of the question.

Good old transparencies would have to do. Arriving at my classroom, the overhead projector was set up as promised. Wonderful! But no light bulb. So I went to the administration and asked for a light bulb: "Oh my! we put in the request three months ago. You mean the bulb has not been delivered yet?" The idea that someone would go out and buy a light bulb was not part of the scenario. Employees did not trust the administration to reimburse them; not to mention the paperwork involved (for just one light bulb). Eventually, a light bulb was rustled up and I gave my class. The next day, the overhead projector was set up, ready for use with a light bulb—but there was no power. "What, I asked my colleague, the school has no generator"? Every self-respecting institution in Port au Prince had a generator in case of blackouts. "Of course we have a generator"—but no fuel. Like our light bulb, a request for fuel was trapped somewhere in bureaucratic hell, and again no one would think of buying fuel with their own money. I gave my class— chalk and blackboard to the rescue: a lesson learned. End of anecdote

The moral of the three anecdotes is that the effects of social distrust filter down into even the most mundane actions. And it is in cities that this distrust hurts the most. The question, of course, is how Haiti got to be this way. This book is not the place to recount Haiti's unhappy history, which involves an unending string of self-proclaimed emperors, strongmen, and dictators, one more corrupt and inept than the next, with an American military occupation (1914–1934) also part of the story. Haiti never completely freed itself from the legacy of slavery. That legacy still hangs in the air two hundred years after the most successful slave revolt in modern history. On the 18th of November 1803, the former slaves vanquished the armies of Napoleon at the Battle of Vertières and subsequently went on to set up the independent Republic of Haiti, an unparalleled exploit of which all Haitians are deservedly proud. The dark side of this historic achievement was that the new nation reproduced and perpetuated the traits of a slave-plantation society—a hierarchical mindset founded on force and coercion—having known no other social order throughout its history. Race has remained a definer of social status[23] in Haiti, with the lighter-skinned former slaves now often playing the role of the old white plantation owners who fled generations ago.

I shall stop here. The remainder of the story tells itself: it is a sad lesson that the roots of urban failure can run very deep. I shall return to Port au Prince; Haiti's tragic legacy of mistrust also left its mark on New Orleans, as we shall discover in Chapter 5.

Buenos Aires—The Urban Costs of National Folly

At this point, the reader will rightly object that I have chosen a rather extreme case of urban failure to illustrate my point. It is difficult to imagine an unhappier place than Port au Prince, putting aside the war-torn cities of the Middle East and Africa. Yet, Third World nations do not have a monopoly on urban failure, as the inner-city ghettos of America and France's *banlieue*[24] attest. But, for the moment, let us travel further south to what was once a rich nation.

The Paris of Latin America

Sometime after my first visit to Port au Prince, I was invited to Buenos Aires for a conference, a city to which I would return three times. I immediately fell in love with Buenos Aires. In those days Buenos Aires was called the Paris of Latin America, and it truly was. This was before the so-called Dirty War of the military dictatorship (1976–1983).[25] I stayed in a small hotel in the inner city (*Microcentro*) whose décor was straight out of an avant-garde French movie, right down to the chain-door elevators typical of prewar Paris. Indeed, were it not for the difference in language, I could easily have imagined myself in Paris. The analogy did not stop there. Here was a city with broad boulevards and vistas more than a match for the fabled boulevards of Baron Haussmann's Paris. The northern neighborhoods (Recoleta, Retiro, Palermo, etc.) had all the sophisticated refinement—and architecture to go with it—of Paris's 16th Arrondissement. Buenos Aires also had its equivalent of Paris's Left Bank in the artsy-Bohemian neighborhoods of San Telmo and La Boca.

The Buenos Aires of the 1970s was a walking city and surprisingly safe. The main central shopping street, *Calle Florida*, was a pedestrian mall not unlike Times Square today, the place where everybody wanted to be and to be seen. Next to my hotel was a dance hall where I discovered the tango, of which I have since become an unrepentant aficionado. And the food! Argentina's rich Pampas produce, at least in my opinion, the best beef I have ever tasted. Add in culinary traditions imported from Italy, Spain, and Central Europe, and the result is a culture of fine dining that can hold its own with the best that France and Italy have to offer, not forgetting the excellent wines produced in the foothills of the Argentinian Andes. The

Buenos Aires of the 1970s was, in a word, a pleasure for the senses, with the feel in every respect of a great metropolis, home to a (metropolitan) population nearing the ten million mark.

When I returned to Montreal after that first visit there and recounted my enchantment with Buenos Aires to my father, he was not surprised. My father had worked as a travel agent in Paris in the 1920s.[26] In those days, as he told it, Argentina was considered as rich as the United States, and Buenos Aires was seen as a worthy rival of Paris and New York. "Rich as an Argentinian" was a common expression heard in the cafés. "Paris is certainly nice," visiting Argentine clients would tell my father, only to add: "*pero Buenos Aires!*" (But Buenos Aires!). The culture and music coming out of Buenos Aires were all the rage in Europe: Carlos Gardel was a superstar and the tango was everywhere. *Porteños* (the popular name for the inhabitants of Buenos Aires) had every reason to be proud of their city, although their sometimes overbearing attitude and their flaunting of their wealth did not always make them easy clients: "worse than Americans," as my father told it, which was saying something.

These were not mere perceptions. Argentina on the eve of the Great Depression was indeed a wealthy nation. Buenos Aires in the late 1920 boasted an income per capita comparable to that of Paris, Vienna, and New York.[27] And like New York, B.A. (an often-used shorthand for Buenos Aires) was the nation's chief port and gateway city, the place where European immigrants landed. B.A. was a cosmopolitan metropolis, its population constantly renewed by Italian, Spanish, and other European immigrants. And like New York, B.A. was home (and still is) to a sizeable Jewish population, is Latin America's largest. Its apparel industry, like that of New York, was the largest manufacturing employer. Buenos Aires was a thoroughly European and Europeanized city, distinguishing it from the rest of Latin America where indigenous, black, or mestizo (mixed-race) peoples often accounted for significant shares of the local population.[28]

B.A.'s European look, high standard of living, and sophistication set it apart from the rest of Latin America. Mexico City, its only possible rival by size in Spanish-speaking America, was simply not at the same level of development.[29] Argentinians, especially the *Porteños*, acquired a reputation, deserved or undeserved, for looking down at other Latin Americans. Argentinian jokes were common currency throughout Hispanic America. Here is an example told me by a Mexican friend: "How many Argentinians can you fit into a Volkswagen Beetle?" *Answer*: "All forty million once you let out the hot air."

Buenos Aires's golden age came to an abrupt end with the Great Depression as beef and grain exports tumbled. Even so, Argentina continued to stand out in Latin America. As recently as 1970—around the time of me first visit—GDP per capita was still about twice that of Mexico's and about a third higher than that of its two neighbors, Uruguay and Chile.

A Third World City

Let us now update to today. The most recent estimates put Argentina's GDP per capita at a mere quarter—give or take a point—of that of the United States and other advanced nations and below that of Chile and Uruguay.[30] Argentina has managed the unenviable exploit of moving backward from the First World to the Third World in the space of just two generations.

Cold data do not adequately tell the story, however, as my most recent visit to Buenos Aires will illustrate. My wife had never been to B.A., and so I wanted to show her the Buenos Aires I loved. I was invited to a conference in Santiago de Chile and convinced her to come along, with the promise of spending a week in Buenos Aires. I reserved a hotel room in what I remembered to be a good location in the *Microcentro* right off *Calle Florida*. The arrival at the hotel, which shall remain unnamed, was the first shock. The hotel was adequate, but the area was very different from what I remembered. I will not burden the reader with unnecessary details; two observations will suffice. *Calle Florida*, my favorite street, was now crowded with informal vendors and beggars, full of tacky shops, conveying a general feeling of neglect. A few blocks away, *Calle Lavalle* and *Avenida Corrientes*, my old haunts for fine dining and evenings out, were now gray and uninviting, with a few lonely restaurants that had miraculously survived, as if Times Square had reverted back to its seedy past. A sense of insecurity hung over the entire *Microcentro*. Going out in the evening was no longer fun. Without wishing to be too harsh, Buenos Aires was visibly going in the opposite direction of New York, losing its center. Discussions with *Porteño* friends confirmed that the middle classes had abandoned the downtown, rarely venturing there anymore for shopping or entertainment. My wife would never see the Buenos Aires I had wanted her to see.

Few sights are more evocative of Buenos Aires's past greatness than number 877 *Calle Florida*, the erstwhile address of *Harrods*, London's upscale department store. Harrods never ventured outside Britain with one sole exception: Buenos Aires. That it chose B.A. over New York or Paris speaks volumes about the city's standing at the time. Harrods opened its store in 1914 on the eve of World War I on north *Calle Florida*, then the most fashionable shopping street in Latin America, in a befittingly elegant Belle Époque building. Harrods's tea salon—very British if you please—became a favored hangout for the city's rich and famous, providing visible (and reassuring) proof of the city's world-class status.

877 *Calle Florida* is now an empty shell, although the proud Harrods shingle still hangs out front. After changing owners several times, the store was finally closed in 1998 and apparently has still not found a new vocation. The Harrods sign is a poignant marker of the city's decline, impossible not to see, almost as if the city fathers, by letting it stand, were reminding *Porteños* of what once was but is no more.

Beyond personal perceptions, Buenos Aires's fall from greatness is confirmed by its unenviable position on various city rankings (most recent; years vary): 62nd (out of 140) on the Economist Livability Index; 91st (out of 201) on the Mercer Quality of Living Index; and 301st (out of 372) on the Numbeo Safety Index.[31] The last-named ranking is especially worrying. Few handicaps do more to undermine public and business confidence than rising crime rates and perceptions of generalized insecurity.

All this of course begs the question of the causes of Buenos Aires's fall from First World to quasi-Third World city. Argentina's economic decline remains somewhat of a mystery. The easy answer is that it is in Latin America. Other Latin American nations have seen their relative standing decline compared to that of the United States and other developed nations. The reasons given, depending on the author, suggest a mix of causes: the Spanish legacy and the Roman Catholic Church; the absence of stable democratic institutions; overreliance on natural resources; sharp social divisions; the weight of (native) Indian culture. None of these explanations is totally satisfactory, although all contain kernels of truth. All excerpt the last reason also matter in Argentina. However, Argentina stands out because of its high initial standing and the magnitude of its fall.

Buenos Aires's Latin American heritage cannot explain why the University of Buenos Aires, the nation's premier university, is outranked by nine universities in Hispanic America, three each in Mexico, Colombia, and

Chile.[32] My last visit to B.A. was preceded by a stay in Santiago de Chile in 2010, my second visit to that city. I was pleasantly surprised by the changes I found. The old city center, though still somewhat grimy and with none of Buenos Aires's grandeur, was considerably improved. The city felt richer and more prosperous, and was generally well managed. The overall impression was that Santiago and Chile were moving in the right direction, an impression reinforced by Chile's positive economic performance in recent years and its reputation for competent and honest government—certainly by the standards of Latin America.[33] Why then was Argentina, Buenos Aires, in particular, not moving in the same direction? I'm not sure I have the answer. My brief attempt at an explanation, as follows, remains highly personal.

The Price of Populism

Starting with my first visits to Buenos Aires in the 1970s, reading newspapers and listening to debates, I was struck by the city's singular political culture. The past loomed large. Posters extolling the former president and strongman, Juan Domingo Perón, were omnipresent. Even more in evidence were posters of his first wife and political companion, Eva Duarte Perón ("Evita"), often pictured in Madonna-like poses looking down at her beloved people waiting to be saved. Postcards of the Perón couple were on sale throughout the city. Like Vienna, the city was bathed in nostalgia but a wistfulness of a different kind. It's almost as if its citizens had rejected modernity and were content to be captives of political ideologies that had long since been abandoned elsewhere. The political movement behind these reverential images was the Justicialist Party (*Partido Justicialista*), whose adherents were generally referred to as *Peronistas* and which remains, arguably, the most powerful political force in Argentina. The Peronista movement and its messianic devotion to the memory of Juan and Evita Perón have no equivalent in the Western world, and its ideology is most probably incomprehensible to non-Argentines. For lack of a better label, I would describe Peronism as an eclectic mélange of anti-establishment populism, protofascism, and left-wing socialism, with generous dollops of anti-American rhetoric and nationalist bravado. It's also highly personalized and emotionally charged, judging by the paroxysms of emotion I witnessed during the funeral of (Peronista) president Néstor Kirchner, who died of a heart attack on October 27, 2010, and was succeeded by his wife, Cristina Fernández de Kirchner.[34]

The full story of the origins of this peculiar political movement and its impact on Argentina would require a separate book. I shall focus on two points: the *Porteño* origins of Peronism, a truly urban political movement, and the irreparable damage done to the Buenos Aires economy. The Great Depression provoked political upheavals in many nations. In Argentina, the collapse of its export-led economy had two consequences: (1) the collapse of its rural wheat and cattle-based economy sent thousands of unemployed rural workers back to the city; and (2) the concomitant collapse of Buenos Aires's meatpacking, milling, and food processing industries created an army of unemployed workers. These two shocks together produced the growing mass of understandably restive urban poor—the so-called *descamisados* (shirtless ones)—which would provide the popular base for Perón's rise to power and electoral victory in February 1946. Perón was much aided by his charismatic wife, Evita, who masterfully played on her working-class roots to connect with the urban poor, who visibly worshiped her.[35] Perón would rule until September 1955 when he was overthrown by a military coup, largely backed by Argentina's moneyed elites dissatisfied with Perón's pro-labor stance, overly generous social policies, and growing personality cult.

The September 1955 coup left a highly polarized polity, from which Argentina has yet to escape, divided between those who dream of the return to a mythical Peronista nirvana of unrestrained social spending and those who are of a more pragmatic bent, many of whom are to the right on the political spectrum. This division would poison Argentine political life for decades to come. Attempts to violently wipe out all traces of Perón's legacy (i.e., the Dirty War of 1976–1983) would follow alternating with periods of Peronista euphoria. Perón would triumphantly return to power in 1973 after eighteen years of exile, only to die in office less than a year later. Nonetheless, the shadow of Juan and Evita Perón has continued to hang over Argentine politics. The majority of Argentina's elected presidents since Perón's death (military dictatorships aside) have sprung from the Peronista mold. In December 2015, Argentinians elected their first non-Peronista president in many years, Mauricio Macri. Only time will tell whether Macri is simply a pause in Argentina's long Peronista Winter or a true break with the past.

Why left-leaning politics (if that indeed is the proper label) took the quasi-messianic Peronist route in Argentina remains a mystery. Social inequality is often pointed to as a cause. Argentina, Buenos Aires in particular, has a long history of social inequality, with sharp divisions between rich and poor and between neighborhoods. But this also holds true for most of Latin America and thus cannot explain why the movement took such an idiosyncratic turn[36] and continued to attract a constant following over more than six decades.

Populist parties are by their nature Keynesian; that is, interventionist and less wary of deficits. Peronista governments were not universally bad. Their commitment to social justice (at least in words) was undoubtedly sincere. However, Argentina's Peronista administrations stand out among nations in their singular propensity for economic mismanagement, with astonishing disregard for the basic rules of sound fiscal management and the proper functioning of markets. I shall not go through the litany of bad economic policies, which includes everything from taxing exports to cooking the national accounts. Rather, I shall focus on a facet of fiscal policy that is of particular significance for metropolitan economies: the management of the national currency. One of the premier functions of a great metropolis, notably those at the top of the national urban hierarchy, is to be a center of finance. The towers of Wall Street, are visible proof of New York's standing. Port cities like New York, London, Amsterdam, and Shanghai are natural centers of finance and business intermediation (freight forwarders; insurance carriers; accountants, etc.). With its size and preeminent position in South America, one would normally have expected Buenos Aires to emerge as a major financial center for South America.

That did not happen. Buenos Aires does not even appear on current international rankings of financial centers.[37] An essential attribute of a successful financial center is the confidence people place in the national currency, which is one reason why a small city like Zurich punches well above its weight;[38] the Central Bank of Switzerland has a well-deserved reputation for rigorous monetary management. A sound currency is built on a least two foundations: (1) an independent central bank protected by law from political interference, meaning that the president or prime minster cannot order the central bank to print money to finance popular programs; and (2) sound fiscal management of the government budget, meaning that like all prudent households spending does not outrun revenues or, alternatively, the household's ability to assume debt (i.e., meet prospective interest payments). Argentina has failed miserably on both accounts. In 2002, Argentina staged the biggest default on sovereign debt in recent history, defaulting on more than $100 billion in loans. The negotiations that followed resulted in a settlement that left lenders with a severe loss, not the sort of behavior that breeds investor confidence.

However, it is the repeated bouts of hyperinflation, the everyday face of fiscal mismanagement, that are the prime hallmarks of Argentina's turbulent economy, felt by ordinary Argentinians. Argentina's monetary history is a sad lesson in political incompetence, with on-again and off-again periods of economic crisis since the 1950s. It took approximately 100 billion 1982 pesos to buy one new peso in 1992. At its summit (1989), the annual inflation rate approached 5000 percent. One would think that such painful jolts of hyperinflation would act as an antidote, but quite the contrary: Argentina's governments seem to be addicted to inflation, with the last Peronista administration under the Kirchners (2003–2015) being no exception. Between 2005 and 20015, the peso lost 85 percent of its value. Equally revealing was the Kirchner government's refusal to acknowledge reality, manipulating official statistics. Argentina had the dubious distinction of seeing its published statistics rejected by the International Monetary Fund (IMF), its national statistical agency having lost all credibility. On a more comical but nonetheless sad note, President Cristiana Fernández stubbornly refused to allow the Central Bank of Argentina to issue anything higher than a 100 peso banknote, which was worth about ten U.S. dollars (June 2015). Banks and businesses had to handle ever-growing volumes of cash, making transactions unwieldy and unsafe. ATM machines were hard put to remain stocked.[39]

Let me stop here; I think I've made my point. Buenos Aires has, for reasons that should now be clear, failed to spawn a dynamic financial sector consistent with its standing as a metropolis. The reader will have guessed by now that Buenos Aires would rank very low on Pillar 1. Hopefully, the new Macri government will undo many of the worst practices of the past. The national statistical office is slowly winning back its credibility, now publishing accurate inflation data, which at the time of writing was still high. Building the confidence and credibility necessary for a financial center is a matter of generations.

Two Colonial Cities, Two Diverging Paths

A final question needs to be addressed. Surely the effects of globalization, imperialism, and the legacy of colonialism cannot be ignored. The view of Latin America as a victim of imperial exploitation and the United States as the favorite culprit is deeply ingrained in the Latin American psyche. It is an article of faith among left-leaning (and even not so left-leaning) intellectuals.[40] It is a polemic I will disregard; instead, in an attempt at an answer, I shall compare Buenos Aires with Montreal, another metropolis of the Americas with colonial roots and a remarkably similar pre-1930 economic history.[41]

On the eve of the Great Depression, Montreal and Buenos Aires had about the same income per capita[42]; they were two rapidly growing metropolises in two New World nations with rapidly expanding economies. Canada, like Argentina, grew rich in the late 19th and early 20th centuries through the exploitation of natural resources, exporting similar products (wheat, notably). Montreal, like Buenos Aires, was the great port city through which exports moved, destined for European markets. It was the terminus for a vast rail network leading into the interior, linking the city with the Prairies, Canada's counterpart of Argentina's Pampas. In both cities, industries dependent on the exploitation of the nation's rich resources, notably food processing and the manufacture of rolling stock, were major sources of employment. If imperialism is to be a criterion, Montreal in the 1920s was no less colonial than Buenos Aires. Canada was still formally a Dominion within the British Empire, and the city's economy was dominated by an Anglo-Scottish elite with close links to London. The leading trading houses, banks, and railway companies were largely financed by British capital,[43] not all that different from that of Buenos Aires at the time. Harrods's choice of Buenos Aires was no accident. Its economic elites had equally close ties to London,[44] taking pride in their Anglocentric lifestyle, including a large British expat community. A Montreal banker would have felt perfectly at home in the Buenos Aires of 1928.

Both cities were devastated by the Great Depression. Immigration stopped, and capital investment dried up. Canada also spawned its idiosyncratic populist party—Social Credit—whose ideology essentially came down to printing money to bolster demand, an idea with which Peronistas would have felt entirely at ease. The party had its moments of glory, especially in Alberta and Quebec, but it has since disappeared from the political landscape. After World War II, as happened in Argentina, the United States replaced Britain as Canada's dominant source of investment and trade, fostering outcries among Canadian nationalists (generally on the left of the political spectrum) that their country was in the process of becoming a branch plant economy beholden to American multinationals.[45] A passing Argentine intellectual at the time would have felt entirely at home, sadly agreeing that both nations had fallen victim to unbridled American capitalism.

Let us now do our usual fast forward to the present. Buenos Aires's GDP per capita is now about 30 percent that of Montreal, a two-thirds drop from the 1920s. The figure was still in the order of 60 percent in 1970.[46] While the Argentine economy was treading water, the Canadian economy underwent a major transformation beginning in the 1970s. The expression "branch plant economy" disappeared from the political vocabulary, Canada was now spawning its own multinationals, many of which were Montreal-based. Montreal experienced a social revolution (of which more will said in Chapter 6) that laid the groundwork for a new generation of outward-looking entrepreneurs. To my knowledge, Buenos Aires has not given birth to any world-class multinational corporations. [47] I do not wish to push the comparison too far, though the message is clear. Imperial or neocolonial domination (if those are the proper terms) cannot explain why the two urban economies have diverged. The answer must be found elsewhere, which inevitably leads us back to Argentina's peculiar political legacy.

The Buenos Aires story teaches us that even great cities with all the trappings of a world-class metropolis can fail, given the right (or rather wrong) national policies. A single charismatic leader, in countries where the institutional safeguards are weak, can undermine the foundations that allow cities to create wealth. [48] The Buenos Aires of the 1920s was, by any measure, as cosmopolitan and as creative as New York at the time. Political folly can destroy even the strongest urban economies.

2

Creating Wealth

It Takes a City and Also Much More

This chapter asks a simple question, though the answer is not simple: how is wealth created? If cities are the answer—natural wellsprings of wealth—we need look no further. But we already know that this is not true, as Port au Prince so sadly reminds us. In search of an answer, we shall revisit the foundations of economic growth, a subject on which much has been written, asking, in turn, what role cities—urban agglomerations—play in economic growth.

The term *wealth* is used here in its more restrictive, purely economic meaning, a synonym for development, generally associated with indicators such as income or GDP[1] per capita. By the same token, the terms *growth, development,* and *progress* refer implicitly to sustained increases over time in real[2] income or GDP per capita. Finally, a precautionary note: the next pages may seem somewhat technical, for which I apologize, but unavoidable given the subject matter.

Agglomeration Economies and the (Incomplete) Creation of Wealth

Cities are "engines of growth," to employ an oft-used catchphrase that has become somewhat of a truism among urban scholars. The title of a recent book by Edward Glaeser nicely captures the essence of this confident view of cities : *Triumph of the City: How Our Greatest Invention Makes Us Richer, Smarter, Greener, Healthier, and Happier.*[3] Jane Jacobs, whom we met in the Introduction, laid the groundwork some thirty years earlier.[4] She argued that cities—and only cities—provided the necessary context for economic development. Development is all about improvisation and the continued introduction of new ideas and new products and that, Jacobs persuasively argued, is the very essence of cities."[5] It is in cities, through the diversity of interactions and experiences that only they can provide, that new and better ways of doing things will emerge. It is a powerful idea and one that cannot easily be disputed. It is impossible to imagine economic progress without cities.[6]

To understand why cities (agglomerations) are not enough, we need to return to the concept of *agglomeration economies*: the gains ("economies") firms derive from being close to other firms, workers, and customers.[7] Agglomeration economies are often divided into two classes: *localization economies* and *urbanization economies*. The former identify the gains firms derive from locating close to related industries (i.e., textile mills and clothing manufacturers), whereas the latter identify the advantages of locating in a large diverse metropolis. Localization economies are at the heart of "clusters," a concept popularized by Michael Porter, a business management guru,[8] whose writings focus on the advantages of building sufficient mass and expertise in specific fields. Urbanization economies are sometimes referred to as "Jacobs economies" in honor of Jane Jacobs. The focus of these economies is on the advantages of variety and diversity. Thus, an advertising agency may at various stages need to call on the talents of fashion designers, musicians, computer graphics programmers, actors, and the like, depending on the nature of the ad campaign.

The empirical evidence for agglomeration economies is irrefutable: urban agglomeration and higher densities are positively related to productivity, and so too are wages and income. Wages and incomes are almost always higher in cities than in the countryside and higher in larger than in smaller cities. In a word, cities allow firms to be more productive and larger cities, more so. Productivity, specifically with reference to labor, is at the core of economic progress. I shall spare the reader the technical problems surrounding the measurement of productivity. Productivity, simply put, refers to the (labor) time required to produce a given number of units of output. Whereas it might have taken four hundred hours of worktime to manufacture a car in 1920, today a car rolls off the assembly line in two days (seventy hours); this is a sixfold increase in productivity, without even factoring in the improved quality of the end product (the car). Higher productivity means higher profits and higher wages; that is, assuming that the fruits of higher productivity benefit both owners and workers.

The reasons behind the positive relationship between cities and productivity, *agglomeration economies* in other words, are manifold. Volumes have been written, including highly technical microeconomic treatises, to explain the mechanics of agglomeration economies.[9] The mechanics are not necessarily the same for all industries, nor are they necessarily the same over time. During the industrial era, the nexus between customers and suppliers, especially in manufacturing, was a major driver of agglomeration. It made sense for the auto industry to develop near the steel industry, reducing transport costs. Infrastructure costs could be distributed over multiple users (including railheads, quays, and waterworks), thereby reducing unit costs; the greater the number of users, the lower the unit costs. In today's knowledge economy, access to highly skilled labor and to information has become a powerful driver of agglomeration. Bankers need to be close to other bankers. The need for access to the right people, movers and shakers, increasingly favors hub cities that are well connected to other cities. New York is a prime example.

Whatever the mix of reasons, the great majority of industries in modern economies, unless directly tied to the exploitation of natural resources (agriculture, fishing, forestry, and mining), will find it more profitable to operate in cities. This begs the question of why some cities, despite their size and visible vibrancy, have failed to generate equivalent levels of productivity and income. Port au Prince and Buenos Aires are apt examples.

In other words, agglomeration economies tell only part of the story. Let us therefore take a closer look at the mechanics linking firms and the "economies" that urban agglomeration produces.

Figure 2.1 gives GDP per capita figures, a fairly good approximation of productivity per worker, for seven metropolitan areas around the world.[10] All but one (Vienna) have populations over ten million. Four are in the developed world and three in the developing world. These are all large cities, the economic powerhouses of their respective nations. In each case, GDP per capita for the city is significantly higher than that for its host nation. Buenos Aires's per capita GDP is some 50 percent above the Argentinian average, Mexico City's is about twice the Mexican average, and New York's is some 30 percent above the U.S. average.[11] We can safely assume that the differences in each case between the city and national figures are a fair approximation of the power of agglomeration economies. If such "economies" did not exist, Mexico City's workforce would have been only half as productive and its population correspondingly poorer. All of Mexico would have been worse off if Mexico City did not exist, and Argentina would be even poorer without Buenos Aires. In each nation, its greatest city is manifestly a source of wealth and prosperity.

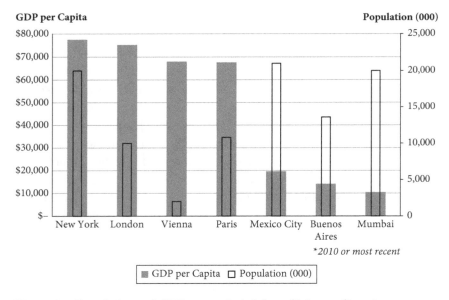

Figure 2.1 Population and GDP per capita*: Selected Metropolitan Areas.

Figure 2.1 also tells us that the GDPs generated by Mexico City and Buenos Aires are well below what their respective sizes would suggest, all else being equal as economists are wont to say. Mexico City with about the same population as New York only generates a quarter of New York's GDP. Stated differently, while the power of agglomeration allows Mexico City to double its productive potential compared to the national average, that potential is well below its full potential, taking New York as a yardstick. Seen from the other side of the looking glass, agglomeration, once everything else is stripped away, explains only a fraction of New York's higher productivity. Figure 2.1 reminds us that Vienna, with only a tenth of New York's population, generates a GDP per capita close to New York's. The meaning is clear: other things besides agglomeration are required to generate New York's or Vienna's levels of material welfare.

Unrealized Agglomeration Economies: A Mexican Story

The corollary of the above is that agglomeration economies are not working as they should in places like Mexico City. To understand why, we need to look beyond statistics at the real-world foundations of agglomeration economies. I now invite the reader to a journey to Puebla, Mexico's fourth largest city, with a metro population of three million. I taught there over a fifteen-year period in the Department of Economics of the *Universidad Autónoma de Puebla (UAP)*. Puebla is one of Mexico's most beautiful colonial cities, with an impressive architectural heritage, a lively downtown, and exceptional cuisine. In short, it is a generally pleasant place, certainly by Mexican standards. Although safety is a growing concern, Puebla is far from the worst case in Mexico, and by Third World standards, it is a reasonably well-managed city.

Yet, wages in Puebla are on average about a third those of Montreal. *Poblanos* (inhabitants of Puebla) do not work less than Montrealers; indeed, they generally work longer hours. Puebla houses the second largest Volkswagen factory outside Germany, with some fifteen thousand workers using state-of-the-art technology and receiving good wages by Mexican standards, but still less than half what comparable workers would earn in a Canadian or U.S. auto plant. Why should the same worker (age, education, technology, and experience) working in the same industry (let's call him Miguel) triple his wages if he were to move to Montreal? Why is Miguel three times less productive in Puebla than in Montreal, assuming wages are reasonable indicators of productivity?

In search of an answer, I and my colleagues initiated a research project, funded by the World Bank, in which we surveyed firms and workers in Puebla and three other Latin American cities, plus Montreal.[12] To ensure comparability, the surveys were limited to two industries present in all cites: apparel and food processing. Much of what follows is based on those surveys.

Interaction Thwarted—The Economic Costs of High Transportation Costs

Lower interaction costs, in both time and money, go to the very heart of agglomeration economies. The fundamental reason that drives (nonprimary, nonagricultural) firms to locate in cities is the need to be close to others.

The notion of interaction costs includes the full range of costs related to business travel, information exchange, and the delivery and reception of merchandise. The principal cost is often time. Time, as the old saying goes, is money. The successful businessman or businesswoman must get to customers first, obtain the best information first, acquire supplies faster, and turn around faster in response to changes in demand. Access to numerous customers allows the firm to realize scale economies, a component of agglomeration economies that lowers unit costs. Producing at full capacity allows a manufacturer of blue jeans, say, to distribute fixed costs such as rent, equipment, and other overhead over the entire line of production, reducing the unit cost of each pair of jeans produced.

Returning to Puebla, let us consider five common concerns in the daily life of a firm: deliveries; customer service; employee reliability; car and truck fleet maintenance; business meetings. Seventy-five percent of firms surveyed answered that deliveries arrived late at least once a week, double the percentage in Montreal, resulting in some cases in production slowdowns or stoppages. Faced with unreliable suppliers, the firm may choose to keep greater quantities of input in stock, but this again involves a cost.

The impact in turn on market reach is not difficult to guess. Unreliable deliveries, whether because of poor traffic management, deficient road maintenance, theft, or other unforeseen hindrances (i.e., police shakedowns), mean that the firms will have difficulty competing for outside markets, domestic or foreign, reducing the potential for scale economies. However, the consequences of poor transport conditions do not end there. Again, 75 percent of firms (in both Puebla and sister cities) answered that poor street and road maintenance increased fuel and vehicle maintenance costs. Almost all responded that employees arrived late for work at least once a week, impacting production runs.

The essence of cities, certainly large cities, is and remains people meeting people; business meetings are the glue that holds the modern city together as an economic unit. Half of the firms in Puebla (with similar percentages in San Salvador and San José) missed a business meeting at least one month due to poor traffic conditions and a significant proportion at least once a week (almost no cases in Montreal). The direct impact of missed business meetings on productivity is impossible to measure, but we can reasonably assume that it is non-negligible, defeating the very purpose of cities as economic engines.

Opportunities Lost: The Economic Cost of Lost Time

This begs the question of the value of time and how it is perceived in different societies. The possibility of circular causation cannot be dismissed. A society that values time will put a premium on punctuality and give greater importance to infrastructures that facilitates punctuality. Punctuality is not a Mexican virtue. Here, I cannot help but again slide into anecdotes. At about the time I was teaching in Puebla, I also visited Seoul, upon the invitation of a research institute. A schedule of meetings was carefully programmed. That was to be expected; after all, this was South Korea, a vaunted Asian Tiger. Less predictable was the almost obsessive attention given to time and punctuality. Meetings began and ended on the dot. One meeting that especially sticks in my mind was scheduled with a researcher in his office. Upon introduction into his office at the allotted time, and after a curt but courteous hello, the researcher placed his watch on his desk in full view and declared "you have ten minutes," and ten minutes it was to be. Seoul has one of the most efficient transit systems I know. Is there a link? I think so.

Back to Puebla. I have still not figured out how Poblanos calculate time. In my classes, I could repeat until I was blue in the face that class began precisely at such or such an hour, but to no avail. Students still wandered in ten, twenty, even thirty minutes late. Bad traffic was more often than not given as the reason. But which is the egg and which is the chicken: bad traffic or the (perceived) low value of time?

The devaluation of time, compounded by deficient transportation infrastructures, not only leads to time wasted but also makes forward planning difficult. I cannot count the hours lost waiting for meetings to begin or for participants to show up, nor can I forget the hours spent waiting for a plumber or electrician who never showed up. The undependability of scheduled meetings encourages short-termism and (as a logical reaction) contingency planning, Why plan ahead for an event if one cannot be sure it will even take place? Every Mexican has learned to have a plan B ready, just in case. Things do end up getting done, but the cost in terms of time used is higher than in "developed" societies.

Resources Wasted: The Economic Costs
of Insecurity

A determinant of the ability of people to interact is security. Public safety and transportation are linked. The ability of firms to hire and retain workers depends on workers being able to travel safely to and from work. In both industries surveyed, women constituted significant proportions of the workforce. Female workers in particular were understandably fearful of using collective transit (i.e., mini-buses) in the early hours or at night. Half of the firms in Puebla indicated that public safety directly affected their ability to retain female personnel. The result was workhours lost, higher worker turnover, and additional worker training costs. Depending on skill levels, average training time varied between twenty and fifty days. In short, every employee lost and replaced entailed between twenty and fifty days of paid workdays at less than full performance.

Insecurity can directly impact the ability of plants to function at full capacity. Over a third of firms indicated that the reluctance of employees to work beyond normal hours due to fear of travel caused them to limit production runs below what was operationally optimal. As a solution, several firms managed their own fleet of mini-buses to ferry female employees to and from work, a cost not all firms were able to bear.

At a more general level, fear of crime or of being molested can directly affect the ability of women to find work, a fact continually brought home to us during focus group meetings with female workers. Women were especially loath to work far from the home. Among the most frequent deficiencies cited was insufficient public lighting near bus stops and public spaces. Public lighting is a good example of a public service that is often taken for granted, certainly in the developed world, to which we might add walkable sidewalks and traffic lights that work. All these were missing in Port au Prince.

Police protection is normally the first public service that comes to mind when one thinks of public safety. Predictably, inadequate or incompetent police service was the most frequent reason given for criminal activity— theft, assaults, extortion, kidnappings—with kidnappings being the most common.[13] Whether in the apparel or food-processing industries, crime and the fear of crime impacted all facets of plant operations: merchandise handling; equipment maintenance; employee performance; financial transactions. Merchandise theft and disappearing equipment were a fact of life. Half of Puebla firms indicated assaults with a weapon in the last month in the neighborhood (a rarity in Montreal).

Providing security entailed direct out-of-pocket costs for firms. Security personnel accounted on average for 5 percent of the wage bill in Puebla compared to less than 1 percent in Montreal. No firm in Puebla would think of making deliveries with only one driver. Other direct costs cited were security devices (e.g., alarms, cameras), high theft and fire insurance premiums (if available at all), and, not least, side-payments to the police.

All the examples given above center on government failure; costs shifted to firms and individuals that prevent them from interacting productively in the city as they should. Crime and violence can also produce a crowding-out effect for public expenditures[14] where the resources of the state are shifted to policing—even if not effective—at the expense of other public services (especially education and health). This is doubly harmful when the state's ability to raise revenues is hampered by mistrust and mismanagement, the subject to which I now turn.

Energies Misdirected: The Economic Costs of Arbitrary Government

Less visible but no less essential for the proper functioning of cities is the proper application of laws, bylaws, regulations, and norms—in short, reasonably competent and honest national and local administrations.

Corruption and cronyism are not unique to developing nations. Most cities in North America have at one time or another known mayors and other city officials whose behavior was far from ethical (see Chapter 5). But let us return to Puebla. Mexico does not have a good track record when it comes to honesty in government. Not surprisingly, the virus starts at the top. Mexico only formally became a democracy in 2000 with the election of the first freely elected president who was not associated with the PRI (the Spanish acronym for the Party of Institutional Revolution), which had ruled Mexico since the 1920s. Prior to 2000, Mexico was basically a one-party state, elections were rigged, the press was cowed, and dissidence was suppressed. Those eighty years of one-party rule have left a legacy of arbitrary governance from which the nation has yet to free itself. Puebla (both the state and the municipality) is no exception. The majority of survey respondents, often plant managers or owners, felt themselves vulnerable to arbitrary administrative decisions relating to such matters as tax assessments, sanitary inspections, and building permits. No less costly was time lost obtaining various levels of approval and outright bribery, which is not unknown.

In addition to side-payments to politicians or functionaries, surviving in an arbitrary environment meant that many firms had extra personnel on their books as informal lobbyists. It helped, of course, if they were relatives of the mayor or governor. In some firms, extra personnel were hired with the simple function of standing in line—saving the firm's spot in the queue—during intolerably drawn-out administrative procedures, often returning day after day to the same office. This is a pastime I've experienced myself. Again, the principal cost is not necessarily financial, but time and the uncertainty bred by the arbitrary use of power by politicians and bureaucrats—time lost, which could have been put to more productive use or what economists call the opportunity cost of time.

In the Mexican winner-takes-all spoils system, each new administration means a complete turnover in personnel, which is an open invitation to cronyism. Each new mayor, governor, or department head is expected to dole out jobs to supporters, relatives, and friends, with little regard for competence. The change in personnel can mean that a project, previously approved, is now forgotten and that negotiations need to start anew. Such a climate hardly encourages long-range planning and investment.

An anecdote: At the request of the then mayor of Puebla, I and fellow researchers undertook a fairly ambitious project financed by the Canadian government involving the aerial photography and digitalization of the old town, with the objective of providing the city administration with a tool for identifying heritage sites, zones in need of repair, and other features not readily visible from the ground. The results were put on a computer disk. We were understandably proud of the end product, as were the city employees who had worked with us. An official event was organized with typical Mexican pomp and ceremony (local press in force, speeches, a mariachi band and all) in which the now famous disk was formally handed over to the mayor. With the project finished, I returned to Montreal in the knowledge of a job well done.

When I next returned to Puebla, the city administration had changed with a new mayor. I was invited to City Hall for a ceremonial dinner where I found myself seated at the same table with the new mayor. The heads of the planning (*urbanismo*) and heritage (*patrimonio*) departments, new appointees all, were seated nearby. I asked my table companions about our famous disk: had they found it useful? Silence! It was obvious that nobody had the slightest idea what I was talking about. The outgoing administration had cleared all the desks and drawers, leaving nothing behind. No one knew where the disk might be or, for that matter, showed any interest.

This spoils system—my little anecdote being but one example—is manifestly not conducive to good governance, a problem compounded in Mexico by the no-reelection rule (mayors and governors can only serve one term). This rule further discourages long-term initiatives and cumulative learning. Finally, the no-reelection rule is also an invitation to theft and/or grandiose expenditures, taking all you can and spend all you can while you can, with little thought for one's successor.

Education Foregone: The Human Capital Costs of Bad Governance

The arbitrary use of power at the local level almost always mirrors national governments, which are either unable or unwilling to enforce the rule of law. Mexico is no exception. The PRI quasi-dictatorship was simply the last in a long line of authoritarian regimes going back to colonial times, with only brief democratic interruptions.

The Mexican public education system provides a particularly troubling example of the costs of authoritarian rule and cronyism. The national teachers union, long a tool of the PRI for doling out patronage and corralling votes, has historically been more concerned with protecting its privileges than ensuring the education of pupils. The results are all too evident in international rankings of student performance. The Program for International Student Assessment (PISA), administered by the Organisation for Economic Co-operation and Development (OECD), tests the scholastic performance of fifteen-year-olds in sixty-five nations. Comparing Canada and Mexico, recently published assessments were as follows:[15] For Mathematics, Canada ranked twelfth after Finland (Mexico was fifty-third after Malaysia); Canada ranked tenth in science before Germany (Mexico was fifty-fifth); and for reading, Canada ranked seventh tied with Taiwan (Mexico was fifty-second).

Nor are universities, institutions I have first-hand experience with, immune from the effects of arbitrary governance. Rectors (principals) have powers and privileges that no American or Canadian university rector would dream of with little or no oversight. Independent audits of university finances are a rarity, and discretionary budgets are common. Rectors can (and do) directly transfer faculty from one department to another without interference. Pay scales are frequently based on one's position in the political hierarchy rather than on academic performance. The predictable outcome is a politically charged environment, faculty constantly jockeying for the rector's favor, and potentially talented teachers sucked into the administrative apparatus. The impact of this misuse of academic talent is, again, predictable. With but one exception—UNAM[16] in Mexico City—no Mexican university ranks in the top five hundred research universities.[17]

The impact of education (or, rather, the lack thereof) on the realization of agglomeration economies is double. Educated individuals will, one would expect, be more productive. More to the point, the same individual will be even more productive if he or she is near other educated individuals. The productivity gains flowing from concentrations of educated individuals are core components of agglomeration economies; provided, that is, that individuals are able to usefully interact, taking us back to the fundamental (economic) reason for cities.

Primary education, like safe streets, is what economists call a *public good* whose benefits are not purely private and whose provision must be paid for, at least in part, collectively. Cities we saw in our journey to Port au Prince are different from rural areas in their dependence on *public goods*: infrastructure, services, and proper regulatory environments that only the state can provide. Public goods share at least one of two attributes that make private provision unlikely or inefficient: (1) users cannot be excluded or individually charged; how, for example, would one charge for street lighting? Private firms may be contracted to produce the service (i.e., mount street lamps, pave streets) but will need to be paid with public funds; (2) the service has network features and/or is subject to scale economies. Power generators can be individually purchased but at considerably higher unit costs than from a power grid. Network services (such as water, power, and sewage) with implicit monopoly features may be provided by private firms and often are, but they require regulatory oversight if they are not to abuse their monopoly powers. In both instances, the provision of the service requires, as the reader will certainly have understood, a functioning state with corresponding taxing and regulatory capabilities, the subject to which we now turn.

Taxes and Services Foregone: The Economic
Costs of Informality

Anyone who has been to a developing city will have witnessed the vibrancy of local economic life, whether the open markets of Africa or the *ambulantes* (street vendors) and back-alley workshops of Latin America. Puebla is no exception. Much retailing and manufacturing functions outside of the formal economy (most probably the majority in Port au Prince). Entrepreneurship is a trait shared by all peoples. Once societies move beyond subsistence economies, markets will spontaneously emerge. Who can fail to admire the resilience and ingenuity of small businesspersons in apparently chaotic environments?

The temptation is strong to romanticize these courageous entrepreneurs who succeed in running their businesses despite a dysfunctional state. That is precisely the point. Informality is the counterpart of a deficient state that fails to provide the conditions for markets to function properly. Informal markets can only go so far in producing wealth. The collapse of the Soviet Union provides a useful reminder that efficient markets, conducive to the creation of wealth, do not miraculously spring forth unaided. They require a well-run state: an independent judiciary; nonpartisan regulatory agencies, plus myriad big and small public services. The catch, to state the obvious, is that such public goods require resources. Judges must be paid, as must law enforcement officers, firemen, teachers, and civil servants, which means *taxes*, whether on income (wages, profits, dividends, and so on), transactions (sales or value-added taxes), or real estate (property taxes).

Informality equals taxes not paid and public revenues foregone. We thus come full circle back to the need for trust and (perceived) honest government, which is woefully lacking in Port au Prince. Taxes diligently paid and good governance are two sides of the same coin. In Haiti, faced with corrupt and kleptocratic officials, tax avoidance becomes the norm, almost a duty, with corruption and tax evasion reinforcing each other. Why pay taxes if services are not provided? In the absence of a trustworthy state, "taxes" will also often be informal and be paid to corrupt officials, part of protection rackets run by representatives of the state. In Puebla not so long ago, a mayor was caught negotiating the issuance of permits and police protection with competing informal street vendor syndicates, with the proceeds split between his honor and the local police chief.

There is nothing romantic about informal markets. The lack of a strong legal framework (including property rights and binding contracts) makes it difficult to raise capital and undertake long-term projects. Again, outlaw elements will often step into the void providing a façade of governance, but they simply reinforce the general sense of vulnerability and mistrust of the state. Anyone who has worked with informal urban settlements will have witnessed the multiplicity of unauthorized arrangements that allow communities to survive despite their precarious legal status. In the best cases, often with the help of nongovernmental organizations (NGOs) with outside funding, informal communities will succeed in building tolerable environments. Without such outside help, many neighborhoods in Port au Prince would today lack schools, clinics, sanitation, and other basic services that the state fails to provide. However laudatory the work of many NGOs may be, the services they provide remain stopgap measures in the absence of a functioning state.

Mexico has a singularly poor record of collecting taxes: combined taxes at all levels of government account for some 23 percent of GDP compared to 32 percent in Canada.[18] Mexican public authorities are poorer on average than Canadian authorities not only because Mexico is poorer, but also because Mexican public authorities are proportionally less successful in collecting taxes. Most Mexican municipalities raise only very meager local revenues. Comparing what Poblano home owners paid in local property taxes, I calculated that they paid (proportionally) between three and five times less than I did in Montreal, even after factoring in differences in living standards. In Puebla as in other municipalities, the main sources of revenue are transfers from the state and federal government, in turn reinforcing their dependence on senior governments.

Property taxes require functioning land markets, which are taken for granted in most of the industrialized world. However, there is nothing natural about real estate markets. First, land titles need to be clearly defined and recognized. In Puebla, as in many developing cities, such titles remain nebulous because of competing claims and the indigenous legacy of communal land ownership, with the corresponding inability of the state to enforce an accepted regime of property rights and transfers. Transactions remain informal or semiformal, with property titles more or less recognized, depending on the degree of advancement of land regularization and accreditation.

Land titles are only part of the story. Properly valuing land for taxing purposes requires: (1) functioning real estate markets; (2) up-to-date cadasters; (3) reasonably trustworthy assessments of property values; and (4) perceived fair collection of property taxes. This is a tall order. Property taxes are low in Puebla not only because of the difficulty of valuing real estate but also because of a tradition, difficult to undo, of politically negotiated tax rates. Puebla is gradually putting a computerized cadaster and land valuation system into place, but the road ahead is long, fraught, as always, with politics.

Finally, informality not only deprives public authorities of needed revenues but also hampers entrepreneurship. In the absence of recognized land titles, local residents cannot use their property as collateral for business start-ups or other productive uses. The absence of secure land titles makes it difficult to develop functioning mortgage markets. The impact in turn on the Mexican financial sector is not difficult to understand. This is one reason why Mexico does not have world-class banks and why Mexico City is not a global financial center. Mexico's traditionally high interest rates, a result both of weak macroeconomic management and higher perceived business risk, impose an additional cost on firms.

* * *

The message from this brief Mexican journey is simple. It is the cumulative impact of (good/ bad) governance at all levels—starting at the top—that determines the productive potential of cities; that is, above what pure agglomeration economies would predict.

Revisiting the Foundations of Economic Growth

We have still left our opening question hanging: what are the ultimate drivers of economic development; what sets the process in motion? And how does agglomeration fit into the picture? Our Mexican journey provided a first answer: the public goods that allow cities to be productive are very demanding, conditional on institutions that require high levels of social organization. That answer only tells part of the story; it allows us to understand differences at a given moment in time (the reader may wish to return to Figure 2.1) but not why economies grow (or fail to do so).

History provides a clue. Going back in time, we see that cities—even great cities—were not necessarily harbingers of economic growth. Athens—the unparalleled center of learning of the ancient world—did not trigger an industrial revolution; nor did the great cities of ancient China. The Alexandria and the Rome of antiquity housed populations of one million, impressive technological achievements for the time; but, again, neither sparked an economic revolution. These were lively cities full of busy markets, squares, and bustling streets. The world was never to see such cities again for more than a thousand years. Our planet remained overwhelming rural—over 90 percent of the population toiling on the land—until well into the 19th century. Then, suddenly the Industrial Revolution erupted and cities exploded. This begs the question: what was missing before?

A Brief Journey Back to the Industrial Revolution

This is not the place to go into a long treatise on the roots of economic growth or why the Industrial Revolution took off in Great Britain in the 1700s. The number of books and articles on the subject could fill several libraries.[19] Despite the diversity of sources, a large measure of agreement exists among students of economic growth. In the simplest terms, long-term growth in real income or product per capita is always dependent on ongoing technological progress and ensuing productivity gains per worker. Sustained economic growth means constant, repeated, technological change and new ways of doing things. Use of the word *revolution* by economic historians is no accident.

The story of the Industrial Revolution has been told many times.[20] The problem is getting from A to B. Societies do no change overnight. Numerous changes occurred at about the same time in mid-18th century England, which until then had been an overwhelmingly rural society. Among the most significant changes was the enclosure (privatization in today's vocabulary) of common village fields into individual landholdings, followed by the introduction of improved agricultural techniques: most notably, better irrigation; new crop rotation methods; more effective insect control; sturdier farm implements made out of new metals The social consequences were not always pleasant, often throwing poorer laborers off the land. However, in terms of cold economics, the growth in agricultural productivity freed workers to move to other, more productive sectors, allowing the British economy to produce more goods and services (with the same quantity of labor).

The enclosures in 18th-century England of common fields provide a useful reminder that institutional change is often a necessary forerunner of technological change. Long-term productivity growth is often the outcome of an accumulation of small improvements, but which presupposes the presence of an entrepreneurial class and labor force receptive to change and willing to learn.[21] The values transmitted by society need to send the right signals. Innovation does not occur in a vacuum.

Other innovations were to follow. Until the mid-1700s, cloth manufacture was generally done in the home. The sorting, cleaning, combing, and dyeing of wool and spinning into thread, then the weaving into cloth, was a long, tedious process and extremely inefficient. All this changed with the arrival, among other new technologies, of John Kay's flying shuttle, enabling one weaver to do the work of two; Lewis Paul's roller spinner, making spinning more efficient; and James Hargreaves's spinning jenny, allowing the operator to simultaneously spin dozens of threads.[22] By the 1790s, twenty thousand new spinning jennies were employed across England, resulting in the appearance of factories, a new presence. Some of these factories employed hundreds of workers, taking thousands of men and women (and often children) out of the home.

The impetus behind these new technologies, many of which required prior knowledge of the principles of physics, was an institutional legacy that placed a high value on education and learning, especially science and scientific inquiry. That, arguably, was the most revolutionary change of all. Ultimately, the Industrial Revolution had its roots in the great thinkers of the European Renaissance (e.g., Galileo, Bacon, and Da Vinci) who challenged established religion and superstition. Economic development, the reader will have guessed by now, is not only about economics. Economic growth—with all the good and ill it can bring—will often mean head-on collisions with established beliefs and customary ways of doing things. Some societies have found the transition easier than others.

If the innovations that allowed firms to produce more efficiently were to bear fruit, access to markets was a parallel condition. Trade and the specialization and scale economies it brings have been sources of wealth since the beginning of time. England in the 1700s provided a fairly large politically unified market with uniform norms, institutions, absence of trade barriers, a fairly advanced (and comparatively safe) internal transport system and, especially, an absence of war. It is perhaps these last two attributes—a unified trade area and political stability—that best explain why England, not Holland, would become the cradle of the Industrial Revolution, even though Holland at the time was more urbanized, and Amsterdam, Rotterdam, and other Dutch merchant cities were no less sophisticated and cosmopolitan (and perhaps more so) than the cities of England.

A Word on Culture

Institutions ultimately mirror national cultures. Looking around the globe at the economic success (or failure) of different societies, we find it impossible to ignore the weight of values and beliefs, often shaped by religion. In his now classic work, *The Protestant Ethic and the Spirit of Capitalism*,[23] the German sociologist Max Weber pointed to the Protestant Reformation of post–1500 Europe as the necessary forerunner of the Industrial Revolution. Weber argued that the emphasis this new religion placed on individual achievement—including material achievement—as the road to salvation opened the door to a cultural revolution, laying the groundwork for the economic revolution to follow. Whatever one may think of Weber's thesis, the Industrial Revolution took off in Protestant England and Presbyterian Scotland and rapidly spread to Western European nations with Protestant majorities or nations heavily influenced by the Reformation.[24]

The most economically successful nations (that is, outside Western Europe and its offshoots), all share a common cultural heritage: Japan, South Korea, Taiwan, Singapore, and China are all children, to various degrees, of a mixture of Buddhism and Confucianism. I do not know enough about either philosophical strand to intelligently comment on their value systems. Rather, let me tell another anecdote from my visits to South Korea. A Korean colleague and I were in a cemetery in Seoul. I commented on the numerous families piously standing in front of tombstones, seemingly reporting—or so it looked to me—to the deceased ancestor. They were indeed "reporting" to the deceased ancestor, my colleague confirmed, each son or daughter recounting with appropriate filial respect their achievements over the bygone year. Woe to the son or daughter who had failed to meet his (or her) objectives! I'm sure that I was not the only one to see an analogy with a CEO presenting his or her annual report to the board of directors. Let me change continents and go back to my early youth in

New York. On our annual family visits to Jewish friends and relatives, the matron invariably greeted me with (the exact wording depending on the year): "what were your grades this year; what colleges did you applied to; were you accepted?" The values societies transmit to their young are never neutral.

I do not wish to overplay the culture variable, if only to avoid being accused of simplistic stereotyping. There are limits to purely cultural explanations of economic development. If culture alone were sufficient to explain differences in wealth, then North Korea would be rich. Political systems also matter.

The takeaway from this short foray into the economics of growth should by now be evident: sustained increases in real income and wealth necessarily mean constant technological and social change, which in turn is contingent on the presence of solid political institutions. But with that we have still not fully answered the second part of our second question: what is the role of cities (agglomeration) in economic growth?

Cities: Mothers or Children of Economic Growth?

No nation has grown rich without also urbanizing. The root causes of urbanization—the shift of populations from the country to city—are well understood. They are no different today than they were at the time of the Industrial Revolution: rising productivity in agriculture drives workers off the land. Where once it took a farmer twenty days of work to produce one bushel of wheat, it now takes one day. This is a twentyfold increase in productivity—close to what actually happened in much of the Western world during the 19th and 20th centuries, not only in agriculture but in other industries as well.[25] The consequences of rising productivity (and thus also incomes) for the growth of cities brings us to one of the basic laws of economics, called Engel's law: households spend proportionally less on food as incomes rise. The average American and Canadian household today spends less than 10 percent of its income on food compared to over 50 percent in the mid-19th century. As societies grow richer, relative demand for foodstuffs will fall; at the same time, less and less labor is needed to produce the same quantity of food. The outcome is as predictable as it is inevitable: demand for agricultural labor will fall. The lot of those first

agricultural laborers thrown off the land in 17th-century England has repeated itself since a thousand times over and continues to do so in developing nations today.

This is where agglomeration economies come back into their own. As
incomes rise, demand will shift to nonprimary goods and services. For production not tied to the land, firms will find it more profitable to locate close
to other firms—in urban agglomerations—for all the reasons explained
earlier. Jobs will shift to cities, and people will inevitably follow. Richer nations will have higher shares of their population in cities. The positive statistical relationship between GDP per capita and urbanization levels is well
documented. Cities today account for over 80 percent of the population
in the United States, Japan, and Western European and other developed
nations, compared to less than 20 percent in many sub-Saharan African
nations.

The positive relationship between urbanization levels and GDP (or income) per capita might lead the observer to conclude that the first causes the
second. But correlation is not causation. The direction of causation, the evidence suggests, is in the opposite direction. There is little evidence that initial higher levels of urbanization produce subsequent higher rates of income
or GDP growth.[26] Indeed, nations with initially lower levels of urbanization
will tend to see incomes grow faster as they catch up with richer nations.

How then should we view the relationship between economic growth and
the growth of cities? Urbanization—the shift to cities *in general*—is essentially an adjustment mechanism by which firms, workers, and households
respond to changes in productivity and in demand. This is no different from
the continuing movement of workers from one industry to another. The
only difference—a major one, admittedly—is that the shift from land to city
requires workers to physically move from one place to another. The productivity gains thus realized are, in the language of economics, the expression
of a more efficient allocation of resources—workers in this case—between
land and city.[27] These productivity gains are "static," in the language of economics, in that they do not imply changes in technology. The observed
gains, a measure in principle of the impact of agglomeration economies,
tell us that—given current technologies—labor is more productive (so
allocated) than previously on the land.[28]

The preceding analysis, though somewhat abstract, conveys an essential message: The growth of cities in the modern era is as much a reaction

to change as a trigger of change. The ultimate sources of change, as I have argued, are rooted in the institutions (broadly defined) of society at large and defy simple explanations. That said; the existence of feedback effects and circular causation cannot be excluded. The growth of the population in cities may in certain cases further fuel technological change and ensuing increases in productivity; but this is not the same as a necessary causal relationship between cities (their growth) and innovation. The evidence suggests that cities alone are not enough. Simply put, the agglomeration of people and firms is not a sufficient condition to trigger technological progress and sustained increases in productivity.

What Jane Jacobs Missed

This conclusion, the reader will have surmised, collides with the Jane Jacobs view of cities as the drivers of technological change and innovation. Let us thus take a closer look at the necessary conditions for *productive* innovation, and I emphasize "productive" for a reason. The core of Jacobs's prime mover thesis is that cities "and nothing else" provide the context for *improvisation*, the trigger, as Jacobs puts it, that sparks economic development. As she explains:

> If one wanted to define economic development by a single word that word would be "improvisation. . . . development is a process of continually improvising in a context that makes injecting improvisations into everyday life feasible. Cities in volatile trade with one another create that context. Nothing else does. . . .[29]

I shall take the liberty of using improvisation as a synonym for innovation. Thus reformulated, Jacobs's first sentence is not wrong: few would argue with the idea that innovation is an essential step on the road to economic growth. Also, few would argue with the notion that cities are natural venues for the circulation of ideas, facilitating innovation. This, however, leaves unanswered the question of why some cities are visibly not generating the innovations needed for economic growth. Let us then be more precise and add the adjective "productive" to innovation, innovation that leads to sustained increases in worker productivity.

No one is inherently more creative than another; innovation and creativity are inherent traits of the human species. Even the most primitive societies have produced beautiful works of art. One does not need to be an anthropologist to recognize the inventiveness of many tribal societies. The principal scarce resources in human existence have always been time and energy (health). This is as true for tribal societies as for city dwellers. The question then becomes: where will city dwellers direct their time and creative energy? The priories will not necessarily be the same everywhere. The inhabitants of dysfunctional cities (think of Port au Prince) may be highly innovative—they have to be—but their energy will be channeled into solving the problems of everyday existence, problems that should not be problems at all. This does not leave much time, if any, for "productive" innovations. Jacobs's error, as many others, is the implicit assumption that city dwellers live in conditions that allow them the time and provide them the knowledge base and incentives to improvise "productively." The evidence tells us that this is not universally the case.

Of course, entrepreneurs in cities "improvise and innovate"; the great majority probably do because innovation is inherent in the very act of running a profitable business. But, we may ask, innovate to what end? Tax evasion can be very innovative. No matter how technically innovative our entrepreneur is, his or her creative talents will be misdirected to lobbying and bribing officials if, say, the government plans to impose punitive import or export taxes, so that his or her prospective product will never be produced. I ask the reader to simply revisit the list of obstacles that can prevent cities from functioning properly to understand why potential entrepreneurs will be applying their innovative talents to endeavors of questionable productive value. An institutional environment that promotes "productive" improvisation requires not only a functioning city, but also legal instruments such as copyrights, patents, and incorporation rules that protect (and reward) innovators, not to mention a value system that prizes learning and enterprise.

The question, however, remains: which is it—do cities or the values of the wider society provide the *initial* jolt that allows productive innovations to take off? Trying to unravel the two may be impossible. The problem from a research perspective is that Jacobs's thesis which puts cities first is impossible to test. It can neither be verified nor refuted scientifically. We cannot run a laboratory test through which we invent a society without cities but with the appropriate institutions, and then observe whether it spawns cities and wealth or, alternatively, a society with poor institutions but with cities, and then observe if it subsequently spawns an era of innovation and development. We have already seen that the great cities of antiquity were not sufficient to trigger sustained eras of productive innovation. But perhaps the modern era is different?

A Short Excursion to Tel Aviv.

Israel—the post–1900 Jewish settlement of Palestine and subsequent new state—provides an almost perfect natural laboratory in the modern era for testing the first scenario: a society with "good" institutions but no city.

Palestine at the turn of the 20th century, then an Ottoman province, was overwhelmingly rural and Arab. Tel Aviv did not yet exist: in the words of one commentator, it was "a sand dune."[30] Tel Aviv was founded in 1910 next to the Arab city of Jaffa. The first waves of Jewish settlers, most of whom came from Central and Eastern Europe, were on the whole well educated but had no automatic bias in favor of cities. Indeed, early Zionism extoled the virtues of rural life and self-reliance, with many of the first arrivals settling in Kibbutzim (collective farms).

Let us now do a fast forward to today. Political events and wars aside, successive waves of settlers and their offspring have spawned a technologically advanced and prosperous society. Israel today has a GDP per capita comparable to that of South Korea, and Tel Aviv is now a metropolis of some four million inhabitants. We can reasonably conclude that Jewish Israeli society gave birth to Tel Aviv and not the other way around. The institutional preconditions for the creation of a prosperous society were embedded, so to speak, in the cultural baggage those early settlers and their offspring brought to their new homeland. The creation of a great metropolis like Tel Aviv was a necessary parallel condition for that cultural baggage to fully bear fruit, that is, for the realization of agglomeration economies, but it is difficult to argue that the city came first.

The Social (Non-Jacobian) Roots of Innovation

The city life Jane Jacobs extolls points to cities like New York, Paris, and Toronto, not to small-town America. The implied message, with its emphasis on the virtues of diversity, is not only that "only" cities provide the necessary context for productive innovation, but also that the cities in question are necessarily big. Jane Jacobs moved in 1968 from the quintessentially mixed urban neighborhood of New York's Greenwich Village to Toronto's Annex, a similarly cosmopolitan neighborhood. Although my tastes are not all that different from those of Jacobs, I cannot help but feel that there is something elitist about the jump from big city life to innovation—as if *only* big cities provide the environments in which intelligent, innovative, and creative pursuits are possible.

This is not the place for a treatise on the definition and origins of innovation, a concept about which much has been written. The focus here is on the relationship with city size. I shall limit my use of the term *innovation* to its accepted technical definition: "the introduction of new methods, processes or products that raise worker productivity and thus foster income growth."[31] The implicit postulate behind urbanization or Jacobs economies, discussed earlier, is that diversity promotes higher productivity and, ultimately, growth. However, we already know that the statistical evidence for a positive relationship between urban size and growth is lacking. How then are we to reconcile this with the presumed innovation-inducing virtues of big cities?

The first answer is the non-exclusive impact of many innovations; that is, their productivity and growth-inducing effects are not limited to the place where they first originated. Once a new innovation becomes known—the Internet is a prime example—its use will spread. More to the point, the city that first adopted the innovation will not necessarily be its prime beneficiary. The Internet again is an apt example, which was initially developed in laboratories in California (UCLA and Stanford) in the 1950s. Its primary beneficiaries today are places like New York and London, centers of finance and entertainment. Going back a century, Alexander Graham Bell, inventor of the telephone,[32] made the first long-distance call (to Paris) from his hometown of Brantford, a small town in Ontario, Canada. It is difficult to argue that the telephone primarily benefited Brantford. The Bell Telephone Company would eventually be incorporated in the 1870s in Boston, Massachusetts. In short, there is no necessary relationship between the origins of an innovation and its ultimate beneficiaries.

The second answer involves the absence of a proven relationship between the size of cities and innovation, an object of continuing debate among scholars.[33] If patents are used as an indicator of innovation, the results for the United States and Europe point to a positive relationship, with patents proportionately more frequent in larger cities.[34] However, the use of patents as an indicator is problematic for a number of reasons, including the over-representation of larger firms and major product innovations. The evidence also suggests that new industries tend to emerge first in larger cities. This is referred to as the nursery city hypothesis: new industries first appear in big cities and then move on to smaller cities as production processes become more standardized.[35] There is also survey evidence that product and process innovation occurs in all types of milieus. Richard Shearmur, a Canadian economic geographer, cites several studies that point to the absence of a systematic relationship between innovation and location.[36] Reporting the results of a study of small and medium-sized manufacturing firms in New York State, Shearmur found that these firms were as likely to innovate in rural as in urban areas.[37]

Another part of the riddle is the implicit postulate that innovation nec-essarily entails frequent dealings with a large range of actors outside the firm. This may well be the case for certain types of innovations but does not automatically hold for all types. Specialized cities may be hotbeds of in-novation for particular industries; Basel, Switzerland, for pharmaceuticals and Akron, Ohio, for rubber are two examples. A more telling example is the Swatch, which was invented and marketed in the 1980s in reaction to the invasion of Japanese quartz watches, which threatened to destroy the age-old Swiss watch industry. The Swatch was developed in and around the small town of Biel (population: fifty thousand) in the Swiss Jura region where the Swatch group maintains its headquarters to this day.

Some innovators may shirk dense and diverse environments. It is doubtful that those valiant innovators in the Swiss Jura wanted their Japanese competitors (or any other competitors) nearby while developing the Swatch. The lone inventor experimenting in his or her backyard garage is part of North American lore. The Ski-Doo, the first commercial snow-mobile, was the brainchild of Joseph-Armand Bombardier who began experimenting with the idea of a snowmobile in the 1930s in his garage in the small Quebec town of Valcourt (population: two thousand). There was a need in rural Quebec for a versatile cross-country vehicle in the winter. Like Alexander Graham Bell, Bombardier not only had a knack for me-chanics but was also an astute businessman. His company would go on to become a multinational corporation, a major player in the field of aero-space, high-speed trains, subways, and other transportation equipment. It still maintains plants in Valcourt as well as a museum honoring its founder, but its chief engineering division and head office have moved to Montreal. Therein lies a lesson: cities of different sizes fulfill different roles in the economic development game; which leads us into the closing section of this chapter.

Why We Need Big and Small Cities

Most readers probably have never heard of Drummondville, Quebec, a small city located 100 kilometers east of Montreal. Not so long ago, Drummondville was the archetypical example of a one-industry town. Taking the year 1971 as our benchmark (population: fifty thousand), we find that clothing and textiles accounted for some 90 percent of the city's economic base, as measured by employment (i.e., industries whose products are exported outside the region[38]). As recently as 1990, employment in the same industries still represented some 70 percent of its economic base. Drummondville's industries were built on two advantages: location and relative costs. Its proximity to Montreal facilitated input–output relations with Montreal's apparel industry, while the proximity of the port of Montreal reduced shipping costs for imported cotton. Wages were on average a quarter below those in Montreal, providing an essential advantage for an industry where wages are the principal cost item. But the textile and garments industries were destined to decline. Like the situation in so many other small towns, Drummondville's textile and clothing industries were devastated by competition from low-wage developing nations as trade opened up, culminating in the abrogation in 2005 of the so-called Multi-Fiber Agreement. Three thousand textile and clothing jobs disappeared, producing a veritable bombshell for a town its size.

Today, some three decades years later, Drummondville is the very model of a diversified local economy with a wide range of manufacturing industries, registering high job growth and low unemployment. Drummondville's population has doubled, now approaching the one hundred thousand mark. Its economic base is still almost exclusively in manufacturing; but the loss in textiles and clothing was more than compensated by job growth in industries such as machinery and metal products, food processing, wood and paper products, and electronic equipment. All these industries are what might be called midtech industries that require a competent and diligent labor force, competitive wages, space (i.e., well-serviced industrial parks), and access to road and rail. All this Drummondville could offer.

However, there is more to the story than location and low wages. Many of the new plants were imports, but many, too, were homegrown. Armand Bombardier, whom we met earlier, was not an exception. Cascades, a manufacturer of paper products, was founded by the Lemaire brothers from the neighboring village of Kinsley Falls. Cascades began as a classic paper mill but has since grown to become an international player with eleven thousand employees worldwide and plants across Europe and North America specializing in the recovery of recyclable products and the manufacture of green packaging products and tissue paper. The Lemaire brothers were among the first in the 1960s to introduce production processes using 100 percent recycled fibers. The company has since acquired a reputation as an innovator in the application of green technologies. The Lemaire brothers also innovated in management practices, including profit-sharing plans. The company has acquired a reputation for excellent labor relations and correspondingly high labor productivity. Like Bombardier's company, the Lemaire company's ascent to multinational status has meant a move up the urban ladder. Although its head office is formally listed as being in neighboring Kinsley Falls, its principal administrative offices are located on appropriately fashionable Sherbrooke Street West, Montreal.

Most manufacturing in Drummondville is in midtech niche products we rarely think of but need no less to be produced somewhere. Three homegrown examples are Airex Inc. (which designs and manufactures dust collection and industrial ventilation systems); Jaro Inc. (which manufactures telephone booths); and Stelinex Inc. (which manufactures custom-made stainless steel wires). The town is also home to several foreign-owned plants. German-owned Siemens Corporation (electronics) established a plant in Drummondville in the 1980s, specializing in the manufacture of electric distribution panels and security plugs. The French-owned building-materials giant SOPREMA recently established its largest North American plant in Drummondville to manufacture polyisocyanurate insulation boards. Both of these plants are located in Drummondville, but their Canadian administrative offices and distribution facilities are located in the greater Montreal area.

The lesson from Drummondville is that the efficient realization of the full production process from conception and manufacture to marketing requires different locations with different attributes, which is why small cities exist.[39] Some things are more efficiently done in smaller places. Why assemble telephone booths or fabricate bathroom tissues in a big city where labor and real estate costs are higher, not to mention constant traffic congestion, when both can be produced more cheaply in a smaller city? The nation as a whole gains if these two goods are produced outside big cities. Going back to the very roots of innovation, we need to distinguish between the origins of the initial spark (idea, invention, etc.), which need not necessarily have occurred in a big city or in any size city for that matter, and the material realization of the innovation as a marketable good or service, which will necessarily require an urban setting.

In this chapter, we have seen that cities *in general* will grow as nations grow richer; that is, as they undergo urbanization. That phase is now over in rich nations; the shift to cities is largely complete. Even so, the pieces on the national chessboard will continue to move. Each new technology means that some cities will gain a new advantage and others will lose. Our valiant manufacturer of telephone booths in Drummondville will probably soon need to find a new niche as smart phones replace landlines. On the other hand, consumers will most likely always need toilet paper, which is good news for Cascades.

* * *

We have come full circle from the great cities of antiquity to small-town Quebec. How should we now view the role of cities in economic growth? Before the advent of the Industrial Revolution, a prominent school of thought known as Physiocracy argued that the wealth of nations was derived from the land and from agriculture. This was not an unreasonable thesis since the vast majority of productive activity took place in rural areas. But today, agriculture, farming, and fishing account for less than 3 percent of employment in most wealthy nations. Almost all production today takes place in cities—cities of all sizes. Saying that cities create wealth is today analogous to saying that the economy creates wealth.

In the end, extolling the economic virtues of agglomeration (cities *in general*) is not very helpful in understanding the creation of wealth; it is no more useful than the views of those early Physiocrats on the virtues of land. The question is not whether agglomeration creates wealth (it can do so), but rather to ensure that it does, which is another way of saying that the creation of wealth *in* cities is more than only a city story. In the next chapter, we return to the industrialized world, starting with the United States. We examine how national or state policies have shaped cities, focusing on cities as social constructs where people need to interact both productively and peacefully, at least reasonably so, if cities are to create wealth and a livable environment for the majority.

3

Shaping Cities and the Social Relationships Within Them

Cars, Boundaries, and the Provision of People Services

In the previous chapter, we examined the institutions that allowed cities to become places where wealth *could* be created. We discovered that those institutions are very demanding and are at the root of the underperformance of all too many developing cities. We have said little so far about the shape of cities (urban form and urban structure, the technical terms used by economic geographers) or the conditions that allow (or do not allow) city dwellers to live together in reasonable peace and harmony. Here we return to the developed world.

National Governments Shape Cities

American cities are as a rule less dense and more sprawled than comparable cities elsewhere. That outcome is no accident, but rather the result of a particular mix of institutions and policies. It is to be expected that cities in older developed nations will be more compact, with correspondingly well-developed public transit systems. Cities like Paris and Vienna began to grow well before the advent of the automobile. Vienna attained its current population size before the first cars appeared. Its narrow inner-city streets and pedestrian squares are the outcome of a city where walking and horse carriages were the principal means of locomotion. History also explains why East Coast American cities like New York and Boston and other earlier settled cities are denser with stronger centers than cities that developed later. Los Angeles and Houston are examples of cities built around the car.

However, late settlement cannot alone explain the difference. American cities are also, on average, more car-dependent than Australian and Canadian cities. Sydney and Melbourne, like Canada's three largest metropolitan areas (Vancouver, Toronto, and Montreal) all have well-developed transit systems with strong downtowns—which begs the question: why do American urbanites consume on average more land and use proportionally less public transit? Are Americans inherently more in love with cars than other people; is love of the automobile a peculiarly American trait, so to speak? My experience living in France is that the average Frenchman is no less attached to his car than the average American, and perhaps even more so. For an answer, we need to look elsewhere.

Killing Public Transit: Step 1

The answer most economists give is simple: the "incentive system" in the United States encourages people to drive and to consume urban land. This is shorthand for the myriad rules and price mechanisms that incite people to do one thing rather than another. Let's start with the consumption of urban land. U.S. tax law allows new homeowners to deduct the interest on their mortgage. The home mortgage interest deduction[1] has been in place for several decades and is probably impossible to repeal, understandably popular with homeowners. Besides depriving the U.S. Treasury of a pretty penny (estimates put the annual revenue foregone in the hundreds of billions), the deduction constitutes an explicit subsidy to the middle and upper class, who are more likely to be homeowners. More to the point, the deduction is an incentive to purchase bigger houses and to consume correspondingly more land. By the same token, the deduction favors suburban expansion over central city consolidation. In a word, Americans are being subsidized to consume more space.[2]

Let us now turn to the incentives to use a car to commute to work. In June 1956, President Dwight D. Eisenhower signed the Federal-Aid Highway Act, creating the Interstate Highway System. The federal government shouldered about 90 percent of the capital costs of new highways. That in itself is not particularly noteworthy. Other nations have nationally funded highway systems. The system launched by President Eisenhower, however, differs from that in other nations in three respects. First, it provided no equivalent funding for public transit, precisely at the moment in time (the 1950s and 1960s) when mass transit was coming under threat. Unlike the United States, most European nations invested predominantly in rail and urban transit in the years following World War II, in part to repair the damages of war.

Second, federal highways were to be free—there would be no tolls—the highways were appropriately called freeways in California. Tolls have since been introduced in some parts of the system, but American highways remain largely toll free, notably for highways *within* urban areas.

Which brings me to a third (and major) attribute that sets the American system apart: Highways became major modes (sometimes the dominant mode) of *intra*-urban transport, crisscrossing city centers and becoming the favored mode of transport for commutes between home and place of work. Limited-access divided highways rarely penetrate the city center in European cities.[3] It is impossible to cross or to enter central Vienna without using city streets. A Viennese suburbanite cannot use a highway to go downtown. Divided highways are essentially seen as a means of travel *between* cities—say between Paris and Lyon, not within cities. Paris, like many European cities, has its outer-ring artery (*la périphérique*) that allows drivers to circumvent the city proper, but the driver cannot continue into the city without descending into its winding streets and boulevards.

I do not know what motivated American urban planners to adopt a philosophy of *intra*-urban rather than *inter*-urban highway construction, the former all too often becoming unsightly elevated eyesores cutting across old neighborhoods. Some blame must go to the powerful automobile lobby (the big three: General Motors, Ford, and Chrysler), which had come to dominate the American industrial landscape. The automobile industry was at the heart of America's postwar industrial revival. Anything that encouraged consumer demand for automobiles was good for the economy. Canada was not immune to similar pressures; several intra-urban highways were built in Canadian cities, notably the Gardiner Expressway in Toronto and l'*Autoroute métropolitaine* in Montreal, the latter part of the federally funded Trans-Canada highway system. However, these were exceptions rather than the rule. Vancouver never allowed a highway to penetrate its central core, reflecting Vancouver's environmental consciousness long before the environment became a fashionable issue. No Canadian city, and certainly no European city, comes close to reproducing the cobweb of divided highways that crisscross urban areas like Dallas, Houston, and Los Angeles, where they remain the dominant mode for high-speed intrametropolitan travel.

The incentives to use one's car to commute do not end there. Gas (petrol) prices at the pump vary across nations, the basic reason for the difference being not the cost of extraction or production, but rather taxes. Precise price differences differ across jurisdictions (states, cities, etc.) and fluctuate over time, but average gas prices in American cities are as a rule about half those in Western Europe, and sometimes even lower, and are generally 10 to 20 percent below the price in Canada. In some European nations, taxes account for 75 percent of the pump price, about a third in Canada, but below 20 percent in most U.S. jurisdictions. In short, low gas taxes and largely "free" federally funded intra-urban highways, taken together, constitute a powerful incentive to *use* one's car over other modes. The emphasis here is on *use*, not ownership; Canadians, Australians, and Europeans are all as prone to own cars as Americans; they just use them less to commute.

I am not against cars. Our family car allows my family freedom of movement that would be impossible otherwise, and I am certainly not about to give up my car. However, I commute to work using public transit. Even in Montreal, however, the majority of workers commute by car, except those who work in the central business district (CBD). Montreal is not all that different from many other cities. The principal reason, besides the absence of satisfactory alternatives (especially in the more outlying suburbs), is that drivers in Montreal are not paying the "true" price (to society) of their choice. Roads, boulevards, and streets are "free," as in almost all cities. Street pricing and tolls are the exception not only because of technical limitations (this will be less and less true in the future), but also because road-pricing is a hard sell, naturally unpopular with urban electorates. Elementary economics tells us that when something is free, it risks being overconsumed. This is no less true for highways, roads, and streets, which is the principal reason traffic congestion remains a worldwide problem. In almost all nations, the use of cars is subsidized (underpriced), the bill paid by society as a whole.

Killing Public Transit—Step 2

The United States stands out in the size of the subsidy, a massive transfer to urban American drivers. Putting aside the environmental consequences of higher CO^2 emissions, the most consequential long-term effect of underpricing car use following World War II was the destruction of public transit—almost total in some places—which brings me to the subject of modal split: the competition between transport modes—bus, subway, car, bicycle, walking, and so on. The use of one mode necessarily excludes the use of others; one cannot both drive to work and take the bus. Perhaps early urban planners in cities like Los Angeles and Dallas did not fully comprehend this principle: by building *free*ways, keeping fuel prices low, as well as other incentives for car use (i.e., free or cheap parking spaces), they were directly undermining transit services. Until the mid-20th century, transit services—streetcars, trolleybuses, rail, and buses—were highly profitable undertakings, often owned by private companies. In 1930, Los Angeles's big bus conglomerate carried some twenty-nine million riders a year.[4] Demand was assured since the majority of the population did not (as yet) own a car and were captive clienteles. the most profitable routes highly coveted by transport providers (bus and tram line owners). The allocation of routes by municipal authorities was often an object of political horse-trading and a potential source of graft. Regrettably, this is still the case in most cities of the developing world where car use remains beyond the means of the majority. The most lucrative bus and mini-bus routes in Puebla, for example, remain highly sought-after political prizes.

With the arrival of the automobile, almost everywhere, public transit ridership and profitability plummeted as car ownership grew. Every new driver was a fare lost. The switch to car use set in motion a self-reinforcing cycle of falling revenues and falling demand for travel by bus, streetcar, or other transit modes. Transport companies either went under or simply ceased to operate. Every city has its story to tell, but the sequence of events was fairly similar everywhere. Where the stories differ is in the reaction of public authorities. As streetcar, rail, and bus companies increasingly fell into the red, operators lobbied governments for funding. Unable to operate without public subsidies, the once private companies were, almost everywhere, eventually taken over by local government. Montreal municipalized tram and trolley bus services in 1951, tearing up tram lines. Toronto did not make the same mistake; it was one of the few North American cities to keep its streetcars, which are still in use today. In the United States, several cities (e.g., New York, Boston, and San Francisco) municipalized public transit systems. The New York Transit Authority began operating subways and bus lines in 1953.[5] Once a largely private industry that paid taxes, transit now became a public service, a burden that absorbed tax dollars. Maintaining a public transit system had now become a political choice, requiring public support, as it remains to this day.

In the face of rapidly falling ridership and growing demands on the public purse, public transit was left to decline to the point of no return in many American cities. Here we come to a second infernal circle that is difficult to reverse once set in motion. Cities that grew around the car necessarily produced less dense patterns of urban development, making it more diffi- cult to maintain transit services unless they were highly subsidized, leading in turn to further reduced services and further decline in ridership, and so on until transit services basically collapsed. This outcome was not neces- sarily universally bemoaned. In many places, urban planners at times saw the car as the "modern" solution to urban mobility. Highways were the fu- ture. The construction of wide car-friendly boulevards and urban highways began in Los Angles before the Federal Highway Act of 1956. In the decades that followed, the battle between the car and transit was (and has remained) an uneven one, with the former highly subsided (but largely hidden) and the latter needing up-front public funding to survive.

The extended sprawl of many American cities and corresponding lack of transit services was, in short, not accidental. The principal actors at the time were undoubtedly not fully aware of the long-term consequences of their choices. The first to suffer would be the poor and minority populations who could not afford a car, an inducement to concentrate in inner-city neighborhoods. Nor could policymakers have necessarily foreseen the dev- astating impact of car dependency on the health of downtowns.

Resuscitating Public Transit?

As the negative consequences of disappearing public transit became in- creasingly apparent, with mayors calling for federal intervention, the plight of public transit slowly began to improve. Starting in the 1970s, some twenty years after passage of the Federal Highway Act, Congress began to make federal funds available for public transit based on various cost- sharing formulas with state and local authorities.[6] Almost every American metropolitan area has sought to revamp its transit system with the aid of federal funds. However, in all too many places the damage was done; sprawl and hollowed-out downtowns had become too far advanced to be reversed. Once ridership falls below a certain threshold, revival becomes nearly impossible. Use of public transit is also in part a matter of habit, which is difficult to revive once lost. Buffalo is representative of what occurred in many places. A light rail system was inaugurated in 1985 (Metro Rail) at the cost of some half a billion dollars largely federally funded, with the main line running from downtown to suburban Amherst. The rail cars are admirably modern and clean, but ridership has not followed, even declining in recent years.[7] There is little evidence that Metro Rail has been instrumental in resuscitating the downtown or reviving the regional economy.

The American taxpayer is in the end paying twice for the uneven battle between transit and car: first, by subsidizing car use and second, by paying to repair the damage done. Had earlier policies been less one-sided, the American taxpayer would be paying less today to restore public transit.

Again, I do not wish to leave my reader with the wrong impression. I am not against suburbs. Suburbanization is the inevitable outcome of rising incomes and urban growth. Young families understandably aspire to a home with more than one bedroom and ideally a yard where their children can play. Family-oriented housing is of course more difficult to provide in a center-city setting. As the experience of other nations demonstrates, however, suburbanization need not automatically mean the death of public transit, although suburbanites will often use their car to commute to work. The difference is in relative proportions. Transit shares in Canada's three large metropolitan areas have historically been in the order of 20 to 25 percent, compared to shares below 5 percent in Dallas, Cleveland, and Atlanta.[8] Transit and private vehicles will always be in competition. The challenge is not allowing the second to completely undermine the first.

But does urban form really matter? Do more or less dense, more or less transit-oriented urban forms affect a city's ability to generate wealth? On the one hand, there is no hard scientific evidence of a causal relationship between urban form and income per capita or other indicators of wealth. On the other hand, San Francisco, Boston, and New York, three relatively compact urban areas by U.S. standards with strong downtowns and good transit systems, systematically register at the top on various measures of income and wealth.[9] This brings me to the role of strong centers not only in creating wealth but also in shaping urban environments that are reasonably socially cohesive.

Why Downtowns Matter

Rare are the successful cities that have lost their downtowns, although they may have gone through difficult periods as did Manhattan in the 1960s. Downtowns have always mattered. They matter even more in modern economies driven by the production and exchange of information. A recent Federal Reserve Bank of Cleveland study for U.S. metropolitan areas found a strong positive relationship between central (near-CBD) population density growth and metropolitan per capita income growth.[10] Chicago's central neighborhoods in and around the Loop have grown faster in recent years than the metropolitan area as a whole. Information-rich activities are naturally drawn to dense central neighborhoods that are conducive to face-to-face meetings, which t, as we have seen, are at the heart of New York's revival.

The role of downtowns and central neighborhoods is as much symbolic and affective as economic. For most people, the monuments, architecture, and look of downtown come to embody *their* city: Times Square and Fifth Avenue in New York; the Eiffel Tower and the banks of the Seine in Paris; *Calle Florida* and *Teatro Colón* in Buenos Aires. Like a canary in a coal mine, the health of downtown is a barometer of the city's health. In Chapter 1, I pointed to the decline of *Calle Florida*, which has now been largely abandoned by its middle class, as the sad symbol of Buenos Aires's decline. Then Mayor Rudy Giuliani of New York knew what he was doing when he chose to clean up Times Square in the 1990s, a cleanup that became the visible symbol of the city's rebirth. Most New Yorkers today are justifiably proud of their city, very different from their perception not so long ago. One of the first things Charles de Gaulle did upon becoming president in 1959 was to order the sandblasting of the thousands upon thousands of buildings of central Paris that had become covered in a gray-like grime, the result of decades of neglect. This was a colossal and costly undertaking; but it gave Parisians renewed pride in their city.

New York also taught us that strong centers make good business sense. Strong centralities produce economic rents (which can be taxed), as any mayor knows; which is why mayors around the world fight so hard to protect their downtowns. Centralities are always human-made. Buffalo's downtown, we shall discover in Chapter 4, lost its centrality and the location rent that went with it, and as a result, the whole region is paying a high price. Downtown office rents per square foot are on average 50 to 100 percent higher in Manhattan than in suburban locations. In Buffalo, by contrast, rental prices downtown are no higher than un suburban Amherst,[11] a good approximation of the location rent foregone. Higher real estate values mean higher revenues for local governments.[12] The restoration of New York City's fiscal health, following its self-inflicted fiscal crisis, would not have been possible had it not had a strong central fiscal base to fall back on. New York is able to keep Manhattan reasonably safe and clean because the center generates the revenues allowing it to do so.

The object of this book, need I remind the reader, is the *urban region*, the *city* with all its component parts. The whole body needs to be healthy for the city to work. The word <u>*suburb*</u>, by its very meaning, says that the *urb* in question is part of a greater whole. The suburbs of New York, Montreal, or Paris would not, and could not, exist if the initial central city had not first emerged and grown. The economic value of a healthy center extends to the whole urban region, as does its social value. In regions with revenue-sharing mechanisms, the fruits of centrality will be shared across the urban region, a pillar that is unfortunately lacking (or weak) in many American cities. When a center fails, as it did in Buffalo, the suburbs will bear the costs as much as the center, not only in rents and jobs foregone, but also in higher unit infrastructure costs, notably for transit, making it difficult, if not impossible, to maintain bus, rail, etc. services unless highly subsidized. Cost-efficient transit systems and strong downtowns are two sides of the same coin. The employment densities of Manhattan or downtown Montreal are impossible to achieve without transit, if only because of the impossibility of packing so many cars into a small area. Montreal's downtown generates three hundred thousand jobs in an 18 square kilometer area. Bringing in three hundred thousand commuters every day by car is logistically not viable—that is, unless downtown is transformed into a giant parking lot, which of course defeats the very purpose of a dense center.

The ideal scenario—every central city mayor's dream—is a virtuous circle in which a dense center allows the city to maintain a high quality (nonsubsidized or almost) transit system, which in turn serves to further strengthen downtown. Cities like Vienna and London are not far from this ideal, but for many others, as we have seen, the circle goes in the opposite direction: deteriorating public transit followed by a collapsing downtown. Once both have collapsed, the road back is not easy.

A Strong Center Is More than a CBD

Up to now, I have implicitly conflated central business districts (CBDs) and central neighborhoods when speaking of downtowns. The two are not the same thing, however. Greenwich Village in Manhattan or The Annex in Toronto are central, but they are not in what is commonly understood to be the CBD, which is typified by soaring office towers, luxury hotels, and businesspeople racing to and from meetings. Few people actually live in CBDs; most of them empty out after working hours. Every metropolis, at least in advanced economies, will have its CBD or financial district. New York has Wall Street; Toronto Bay Street, and London the City. In some U.S. metropolitan areas, this is all that is left of downtown, a cluster of office towers that grow dark after 6 PM.

What distinguishes a true downtown, beyond the strict limits of the CBD, is people—people on the street; it is the destination for residents and visitors alike for entertainment, shopping, and just plain people-watching. In New York as in London, the hearts of the city's shopping and entertainment—respectively, Fifth Avenue and Times Square and Oxford Street and Piccadilly—are located at some distance from the financial district. Toronto is no exception, with Bay Street near the Lake (Lake Ontario) and Midtown with its shops, cafés, and theaters further north. Further out, the visitor will find what I call "central neighborhoods," which are often gentrified or in the process of becoming so. These neighborhoods are not typically major employment nodes as such. It is the *proximity* of jobs in and around the CBD that makes these neighborhoods (architectural attributes aside) attractive to diverse educated populations. Universities and other institutions of higher learning bring students. Corporate activities bring business travelers. One of the best indicators of a dynamic center is the location of the best hotels and the best restaurants. Restaurants, like theaters, hotels, and bars, mean people on the street at night, which is the first rule (with lighting) of keeping sidewalks safe. The emergence of lively central neighborhoods is ultimately dependent on the accessibility, within reasonable distance, of a diversity of employment possibilities that only a complete downtown (CBD and more) brings.

Jane Jacobs's Revenge: The Resurgence of Central Neighborhoods

Some sixty years ago, well before the famous urbanist decided to delve into economics, Jane Jacobs published *The Death and Life of Great American Cities*.[13] Like so many urban planners since, Jacobs bemoaned the irreparable damage inflicted on city life by divided highways ripping through old neighborhoods, destroying housing, to be replaced by soulless highrise apartment buildings. Add in the race factor and white flight and all the ingredients for decline were in place. In the 1960s, Jacobs rightly feared for the systematic destruction of many great American cities, above all central cities; this was not very different from my own reading at the time. Jane Jacobs, a staunch urban activist, became famous, among other causes, for her fight (which she won) against a planned Lower Manhattan Expressway, eventually leading to her arrest in 1968 during a particularly rowdy demonstration. A year later, she moved to Toronto to The Annex, which was not unlike her home neighborhood (Greenwich Village[14])—it was walkable, with attractive three-story townhouses, shops, cafés, and a socially diverse population. Jane Jacobs and I thus have at least two things in common. Both of us at the time were not optimistic about the future of American cities, and both of us moved to Canada in the same year.

Jane Jacobs was right, of course, regarding the need for people-friendly neighborhoods where people can exchange, meet, and socialize, which is at the very heart of what makes a city tick. There is no need to return to a technical discussion of agglomeration economies, the economic gains from the spatial concentration of peoples and firms. For these gains to be realized, cities—Jacobs correctly warned—need to be properly designed and planned. Undoubtedly influenced by her personal experience in Greenwich Village and The Annex, she was also right in observing that only cities can provide such diverse environments. Where she was mistaken, we now know, was in assuming that lively, diverse neighborhoods would naturally give rise to *productive* innovations in the absence of other conditions; which, like so many, Jacobs took for granted and can thus be forgiven for ignoring.

That said, I shall now posthumously allow Jane Jacobs to take her revenge, but only partially. In most mature economies, the locus of "productive" innovation, notably in the information technology (IT) sector, has been shifting from suburban research campuses to the city, giving new life to many old central neighborhoods, a renaissance that surely would have pleased Jacobs.

The Rise of Techno Neighborhoods

The digital economy has given new life to numerous central neighborhoods, Manhattan's Silicon Alley, which we met in Chapter 1, an arch example. This gives rise to the question of why this is happening now and why in some neighborhoods and not in others.

Let us thus return to Manhattan's Silicon Alley, the name given to this jumble of neighborhoods nestled between Midtown and Wall Street.[15] With its old buildings and chaotic streets, and firms often lodged in refurbished warehouses or factories, Silicon Alley presents a very different picture from Silicon Valley, a suburban sprawl of techno campuses and office parks, home to IT megastars such as Google and Apple. Facebook recently inaugurated its ultramodern new campus, which is almost a city in itself, in Menlo Park in the Valley. An equivalent campus is difficult to imagine in Manhattan, if only because of space requirements. Visibly, New York's Silicon Alley is a very different beast from San Francisco Bay's Silicon Valley.

Suburban office parks and high-tech campuses will not go the way of the dinosaur. Firms and research institutions for which space is essential— think of large laboratories—will continue to seek out suburban locations. However, they are no longer the sole focus of the New Economy. Silicon Alley is not the only example of a central neighborhood turning into an IT hub. London has Shoreditch, an old working-class neighborhood just north of the City (financial district) with the equally predictable moniker of Silicon Roundabout. In Boston, the South Boston waterfront area, a short walk from the financial district, is now emerging (following a multibillon clean-up) as a high-tech hub. In Canada, central neighborhoods such as Montreal's Le Plateau, north of downtown, and Toronto's Junction Triangle, northwest of the CBD, have witnessed a literal explosion of New Economy firms in recent years.[16]

To understand what is happening, we need to go back to the massive employment shift out of manufacturing into high-order services, which benefited established CBDs in cities like New York, Toronto, and London, but also devastated many blue-collar working-class neighborhoods, laying the groundwork for what came to be known as gentrification (i.e.

young professionals displacing working-class populations). Gentrification remained relatively circumscribed in most places until the 1990s since CBD employment growth was rarely sufficient to offset the loss in blue-collar jobs and populations. Most large metropolitan areas saw their central populations decline during these decades of combined deindustrialization and suburbanization. Manhattan lost half a million residents between 1950 and 1990, a quarter of its population; central Montreal lost more than a third of its population between 1966 and 199; and inner London lost over a million residents between 1961 and 1991, a third of its population.[17] In all three cities, central neighborhoods started to grow again in the 1990s, attracting jobs and residents. Inner London has seen its population grow by some one million since the mid-1990s, entirely recuperating its former losses.

What happened? First, demographics and tastes changed. The suburban dream has not disappeared, nor should we expect it to. But its lure is no longer what it once was. Why? The first reason is simple demographics: childbearing households, the primary buyers of new homes in the suburbs, are less prevalent. Single-person and childless households account for an increasing share of the population in all developed nations. Automobile ownership has reached its limits and is now stabilized. Although suburbs will continue to grow in many places, the great era of suburban expansion now lies behind us in the developed world. The American urbanist, Alan Ehrenhalt, evokes what he calls "The Great Inversion."[18] Perhaps, in fifty years urban scholars, looking back, will refer to the past era of urban flight as a temporary deviation from the normal evolution of cities.

Edward Glaeser nicely documents the change in preferences of Americans for urban living.[19] Before 1990, the statistical relationship between city size and real wages (accounting for living costs) was systematically positive, as one would expect, but it turned negative afterward. For workers to accept lower real wages in big cities, they must now be receiving something in return, that "something" being the myriad amenities central big-city living offers: restaurants; museums; concerts; learning institutions; and so on. Part of the explanation undoubtedly lies in rising levels of education and increased foreign travel, with attendant consequences for tastes and preferences. For U.S. metro areas, the share of college-educated twenty-four to thirty-five-year-olds living within three miles of the CBD increased at double the rate between 2000 and 2009 as for the cohort as a whole.[20] For

Canadian cities, our own research found that New Economy workers are more likely to live close to the CBD than are comparable cohorts.[21]

How the Internet Fuels the Demand for Face-to-Face Meetings and the Laptop Makes Central City Work Easier.

The second big change is technology which has given us the Internet, smart phones, laptops, e-mail, and yet-to-be-invented digital technologies. One of the many ironies of the digital era is that electronic communication *increases* the need to meet. It happened a century ago with the telephone and is happening again. E-communication creates new needs for meetings and gatherings. I invite the reader to count the number of people whom he or she communicates with electronically on a regular basis and has not also met. Probably not many. E-communication and face-to-face meetings are complements, not substitutes. It is no accident that the demand for business air-travel, conferences, symposia, and trade shows of every imaginable nature exploded with the Internet. E-communication multiplies the need to meet. This is nowhere truer than in the effervescent entrepreneurial milieu of the New Economy.

Let us therefore take a closer look at the kind of city neighborhood in which this new breed of start-ups is evolving. These are generally neighborhoods that have completed the transition from warehousing and manufacturing to residential and (nonmanufacturing) commercial uses. Unlike former noisy, malodorous manufacturing and warehousing facilities, not to mention trucks constantly coming and going, the digital economy allows for the cohabitation of workspaces and residences, facilitating mixed-use zoning. The glue here is the circular relationship between lifestyle choices and firm location, the symbiosis further buttressed by a growing trend toward condominium construction in cities like New York and Montreal: condos (apartments) occupy upper floors, while lower floors are left for workspaces and the ground floor for retailing, facilitating the emergence of mixed-use neighborhoods so prized by Jane Jacobs.

In Montreal, one of the most dynamic digital start-up scenes is centered on St. Lawrence Boulevard north of downtown, an old immigrant neighborhood that still has the flavor of its East European and Jewish past with its delis and ethnic eateries, also formerly the heart of Montreal's apparel industry. Today, like Manhattan's alphabet soup of neighborhoods, it is crammed with cafés, artsy boutiques, and, more to the point, computer gaming software developers and other IT start-ups. Why specifically here? A manager of one of the larger computer gaming firms, housed in a recycled clothing factory, put it this way: "The kids we hire here work at all hours. They want to be able to go across the street for a coffee or sandwich at midnight, flake out in a bar at noon. They don't want to commute too far. Many bike to work." The reference to hours of the day is revealing. Firms like these want to be in twenty-four hour neighborhoods, not single-function districts that empty-out after 5 PM.

Technology also plays out at another level. The progressive miniaturization of computer devices, the laptop and IPhone visible examples, plus high-speed Internet and parallel technologies that facilitate information access and processing (cloud services, mobile hardware, social media, etc.) have meant that the space and financial needs for starting up a business are falling. New Economy firms are starting to resemble financial and other high-order services, able to generate high-income streams with little floor space, enabling them to afford the high rental costs typical of central locations. Often, all that is required are a few PCs, determination, and willing financial backers, the last-named further strengthening the pull of neighborhoods within easy reach of financial districts. It is easier to meet a rich banker or eager venture capitalist in Lower Manhattan than in the New Jersey suburbs. In coworking spaces, which are often located in café-like environments, all the budding entrepreneur needs is a laptop and a good idea, further reducing the need for floor space.

A parallel change is the growing focus on *content*: the entertainment (music, games, shows, etc.) information (news, newspapers, broadcasts) content accessible via digital devices, producing a growing symbiosis with the entertainment, publishing, and broadcasting industries, the traditional foundations of downtown economies. The American sociologist Michael Indergaard has coined the term *digitalization of culture* to characterize the growing interdependence between the arts and technology.[22] The birth of Manhattan's Silicon Alley between Midtown and Downtown, conveniently tucked between the center of the entrainment industry to the north and the financial district to the south, was, again, no accident . Add in abandoned factories and warehousing and packaging facilities, together with an excellent transit system and falling crime rates, and all the ingredients were in place, once the digital economy took off, for the resurgence of Manhattan's central neighborhoods.

As the final exhibit, I now return to Silicon Valley, which may seem self-contradictory, but it is not. The Bay Area techno scene is also undergoing a geographical shift, challenging the Valley on its home turf. A growing number of IT firms have chosen to open up shop in San Francisco proper in neighborhoods such as SoMa[23] and The Mission, both of which are within walking distance of the financial district. Twitter, Uber, and Airbnb, to take three examples, have chosen to locate their new production facilities in central San Francisco. Valley workers also increasingly want to *live* in central neighborhoods, which has given rise to a singular class of commuters epitomized by so-called Google Buses, the popular name given to the fleets of buses hired by Silicon Valley companies such as Google to shuttle their employees between their place of work in the Valley and place of residence in (generally) trendy, but also increasingly expensive, San Francisco neighborhoods.[24]

The growing taste of Valley workers for city living, which has driven up prices, has of course not been universally welcomed by local residents. San Francisco was already one of the most expensive housing markets on the planet, reflecting the flip side of the increasing pull of central neighborhoods. High housing prices are a two-edged sword: indicators of economic rents but also potential engines of social exclusion. Today who can afford to live in central Manhattan? We shall return to questions of housing affordability and social cohesion later in this chapter. For the moment, let us simply remember that the rise of the digital economy, while behind the renaissance of many central neighborhoods, also has a darker side. IT facilitates the concentration of high-paid, knowledge-rich jobs both within and across cities.[25] This is good news for the winners but less so for those left behind. Before digging deeper into the social challenges facing modern urban economies, however, let us take a brief journey to Los Angeles.

Yes, Los Angeles Has a (Strong) Center; But It's Just Different

After reading the foregoing discussion, the reader, especially if he or she is an American, may rightly ask: what about cities like Houston, Phoenix, and

Los Angeles (henceforth L.A.) which have notoriously weak transit systems and endless suburbs and yet are economically successful by any measure? Does this not contradict what I have just stated regarding the importance of strong central neighborhoods? It is a valid question.

As a partial answer, I will recount another city story, this time about Los Angeles, which is arguably the poster child of a sprawled car-dependent metropolis. Yet, I like L.A. I spent a sabbatical year in L.A. with my family in the 1980s and returned frequently afterward to visit my Aunt Silvia (whom we first met in the New York story), onetime actress, now deceased. Silvia's apartment, which became somewhat of a second home for me, was appropriately located in the Hollywood Hills.

Let me start with public transit. Undeniably, public transit in L.A. is a far cry from New York's. Yet, this result was not foreordained. I remember an old classmate of mine from Penn in Urban Planning who had since become a transportation planner for the city of Los Angeles, saying: "Mario, if we had known then how things would turn out, we would have done things differently." Los Angeles is another example of how earlier decisions to focus almost exclusively on urban highways, including the tearing up of existing rail and streetcar lines, produced a low-density pattern of settlement that made it almost impossible, several decades later, to build and manage a cost-effective mass transit system. L.A. has since heroically attempted to turn back the clock, with predictably limited success.

With a first line opening in 1990, the newly created Los Angeles County Metropolitan Transport Authority (Metro, for short) embarked on an ambitious program of subway construction.[26] Los Angeles now has a well-developed subway system with six lines, the largest network in the United States after New York and Chicago. Unfortunately, however, ridership has not followed. A simple comparison with New York drives home L.A.'s dilemma. Recent estimates[27] put Metro's daily ridership at around three hundred and sixty thousand for a metro area population of some fourteen million, compared to five million for New York's subway system for a population of some twenty million. Thus, New Yorkers were on average ten times more likely to use the subway than Angelinos.[28] Part of the difference can be explained by the limited geographic coverage of L.A.'s system, a corollary of the region's sprawled development, with many areas still not serviced. However, L.A.'s entrenched car culture, the result of decades of car dependence, is also part of the answer.

Let me use an anecdote to illustrate the strange relationship between Angelinos and their subway, which they seem to consciously choose to ignore. The family was again visiting with my (now bedridden) aunt in Hollywood. After so many stays in L.A., we had completely assimilated the Angelino ethos. We did everything by car. It never occurred to us to use the subway, although (as we would discover) a metro station—Hollywood and Vine—was within easy walking distance. One day, the family car was unavailable, but my older daughter and I needed to go downtown. We bravely trudged down the hill in search of this mysterious metro station. I asked a saleslady for directions in the first available shop, only to be met with a blank stare as if I had asked her for directions to the moon. I had no better luck in the next shop. In neither case was the individual remotely aware that a subway existed, even though a station was just a few blocks way. We eventually found the Hollywood and Vine station. To this day, this little incident, impossible to imagine in New York, remains with me. No self-respecting New Yorker ignores where the nearest subway station is. Navigating the subway system is a matter of pride, the sign of a true New Yorker. I could only conclude that L.A. and New York indeed represent two very different urban cultures.

A Center Created by and for the Car

Angelenos remain wedded to their cars. Yet, contrary to popular opinion, L.A. has a strong center that Angelenos well understand, even if they do not necessarily identify it as such. This is proof, if need be, of the need for successful urban regions to create centralities, places that facilitate face-to-face contacts and personal relationships, even where they do not adhere to the traditional model of transit-supported centers.

So let us now get into our car and visit L.A.'s "center": an elongated downtown stretching west from the CBD (the formal downtown and financial center) along a 15-mile east–west axis to Santa Monica on the Pacific, about a thirty-minute drive (traffic conditions allowing) or five hours on foot if one were inclined to do so, which of course no sane Angeleno would. Almost everything that matters—the best shops, financial institutions, major consultancies, café and night life—lies along this axis. Nestled south of the Hollywood Hills (with its famous sign) and the Santa Monica Mountains, Wilshire Boulevard is its informal main street, which if one were indeed inclined to walk would be the obvious choice. Within L.A.'s urban sprawl, this elongated downtown is actually quite compact and, as economic theory would predict, generates higher land values; office rents are on average twice as high as in the rest of Greater L.A.[29]

Like any self-respecting downtown, L.A.'s is an assemblage of neighborhoods. Leaving the CBD proper with its office towers, going west, the visitor would first encounter Koreatown, your typical inner-city ethnic neighborhood and then enter Miracle Mile and Museum Row on Wilshire. A slight detour north would take the visitor to the heart of Hollywood, which needs no introduction. Like Times Square, the City has made a major effort to clean up Hollywood; but it still has some way go if it ever wishes to equal its East Coast rival. Then, moving west again to West Hollywood, the visitor would discover L.A.'s own gay neighborhood and just to the south Farmers Market and The Grove with its upscale food stores and cafés. Still moving west, the visitor would enter Beverly Hills, which also needs little introduction, and Rodeo Drive, L.A.'s (even glitzier) answer to New York's Madison and Fifth Avenues. Further west still, the traveler would come to Westwood, home to UCLA,[30] my sabbatical alma mater, with its students and cafés. Finally, driving down Wilshire, the mighty Pacific would open up to the visitor: Santa Monica with its oceanside promenade, pier, and active café scene and night life. Predictably, the geography of L.A.'s New Economy start-ups closely follows its elongated downtown, culminating in Santa Monica and Venice Beach, both of which have high concentrations of IT firms.[31]

The Pacific may be the end of the road, but it is much more than that. The Pacific Ocean is not only the western anchor of L.A.'s elongated downtown, but also a vital ingredient in the region's social glue and self-image. L.A. would not be L.A. without the beach and all that that entails in terms of lifestyle and social interaction. Like New York's Central Park, the 2-mile stretch between the Santa Monica Pier, with its fun rides and food stalls, and Venice Beach to the south, with its boardwalk, sidewalk cafés, and people-watching crowd, performs an essential symbolic and socializing function. This is where Angelenos of all classes and races can mingle and do. A Sunday afternoon on Venice Beach is as animated, as lively, and certainly as cosmopolitan as a Sunday in the downtown of any great European city.

I cannot leave L.A. without a word about its darker side. L.A. is a highly segregated metropolis, both socially and ethnically. The elongated downtown I have just described is largely white, middle and upper class, with mostly single-family homes and obligatory manicured lawns; thanks to Mexican gardeners. L.A.'s sprawl means that millions of Angelenos, many Hispanic or black, have no choice but to own a car, but cars are not necessarily within the means of all. Many are thus forced to rely on the city's woefully inadequate transit system with correspondingly long commutes.

The lesson from Los Angeles is simple, but it also carries a warning: "central" places where people can mix and gather are a necessary condition for success in today's information-based economy. But they alone are not sufficient to ensure social cohesion. People of all races and classes must feel that they belong to their city. It is to this subject that we now turn.

Why Social Cohesion Matters and Why It Is So Difficult to Achieve

Social cohesion is a difficult concept to define, but we all intuitively understand what lies behind the term.[32] We know what it is not: indicators such as income inequality, residential segregation (by race, class, or ethnicity), and crime spontaneously come to mind. We would expect politically fragmented and highly segregated cities with sharp income differences to be less socially cohesive. The evidence largely bears this out. Crime rates, a powerful indicator of social cohesion (or rather the lack thereof), are positively correlated both with higher levels of income inequality and of racial segregation for U.S. metropolitan areas.[33] Terms such as *civility* and *trust* also come to mind: lack of trust is often a major factor holding back Third World cities, Port au Prince a particularly brutal example. Unsurprisingly, Port au Prince is a highly segregated city, with its tiny rich elite holed up in the separate municipality of Petionville up the mountain in the cooler, less polluted hills.

The evidence for a positive relationship between social cohesion and wealth, though necessarily indirect, is not lacking. For U.S. metropolitan areas, Edward Glaeser observes that people living in places with more unequal income distributions and higher crime rates are less likely to declare they are happy.[34] As we have seen, insecurity implies a cost. Evidence, again for the United States, suggests that more unequal and more segregated urban areas not only have higher crime rates, but also exhibit lower income growth.[35] The mechanisms by which social and racial segregation hamper overall income growth are not fully understood, but we again intuitively understand that the presence of ghettos where outsiders fear to tread—but also insulated homogenous rich neighborhoods—are unlikely to produce environments conducive to collaborative behavior, personal improvement, and what I have called productive innovation.

While we know that a minimum of social cohesion, trust, and civility is necessary for the creation of wealth, we do not know what that minimum is. The threshold may be lower than we think. Wealth and crime are not incompatible. Despite equivalent or higher per capita incomes, American cities have higher crime rates on average than Canadian, Australian, and Western European cities. It is partly for this reason that U.S. cities do not as a rule do well on quality-of-life rankings. While the causal link between quality of life and wealth creation is often indirect and difficult to quantify, the relationship in the opposite direction is unambiguous. Ensuring a decent quality of life (at least for the majority) is impossible without wealth and the goods and services it buys, especially public health, decent housing, and education. All the cities that top Mercer's quality of living rankings are also wealthy places: Vienna, Zurich, Vancouver, Munich[36]). As American cities bear witness, however, wealth is not a sufficient condition for social cohesion.

The evidence for the United States suggests that larger urban areas, though generally wealthier, are also on average more unequal and more segregated than smaller places.[37] My own research shows similar results for Canada.[38] Part of the explanation is the concentration of the very rich in the largest urban areas. However, a fundamental obstacle to building socially cohesive cities, especially racially and culturally diverse societies, is human nature itself.

Birds of a Feather—The Natural Desire to Flock Together (and to Exclude)

The propensity of human beings to prefer their own kind is entirely natural. In cities with peoples of multiple origins, individuals and families will naturally seek out neighborhoods where they feel at home, if only for practical reasons: to be close to houses of worship, schools, stores, and to other services catering to their special needs. Among the first things my Viennese parents did upon arrival in New York was to find German-speaking butchers, bakeries, and grocery stores where my mother (who loved to cook) could find all the familiar ingredients for Wiener Schnitzel and Malakoff Torte. Fortunately, Manhattan's German neighborhood was not far, just across Central Park, but it has since disappeared as German-speakers melted into the American mainstream.[39]

The propensity of likeminded people to flock together is by no means all bad. However, it is the bad side that makes the news. One need not cite extreme cases such as the institutionalized segregation of Catholics and Protestants in Belfast or the ethnic cleansing of Sarajevo to be reminded that different creeds and races find it difficult to cohabit peacefully. De facto segregation is a reality in almost all cities with racially mixed populations, and not just in the United States. The propensity of people to flock together by class is no less real. Every city has its richer and poorer neighborhoods. The propensity to segregate is universal, and thus also the propensity to exclude.

How Wealth Facilitates Segregation

One of the many ironies of modern economic development is that greater wealth has increased the potential for spatial segregation. Before the advent of trams in the 19th century and other transport modes that greatly increased our ability to move within the city, notably the car, the most common mode was walking (only the rich could afford horses). In the course of my stays in Puebla, I undertook a study of the city's social geography to discover to my surprise that segregation by class was lower there than in Canadian cities. Many neighborhoods were visibly mixed, although Puebla did have very rich and very poor neighborhoods, the latter often consisting of informal settlements. The greater spatial social mix had four explanations: (1) domestics, still a common feature of life in Puebla, often lived next to (and sometimes in) the employer's home; (2) the absence of a fully developed mortgage market meant that families often kept their home even after their social status had improved; (3) Puebla's Spanish- and Arab-inspired architecture with its high walls and interior courtyards meant that a resident's social status was not easily evident from the outside, with rich and poor often lived side by side. The decisive factor (4), however, was the relative absence of mobility, especially for the less fortunate. Few owned a car, a powerful incentive to live close to employers.

Puebla and other Latin American cities, following in the footsteps of richer cities, are becoming more segregated as incomes rise, housing markets become more fluid, and urban transport improves. The role of the car is double. Not only does the private automobile give its owners greater flexibility to choose (and to create) neighborhoods, but it also becomes an expression of social status and a means of maintaining social distance. I do not wish to caricature, but the private car essentially allows white elites (or those who think of themselves as white) to isolate themselves from the unwashed masses. If the lucky owners can in addition use divided highways (elevated is even better) to move around the city, they can live in the city without ever having to see a poor neighborhood. The reader will by now have guessed the analogy with many Western, especially American, cities: our friendly white-collar worker driving in from his or her manicured suburb to his or her reserved underground center-city parking space without ever having traversed a "bad" neighborhood.

The car as an expression of social superiority is on the decline in rich nations as car ownership becomes universal, but it is still very much alive in many developing nations. A visible expression, all too common in Latin American cities, is the attitude of drivers toward pedestrians, who are unworthy of consideration since they are walking. Only rarely have I seen drivers voluntarily stop for pedestrians. Public transit, by the same token, is for lesser folk. No self-respecting executive or otherwise socially powerful individual would contemplate riding a *collectivo* or mini-bus—a taxi perhaps, but public transport, never.

The most powerful manifestation of social segregation, which is difficult to imagine without the car, is the growth of gated communities, a form of secession by the rich from the rest of society. The decline of downtown Buenos Aires is the predictable complement of the flight of its elites into often self-contained suburban communities. The province of Buenos Aires tax office identifies some four hundred gated communities around the capital, containing ninety thousand homes. Most manage their own utilities and security with CCTV and guards patrolling at all hours. Some are small towns in their own right: Nordelta, a secure mega-complex on the capital's northern edge, is home to more than seventeen thousand residents, who have their own schools, hospitals, and hotels.[40]

Buenos Aires is by no means an isolated case. The first thing a Poblano colleague did after purchasing a car was to move to a gated community (*La Calera*) on the southern outskirts of Puebla, which like its Porteño sister had its own utilities and guarded entrance. I couldn't really begrudge my colleague, for *La Calera* obviously provided much better surroundings for raising his children: landscaped grounds, fully equipped playgrounds, and, above all, an environment in which it was safe to walk and move around. Had I stayed in Puebla, perhaps I, too, would have moved there. Yet, as for all such self-contained communities, this meant not only the formal exclusion of "others," but also the withdrawal from the wider community of resources in the form of taxes paid and concomitant expenditures on public services.

Don't Let the Good People Secede

The core challenge of any political model (and there are many) of regional governance conducive to social cohesion is the shared financing (or not) of public services. The challenge, stated more crudely, is preventing the "good people"—the better-off or privileged group[41]—from seceding from the rest of society, be they wealthier lighter-skinned Haitians seceding to Petionville up the hill or wealthy white Buffalonians (see the next chapter) seceding to Amherst in the northern suburbs. How can society ensure that all share in the financing of public services? And which services? Here we come to the essential distinction between what I call "people" services and urban services.

The Distinction Between People Services and Urban Services

The problem is not municipal fragmentation as such. Almost all major metropolitan areas around the world are politically fragmented, not only in the United States. The fundamental issue is the jurisdictional level at which people services (investments in people) are financed, as distinct from land and building-oriented services (urban services, for short). It is the former—education, daycare, health, and other social services (to which public transit could also be added in many cases) that allow individuals to better themselves, to rise out of poverty, and to advance. Erasing or reducing inequalities across neighborhoods or municipalities becomes problematic where people services are financed via local taxes and consequently tied to the wealth of the local area, be it called a borough, township, municipality or something else.

In many of the cities visited in this book (e.g., Vienna, which we visited in Chapter 1 and Montreal, which we shall meet in Chapter 6), people services are centrally financed via, respectively, the Austrian state and the province of Quebec, with costs borne by all taxpayers. The neighborhood or municipality in which one grows up is not necessarily a determining factor of one's life chances. American cities, at least the majority of them, are different: the financing of most people services is a local responsibility. The main point of contention often centers on primary and secondary education, which, when locally financed, not only produces quality differences across space, but can further exacerbate inequality by triggering population movements, with wealthier inhabitants fleeing to better serviced areas, thereby creating a vicious cycle.

Ironically, one of the principal obstacles to regional revenue sharing is that urban regions that would gain most are also the least likely to have it. Political opposition will be strongest where people services are financed through local taxes and where, correspondingly, social divides are the deepest and thus where so much is at stake, creating a political catch 22. The decentralized financing of people services is arguably the Achilles heel of the American urban model (at least, the majority model). Why would the mayor of a suburban municipality freely consent to reduce his town's school funding for the sake of regional harmony or freely use local tax revenues to finance transit systems that primarily benefit central city riders? He or she wouldn't—that is, unless forced to do so by senior government. U.S. senior governments (states) are generally reluctant to intervene. Regional revenue-sharing arrangements are extremely rare with Portland, Oregon, and Minneapolis-St. Paul, Minnesota, among the rare exceptions.

Is Social Cohesion Possible without Coercion?

The apparent difficulty of the different-colored tribes of our species to live together in peace or of the better-off (whether individuals or communities) sharing their riches unless forced to do so raises a simple but central question: is social cohesion possible without coercion from above? The evidence suggests that the answer is "no." As we shall discover as we move to other city stories, senior governments almost everywhere have stepped in, to various degrees, to limit the freedom of individuals to choose (and to exclude) neighbors. The fundamental question is the degree of coercion and, correspondingly, the willingness of society to accept limits on freedom to ensure social harmony. Here, nations vary greatly. The Netherlands is among the more coercive with an openly directive housing policy that redirects newcomers to chosen locations. This policy is explicitly aimed at producing ethnically diverse neighborhoods, which goes some way in explaining the relative absence of ethnic ghettos in Dutch cities.[42]

Singapore provides a radical example of central government coercion to ensure ethnic harmony. The island city-state counts three major ethnic groups: ethnic Chinese (the majority), Malays, and East Indians; the first have historically higher incomes, and the second are traditionally at the bottom of the social ladder. Upon independence in 1965, Singapore introduced an explicit policy aimed at preventing residential segregation by race. Publicly built or subsidized housing became the dominant form of habitat and still is. Apartments are administratively assigned to prevent members of the same ethnic groups from living in the same building block, even to the point of not allowing an ethnic Chinese couple, say, to rent or sell their flat to fellow Chinese. By all accounts,[43] Singapore's strategy has worked, forging a shared sense of Singapore nationhood. This is no small achievement in a region with a history of interethnic strife between Malays and ethnic Chinese where not so long ago native Indonesians (Malays) massacred several thousand ethnic Chinese in a moment of nativist frenzy.[44] Singapore has been equally forceful in imposing public transit with a combination of road tolls and punitive taxes on the purchase of private vehicles, making cars unaffordable by all but the very rich.

The dilemma is real. Is coercion the necessary price to pay for social peace in ethnically diverse societies? Freedom is a core value of civilized society, including the freedom to choose one's neighborhood and to protect it, which brings us to what has come to be known as NIMBYs[45]: actions by residents to block projects they see as detrimental to their neighborhood, be it via protests, referendums, or other means. NIMBYs have become a major force blocking mixed residential development, not least in American cities. Richard Florida, in his recent book, the *Urban Crisis*,[46] is not incorrect in pointing to NIMBYism as among the chief culprits driving the social divides in American cities. The *New York Times* quotes Diane Yentel, president and chief executive of the National Low Income Housing Coalition[47]: "One of the biggest obstacles that has always existed and that remains in building affordable housing in higher-income, higher-opportunity neighborhoods is local opposition."

Data for the largest U.S. cities over the last fifteen years show that low-income housing projects using federal tax credits are disproportionately built in majority nonwhite communities. The government is de facto helping to maintain racial divides, despite federal law requiring government agencies to promote integration.[48] Why? The reason is that it is simply easier (and cheaper) to build social housing in poor minority population neighborhoods. *The New York Times* cites a federally funded public housing project to be built in an affluent majority-white neighborhood of Houston, but which was eventually abandoned after a particularly rowdy town hall meeting. Residents expressed fears, valid or not, of school overcrowding and falling property values. One resident cited was admirably (but also depressingly) honest, fearing "unwelcome residents who, due to poverty and lack of education, will bring the threat of crime, drugs and prostitution to the neighborhood."[49] It is easy to condemn such fears; the challenge is overcoming them.

It is difficult to see how such opposition can be overcome without placing constraints on the rights of citizens. A bipartisan bill was introduced in the U.S. Senate in early 2017 that would prohibit community residents from vetoing federally funded projects.[50] A similar bill (SB 827) was introduced in the California Senate in January 2018 that would have reduced local control of land zoning near public transit stations; the bill did not pass. The concerns raised by NIMBYs are not limited to the United States. The Quebec National Assembly recently passed a law abrogating the right of neighborhood residents in Montreal and Quebec City to trigger binding referendums on proposed zoning changes and building projects. Community groups predictably see this as an attack on democracy, while mayors defend the law as necessary for maintaining efficient housing markets and preventing NIMBYs.

NIMBYs come in many flavors, but they are almost always defended as a means of protecting the neighborhood from incursions that would alter its "character" and implicitly bring down housing values. Should not citizens have the right to protect their environment and their investments? Unfortunately, the evidence suggests that citizens, given the power to decide, will more often than not oppose (rather than support) new construction and new populations coming to their neighborhood.[51] It is important, however, that one not conflate the two classes of motivations behind NIMBYs, although the two may overlap, especially where race comes into play. NIMBYs motivated by the desire to keep certain types of people out of one's neighborhood are one thing; NIMBYs motivated by the desire to prevent new construction are another. It is the former that was our focus here. We shall cover the latter in Chapter 7 when we address housing prices.

Center/Suburb Divides and the Quest for the "Right" Model of Metropolitan Governance

Finding the right regional governance model remains an ongoing challenge to which no society has as yet found the ideal solution. The importance of formal regional governance structures should not be overstated. It is not a critical factor where people services are centrally and/or regionally financed as they generally are in Europe and Canada. Many region wide services can be effectively delivered via special-purpose agencies without necessarily requiring a formal regional governance structure. Transit is the prime example where costs are shared in varying proportions between riders, local government, and senior government. In the United States, federal grants for public transit are conditional on the region first creating a Metropolitan Planning Organization (MPO), with a governing board drawn from local authorities and typically also including nongovernment actors. This is an unfortunately all too rare example of the federal government stepping in to promote regionalism.[52] At the time of writing, it was far from certain whether the Trump administration would continue the grants.

Total consolidation under a single regional government as in Vienna (see below) is rarely the solution and in any case is not feasible in most cases, if only because metropolitan areas are continually expanding. The challenge is inventing and reinventing models of metropolitan governance appropriate to local context. The range of institutional arrangements is almost infinite.[53] Portland's model is different from that of Minneapolis-St. Paul, just as Montreal's is different from that of Toronto. Whatever the formula adopted, the ultimate test is the prevention of social and/or ethnic divides that undermine the ability of people to live together.

Often, the principal challenge, as we shall see in Paris and many U.S. cities, is the social and political divide between the central city and surrounding jurisdictions. The evidence suggests that urban regions where the central city is undisputedly the dominant player are less prone to center–suburb tensions. New York City had the good fortune, we saw, of annexing its outer boroughs early-on during the urbanization process. A recent study for German cities points to a positive relationship between central-city fiscal health and its regional weight, in essence reducing downward tax competition.[54]

Cooperation between center and suburb is almost impossible to achieve where the municipal border between the central city and suburb is also an "us/them" divide, turning the boundary de facto into a form of institutionalized segregation. Paris, as we shall see, comes close, though it has nothing like the stark black/white boundaries that separate many American central cities from their surrounding suburbs. Detroit is a particularly harsh example.[55] There is nothing subtle about these boundaries, both social and institutional, as visible to the passerby as an international border. Here secession has triumphed, the good people leaving little behind in the way of taxes or anything else for that matter.

The full measure of the public policies discussed so far, whether with respect to city/suburb divides, the provision of people services, public transit, or the health of downtowns, will become clear in the next chapter when we visit Buffalo. There we shall compare its story to that of Toronto. But before that, let us return to Vienna

Vienna's Livability—A Confluence of Chance and Political Will

Vienna, let us recall, is ranked at the top on both the Economist Livability and the Mercer Quality of Living indexes. As we shall discover, Vienna's admirable performance is in large part the accidental outcome of its past decline and the social upheavals it triggered, another of history's many ironies. As such, Vienna's undisputed achievement is difficult to replicate and, by the same token, potentially fragile as the conditions that made it possible fade into the past.

An (Accidentally) Preplanned Metropolis

Vienna is unique among the world's great cities in that regional governance is not an issue. There is no central city–suburb divide (at least not yet), nor is there a need to invent institutions to promote regional cooperation. Vienna is not a fragmented metropolis divided into competing jurisdictions. The city of Vienna is largely coterminous with the urbanized region, its two million inhabitants contained within essentially the same borders as a century ago. Berlin finds itself in a similar fortunate position, for similar historical reasons. The only other possible comparison is Singapore, which is an independent city-state, a single jurisdiction.

Vienna has the added advantage of being a *Land* within the Austrian federation with the full powers of a federated state, with the double status of City and *Land*. It's as if the New York metropolitan area with its twenty million inhabitants were a separate state within the United States, with borders drawn a hundred years ago that shrewdly foresaw the metropolis's future growth.

How did this come about? The story begins in the years before World War I when Vienna was still the rapidly exploding capital of the Austro-Hungarian Empire. Planners foresaw a glorious future for the imperial capital and with laudable foresight planned infrastructures for a metropolis twice its size, including its vaunted tramway network, a model metropolis for the 20th century. The growth of Vienna, we know, came to an abrupt end as the Empire collapsed after World War I. Vienna, however, remained essentially intact, both politically and territorially.[56] Those who would be called upon to govern Vienna in the future would inherit a city with considerable powers and whose territory matched its demographic reality.

This unified structure facilitated the application of policies that were conducive to social equality—that is, were a city administration inclined to do so. This is where the story takes a dramatic turn which would transform Vienna into a unique social laboratory. Vienna was far from an equal society. In addition to the material suffering brought by the war and defeat, Vienna was a socially divided city, with poor working-class outer districts pitted against the richer center and leafier western districts, a divide that would ignite a political revolution.

Red Vienna: Planned Cohesion

On May 14, 1919, six months after the end of the war, the Viennese elected an openly Socialist administration, marking the beginning of what would come to be known as Red Vienna (*Rot Wien*). It would last until 1933. Red

Vienna was to be a great social experiment, a beacon for social reform movements around the world, and the model for a more just and equal society. City Hall recruited the best talents of the day: urban planners, social thinkers, and architects. The new Vienna, city leaders proclaimed, would bring education, health, and generally better living conditions to the hitherto disenfranchised working classes. The centerpiece of Red Vienna was a massive public housing program, which went well beyond the provision of housing. This was an experiment in social engineering. Red Vienna's program was exceptional in its sheer size; some 382 housing estates were built between 1923 and 1933, comprising sixty-four thousand housing units, new homes for two hundred thousand families. Housing estates were deliberately dispersed across the city, and occupants were chosen to promote social mix, although, unsurprisingly, poorer districts tended to be favored, the Socialist Party's political base.

Among the revolutionary features of Red Vienna's social housing program was the architectural quality of the housing estates. These were not the assembly-line high-rises of the Paris *banlieue*. Each housing estate was a signature project overseen by a well-known architect. Most still stand today, many of them now classified as protected heritage buildings. Karl-Marx-Hof, the most famous project in the (former) working-class district of Heiligenstadt, is now a tourist attraction, designed by the well-known urban planner Karl Ehn. It was completed in 1930 with 1382 housing units. Karl-Marx-Hof became a symbol of working-class resistance, stormed by right-wing militias during Austria's brief 1934 civil war as the nation began its slow slide into the abyss.

The objective was not simply to house but to uplift the working classes. Each housing estate incorporated kindergartens, dental clinics, baths, maternity centers, schools, and so on, as well as the mandatory playing grounds and green spaces. The city administration also financed an extensive network of so-called workers libraries and public swimming pools, the latter also often becoming architectural icons. All this was financed by a mix of special municipal taxes named Breitner Taxes in honor of the city councilor who introduced them: taxes were placed on luxury items such as large homes and villas, horse racing, upscale bars and bordellos, champagne, and other "superfluous" expenditures. The taxes were understandably not overly popular among the upper classes. All that came to an end in the 1930s as the First Austrian Republic fell victim first to an authoritarian-clerical regime and then to National Socialism.

Jumping over those dark years, let us come back to the Vienna of today. Although the Socialist idealism of the 1920s is now history (gone are the dreams of fashioning a "new man"), Red Vienna's housing legacy has survived and is now part of Vienna's DNA. All national governments since have continued to support Vienna's unique approach to housing. "Public" housing is in effect a misnomer in the Viennese case; publicly supported housing accounts for close to two-thirds of the housing stock, including a uniquely Viennese institution, *Gemeinnütziger Bauvereinigungen* (Limited-Profit Housing Associations or LPHAs), also a legacy of the prewar period.

Austria's approach to housing has the additional non-negligible effect of keeping housing prices low, a major element in Vienna's continued high ranking on livability. Private builders must compete with the large publicly subsidized construction sector, keeping costs down in the nonsubsidized segments of the housing market.[57] The crux of the Austrian system is the direct funding of builders, including LPHAs in the form of construction assistance grants, thus subsidizing supply, the opposite of subsidies that target demand (households).

Vienna's history, in short, produced a very different attitude toward housing from that found elsewhere, with housing viewed not as a consumption good or an investment, but as a public service like transit or sanitation. More to the point, the presence of "public" housing in almost all segments of the market except the most exclusive, as well as the general quality of construction, has meant that no social stigma is attached to living in "public" housing. Such housing is a normal choice for all but the very rich. Vienna's activist housing policy with immigrant populations directed to geographically dispersed housing is explicitly aimed at promoting social mix.[58] The end result is a metropolitan area that is largely devoid of sharp residential divides—at least, nothing approaching the ghettos of urban America. Homelessness is almost unknown, which goes some way in explaining why Vienna continues to rank high in quality-of-life rankings.

Is Vienna's Success Sustainable?

The integrated regional governance of Vienna was only possible because the city had ceased to grow. Had Vienna continued grow, it would soon have found a large proportion of its population beyond its borders in suburban municipalities. It also is difficult to imagine that Vienna's ambitious public housing program could have kept up with demand under conditions of rapid growth.

Other aspects of Vienna's success are historically grounded and as such are difficult to replicate. The trauma left by the turbulent interwar period and World War II, which prompted the strong desire not to repeat the errors of the past, gave birth to a political culture of consensus, the so-called Social Partnership (*Sozialpartnerschaft*) in which the various bodies representing capital (i.e., Chambers of Commerce), labor (unions), and the state systematically consult and negotiate on major issues. Vienna's imperial legacy also helped. The imperial crown left the city with an impressive network of parks and protected forests, which are now accessible to all classes of society. Vienna's vaunted quality of life, one might say, is in part the outcome of the accidental meeting of two opposites: royal privilege and Socialist egalitarianism.

Vienna's "cohesiveness" was (and still is to some extent) the product of a fairly homogeneous society with shared social norms, which again is an outcome of its past slow growth and relative isolation. The Iron Curtain helped keep "others" out. But no longer: Vienna's immigrant population has grown rapidly in recent years, the natural outcome of its success. Neighborhoods with high proportions of non-native Austrians, often Turks and migrants from former Yugoslavia, have emerged in the city's western inner suburbs, the historical heartland of working-class Red Vienna. These nascent ethnic clusters bear little resemblance (at least, not yet) to urban ghettos but nonetheless bear witness to the difficulty of maintaining the right balance between freedom (the right "to flock together") and spatial equality under conditions of high growth and ethnic diversity.

Austria is not immune to the political winds sweeping much of the Western world. In the October 2017 legislative elections, the right-wing anti-immigration Freedom Party (*Freiheitliche Partei Österreichs: FPÖ*), long politically ostracized, garnered 26 percent of the national vote, entering the government for the first time. The Freedom Party's electoral base, like Trump's Republican base, is concentrated in rural areas and small towns, although its share of the Viennese vote (21 percent) was also non-negligible. Herein lies another warning. The very success of cities like Vienna in welcoming "others" can trigger a backlash, both inside and outside the city.[59] In the end, cities are at the mercy of national electorates.

4

Diverging Neighbors

A Tale of Disastrous Decline and Extraordinary Good Fortune

This chapter tells the story of two cities (metropolitan areas) in two rich nations located not far from each other: *Buffalo* in western New York State and *Toronto* in the Canadian province of Ontario. Both are situated on the Great Lakes, and less than 100 miles separates the two. Yet, a more powerful story of contrasting fortunes is difficult to find, revealing profound differences, we shall discover, in American and Canadian political cultures and how they shape cities. The chief culprits in this case are not so much national as state/provincial governments.

Buffalo: The Perfect Storm

Buffalo's story[1] is not very different from that of other American cities that have fallen on bad times. I could just as easily have chosen Detroit, Cleveland, or St. Louis. As such, Buffalo's saga can be viewed as a metaphor for other cities that have had to confront similar gales.

Figure 4.1 illustrates the magnitude of the divergence with its Canadian neighbor since the 1950s.[2] Toronto and Buffalo at the time were of comparable size, with about one million inhabitants each and two industrial cities with manufacturing accounting for 40 percent of employment.[3] Some sixty-six years later, Buffalo's population is still about one million and has even declined slightly since the 1970s. Toronto's population has exploded, now past the six million mark. Toronto today is a world city. Buffalo, without wishing to be too harsh, has become an economic backwater with persistent high unemployment, a deserted downtown, and seemingly locked into a permanent state of economic stagnation.[4] The ultimate insult came in 2003 when the city of Buffalo was placed in receivership under a state-appointed control board,[5] to be followed two years later by surrounding Erie County.[6]

The City of Light; Buffalo 1900–1950

Figure 4.1 does not fully capture Buffalo's fall from grace. The Buffalo of the 1950s was by right and by history the senior metropolis of the two. The 1960 edition of *Encyclopedia Britannica* devotes a full two pages to Buffalo but barely a page to Toronto. My older Toronto friends still recall a time when Torontonians looked up to Buffalo as a visibly richer and more advanced metropolis. A weekend outing to Buffalo was a move up the urban ladder. The Statler Hotel in downtown Buffalo in the 1950s, to quote a Toronto friend, was "the cat's whiskers."

Buffalo in 1950 was one of America's wealthiest cities, proudly bearing the nickname "City of Light" thanks to the electric power provided by nearby Niagara Falls. Buffalo was the nation's busiest inland port and the largest wheat port in the world, thanks to its strategic location. Access via the Great Lakes to Minnesota's iron ore deposits and to nearby Pennsylvania's coal deposits ensured the profitability of its steel and metal-bashing industries. Location, in short, had truly blessed Buffalo. "Nature has done everything

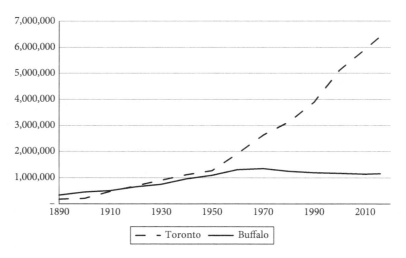

Figure 4.1 Population (Metropolitan Area) of Buffalo and Toronto, 1890–2016.[2]

to favor this locality," boasted Albert Shaw, president of the Canadian Niagara Power Company, in 1893. Shaw, with laudable optimism, predicted that Buffalo would become the greatest manufacturing center in the world.[7] Some sixty years later, Shaw's boast still did not seem out of place. Although not the "greatest" manufacturing center in world, Buffalo in the 1950s was one of America's great industrial powerhouses.

Buffalo's reputation went beyond commerce. The following quotes from the 1911 *Encyclopedia Britannica*[8] nicely convey the city's repute at the time:

> Buffalo is widely known for the beauty of its residential sections. . . . Buffalo today has broad and spacious streets, most of which are lined by trees, and many small parks and squares. The municipal park system is one of unusual beauty, consisting of a chain of parks. . . . the excellent drainage and water-supply systems, make Buffalo one of the healthiest cities in the United States.

The 1960 edition of the same encyclopedia was no less laudatory,[9] praising Buffalo as a beacon of culture and learning with a university, major art gallery, and well-stocked network of public libraries. Buffalo had every reason to think of itself as one of America's great cities[10] and as likely to remain so. The mood in the 1950s was one of unbridled optimism: Buffalo was a city on the threshold of another century of uninterrupted growth. Demographers saw Buffalo soon growing to two million, maybe even three million. Dexter Rumsey, president of the Buffalo Chamber of Commerce, exulted in 1958, "There has never been a time when we could look forward to a more brilliant future."[11] Then it all began to unravel.

An Unassailable Natural Location Advantage

Buffalo is located at what is commonly called a break-bulk point, a geographical obstacle that forces transporters to switch from one transport mode to another, from sea to land, rail to road, and so on. For east–west or west–east trade between the American Midwest and the Eastern Seaboard (or eastern Canadian ports), Niagara Falls constituted a major obstacle together with its downstream rapids, preventing shippers from using the St. Lawrence River beyond the Falls. Until the arrival of railways in the mid-19th century, water constituted the most economical transport mode. The

Erie Canal, opened in 1825, connecting Lake Erie with the Hudson River and thus New York City, immedicably became the principal transport route between east and west. Buffalo, located at its western terminus, was in essence born with the Erie Canal. Raw goods (mainly wheat, grains, and other produce) coming from the West had to be transshipped from lake-faring boats to canal barges in Buffalo before heading east to New York or other eastern or European markets, and vice-versa for goods and manufactured products shipped from the eastern to midwestern and western markets. The arrival of rail did not fundamentally alter Buffalo's "natural" advantage, for Niagara Falls continued to block eastward water transport. Almost all of the major Great Lakes steamship transportation lines had their eastern terminus at Buffalo, a monopoly position that continued well into the 20th century.

Buffalo's favored position as transshipment point between the American West and East meant that it grew as the West grew. The West's wheat and other produce needed to reach markets; Buffalo was the natural intermediary, coming to house one of the world's greatest grain markets. Ancillary industries developed: flour and grist milling, biscuits and other grain-based manufacturing as well as associated service industries: shipping companies; boat repair; insurance and banking; and storage and handling. The grain elevator was first invented in Buffalo (1853) and soon became a dominant feature of Buffalo's landscape. Slaughtering and meat packing was another natural outgrowth of the city's position as a break-bulk point; western cattle was processed, packaged, and then sent to eastern markets. In the opposite direction, Buffalo emerged as a distribution center for eastern manufactured goods destined for western markets. By the end of the 19th century, Buffalo had become a major transport hub. Some fourteen trunk (rail) lines had terminals or passed through the city.

The natural advantage of break-bulk points for manufacturing is a basic rule of economic geography. Since goods have in any case to be physically unloaded and reloaded from one transport mode to another, a costly labor-intensive operation, it makes sense to establish a plant there at the same time. Why bear the cost twice by locating elsewhere? Minnesota iron ore had, in any case, to be unloaded (from boats) in Buffalo if it were to go further east (by train). Coking coal from Pennsylvania needed to be transferred from rail to boat if it were to go further west. It therefore made sense to produce steel in Buffalo. Steel and metal-bashing industries came to account for some 60 percent of total manufacturing employment, a share that remained stable well into the 1970s.[12] Like its lakefront silos, symbols of its role in the grain trade, giant steel mills became the proud markers of Buffalo's industrial might.

The largest plant, which would come to symbolize the steel industry in Buffalo, opened its doors in 1902 in the small (renamed) community of Lackawanna. The Lackawanna plant, bought by Bethlehem Steel in the 1920s, initially employed some six thousand workers, eventually going as high as twenty thousand workers. These were good-paying jobs, laying the groundwork for prosperous middle-class communities, largely blue collar, buttressed by strong labor unions. The steel industry was capital intensive, dependent on scale economies and in turn on large markets. Large, highly capitalized plants meant that employers could afford to pay high wages, as labor constituted only a fraction of total production costs. Other highly capitalized high-wage industries, mainly rolling stock manufacturing and later automobiles, came to locate nearby. This, of course, was a boon for the workers who had been hired and for local merchants who profited from their spending power. However, the dominance of metal-bashing industries meant that Buffalo was now a high-wage economy, a fact that would later come to haunt it—but I'm jumping ahead of the story

Let us now move to Buffalo's third "natural" advantage: electric power. With the invention of the technology for generating power via water-powered turbines, Niagara Falls provided the region with an additional advantage for attracting industry. New industries were emerging that required large inputs of electric power: aluminum smelting; petrol refining; chemicals. During the first half of the 20th century, numerous plants opened in the municipality of Niagara Falls. The chemical industry came to occupy an important place in the regional economy, a fact that would equally come back to haunt it later. Finally, we should not forget the symbolic value of the Falls, not only as a source of electric power but also as a non-negligible source of tourist income. Niagara Falls proudly touted itself as the "The Honeymoon Capital of the World," a favorite destination for foreign and American tourists alike.

Buffalo's urban landscape reflected its wealth and industrial might. At the center of its "beautiful residential sections and broad and spacious streets" was a strong central city and downtown with a lively theater district, busy shops, and office towers. Among the most emblematic was the Larkin Building, completed in 1906 and the head office of the Larkin Company; which initially made soap but evolved into one of America's largest mail-order businesses. The Larkin Administration Building, designed by Frank Lloyd Wright, one of the greatest architects of the time, was hailed by the visiting state architect of The Netherlands as "without equal in the whole of Europe." It soon became the proud symbol of Buffalo's corporate glory. Mies van der Rohe, another of the century's great architects, called the Larkin Building a masterpiece.[13] Buffalo's downtown remained vibrant well into the 1970s, accounting for some 25 percent of the city's property and sales taxes.[14]

Without wishing to overdo the hype, the Buffalo of the 1950s (recall, I am as always referring to the metropolitan area) seemingly had it all: a major transport hub; a strong industrial base, an international tourist destination, a vibrant downtown, and an attractive, livable city with a strong sense of civic pride. Let us now see how each of these assets unraveled, starting with technological change.

The First Gale Wind: Buffalo Loses Its "Natural" Location Advantage

If the Buffalo story teaches us anything, it is that no advantage, no matter how seemingly "natural," is God-given or immune from human intervention.[15] Indeed, Mark Goldman argues in his seminal book[16] that Buffalo's perceived natural location advantage was at the root of its demise, producing a corporate and civic culture of overconfidence, its location advantage becoming an article of entrenched faith. Year in and year out, boosters touted Buffalo's *centrality*,[17] its destiny assured by geography, an unalterable fact inscribed on the map of North America. How could geography change? But change it did, in the year 1959 to be precise. The name of that first gale wind in what was to become a perfect storm was the St. Lawrence Seaway.[18]

The idea of building a water passage—a series of canals and locks—to circumvent Niagara Falls and numerous rapids along the St. Lawrence River had been in the air since the end of the 19th century. As always, there were proponents and opponents. A project of this scale would require broad support, not least of which from the Canadian and U.S. federal governments and the provinces and states along the proposed route. A simple look at the map explains who was against and who was in favor. The port cities of the Eastern Seaboard (New York, Philadelphia, Baltimore) were against the project, together with rail, shipping, and other commercial interests, which constituted a powerful lobby. A direct passage between the Midwest (Chicago, Detroit, Duluth) and the Atlantic would mean that goods could now be shipped directly to European and other international markets, bypassing New York and other Atlantic ports. By the same token, freighters coming from Europe (Japan, Africa, or elsewhere) would sail directly up the St. Lawrence and the Great Lakes to deliver their goods to Chicago, Cleveland, and other midwestern cities. These fears, not totally unfounded, were successful in blocking the construction of a passageway until the 1950s.

Several factors eventually tipped the balance in favor of the seaway. As the U.S. economy shifted westward, the West's political and economic clout grew. The 1950s was the golden age of the Midwest economy: the automobile industry was king, voracious consumer of steel. The term *Rustbelt* still lay far in the future. Steel mills needed access to iron ore. The spark that triggered the steel industry's (and thus also the powerful automobile lobby's) push for a seaway was the discovery in the early 1950s of rich iron ore deposits in Labrador, which was accessible via the Quebec ports of Sept-Îles and Port-Cartier on the Gulf of St Lawrence. At the time, it was also feared that the Messabi Range iron ore deposits in Minnesota would soon run dry. Access to the Labrador deposits was seen as a matter of life and death for the Great Lakes steel industry. Simultaneously, the wheat lobbies in both Canada and the United States pushed for direct shipping access to international markets, circumventing the clogged ports of the East Coast. The seaway would allow western wheat to move east unobstructed and allow Labrador iron ore to move west, a winning proposition for both sides. The final card that forced the U.S. administration's hand was Canada's threat to go it alone.

Congress authorized the construction of the Seaway in May 1954, and the formal agreement between the United States and Canada was signed in August of that year. Finally completed in 1959, the St. Lawrence Seaway would be the largest navigable inland waterway in the world, the biggest civil engineering project ever attempted in North America, dredging 360 million tons of rock and installing seven locks on the St. Lawrence.[19] The project was more than just a waterway; it was also a power project, which was a prime factor in its approval, resulting in the construction of a massive power dam bisecting the international border between Cornwall, Ontario, and Massena, New York, the world's largest joint power facility at the time.

Let us now return to Buffalo on the eve of the completion of the St. Lawrence Seaway. In one fell swoop, the Seaway would undercut Buffalo's two "natural" advantages: its position as break-bulk point between East and West and as provider of electric power. Should not the city fathers (and mothers) have foreseen what was coming? Looking back, the consequences of the Seaway should have been obvious. With hindsight, one can only wonder at the shortsightedness of Buffalo's elites and, more to the point, at their failure to plan and to prepare in the face of the coming storm.[20] The Seaway was hardly an unforeseen event.

The failure of local elites to correctly see what was coming had its roots, in part, in a mistaken perception of the consequences of the Seaway. It is in the nature of businessmen and politicians to paint rosy pictures of the future; nobody likes harbingers of doom. The mistaken perception was in part due to a misunderstanding of the Seaway's carrying capacity. Here, much of the blame must go to the two national governments (the U.S. and Canadian) and the promoters of the project for not honestly explaining the Seaway's function. Instead, Buffalo's city fathers were carried away by the hype of a "Super Seaway" that would welcome ocean liners out of Europe proudly sailing up the St. Lawrence to Chicago, Toronto, and (yes) Buffalo. That never happened, but one cannot totally blame Buffalo's leaders for falling victim to such visions of future glory.

The result on the eve of the opening of the Seaway was a generalized mood of optimism, even euphoria, which, seen through today's eyes, seems almost otherworldly. Three quotes, which I unabashedly borrow from Thomas,[21] nicely convey the mood of the times:

> I'm for the seaway because I'm for Buffalo. I'll tell you this: Smart men will see the potential here and move in, and 10 years from now, Buffalo will enter a period of great growth. I don't know anything that can stop it. — Melvin Baker, Chairman, National Gypsum Co.
>
> We're counting on this seaway to open us up to the world. —Fred Schoellkopf, President, Niagara Share Corp.
>
> Buffalo is in the most favorable position of all the cities on the waterway. —Frank Sedita, Mayor of Buffalo.

Ocean liners did not steam up to Buffalo and open her up to the world. Exactly the contrary happened. Shipping to and from Buffalo collapsed, and with it industries associated with the movement of grain. The Seaway was not designed for ocean-bound shipping, but rather for bulk cargo (principally grain and iron ore) carried on Lakers specially designed for that purpose. The commerce that was destroyed (or rather, rerouted) was precisely the trade in which Buffalo had specialized for over more than a century. Henceforth, American wheat out of Duluth and Canadian wheat out of the port of Thunder Bay would be shipped directly to the new grain ports of Port Cartier and Sept-Îles on the Gulf of St Lawrence, bypassing Buffalo. The iron ore of Labrador would move in the opposite direction, going directly to the steel mills of the Great Lakes, again bypassing Buffalo, its "natural" monopoly for east–west trade irretrievably lost: end of story.

It is small consolation that, in one of the ironies of this extraordinary saga, the rationale for construction of the Seaway has since proven to be false. The Messabi Range iron ore deposits have not run dry. The Labrador deposits are no longer being mined (too expensive). In short, the Seaway is no longer needed for the east–west shipment of ore. The Seaway today is underused and would probably not have been built under current conditions. For Buffalo, however, the damage was done.

The Second Gale Wind: The Collapse of Steel

Misfortune seldom strikes only once. A second gale wind would soon hit Buffalo. The second gale—the death of the steel industry—was more directly technological and, unlike the first, not particular to Buffalo, hitting all the great cites of what we today call the Rustbelt. Nor was it particular to the United States: the story was not all that different for the once great steel-bashing cities of Europe. The giant Krupp steel works near Essen were no less massive and no less impressive than Bethlehem Steel's plant in Lackawanna.

The steel industry provides a useful lesson of the relationship between technology and work cultures. Every industry, every technology, produces a distinct social environment. The steel industry in Buffalo, as elsewhere, relied on massive blast furnaces, coke-fired ovens, and rolling mills, requiring large infusions of capital, which predictably produced an industry dominated by a few big firms, US Steel, Bethlehem Steel, and Republic Steel being among the largest at the time. This oligopolistic relationship benefited not only owners and shareholders, but also workers able to appropriate a share of this monopoly rent in the form of high wages, thanks in no small part to strong steelworkers unions, which often worked hand-in-hand with management.[22] In essence, industry leaders avoided strikes by buying labor peace. The hourly manufacturing wage in the early 1980s was higher in Buffalo than in New York City: $11.38 compared to $8.08.[23] As late as the 1990s, the average manufacturing wage in the Buffalo area was still 25 percent above the U.S. average.[24]

This cozy relationship to the benefit of both parties held fast as long as plants remained big and oligopolistic rents were unthreatened. All this started to unravel in the 1960s. Three things happened, although they were not perceptible at first: changes in the technology of steel making; the entry of more efficient foreign competitors; and the relocation of the automobile industry, the industry's chief costumer. Starting in the 1950s, a new class of steel producers entered the market using a new technology: electric rather coke-fired furnaces, which were less reliant on scale economies.[25] These minimills gradually became the industry norm. No major U.S. steel company built a new plant after the mid-1960s, and no new blast furnace was built after 1979. The new minimill companies were more flexible in their location choices, generally avoiding large steelmaking cities like Cleveland, Pittsburgh, and Buffalo with histories of high wages and strong unions. The writing was on the wall for large steel mills. The predictable agony began in 1971 when Bethlehem Steel laid off nine thousand workers; in 1978, Bethlehem laid off a further thirty-five hundred workers.[26] The final dagger was hurled on December 27, 1982, arguably the darkest day in Buffalo's now perfect storm, when the Bethlehem Steel Corporation announced the shutdown of all its local steelmaking operations, laying off the remaining six thousand workers.[27]

It is not necessary to list all the plants that closed during the terrible decades of the 1970s and 1980s to understand the disaster that befell the city. The *Buffalo Evening News* reported in 1976 that no less than thirty-eight manufacturing firms (about ten thousand jobs lost) had shut down in the preceding five years, with a predictable fall in payroll earnings and property taxes.[28] Robert Crandall puts the total number of manufacturing jobs lost between 1954 and 1997 at one hundred thousand, a drop of nearly 50 percent, which is as good a barometer as any of the scale of the disaster.[29] The chemical industry was decimated, losing 75 percent of initial employment, falling from twelve thousand jobs in 1954 to three thousand in 1997,[30] a consequence in part of the region's loss of comparative advantage for the production of electric power. The collapse of rail, the combined result of the competition from trucking, and Buffalo's lost position as a break-bulk point meant the disappearance of a major customer for steel, but also that of a major employer in its own right. By 1979, six of the seven large northeastern railroads had collapsed, accounting for 20 percent of the city's land use.[31] They ceased paying property taxes with a predictable impact on the city of Buffalo's finances. Falling revenues in turn blocked access to bond markets, further crippling the city's ability to provide services and undertake capital projects.

Let us now turn the automobile industry. The reasons for the near collapse in the 1970s of the once powerful U.S. automobile industry are well known: their failure to compete with Japan's more efficient automakers and adapt to the shift in demand toward smaller, more fuel-efficient cars. More important for Buffalo, however, was the shift in the location of new plants. The Japanese (but also Korean and German) transplants tended to locate further south in states with right-to-work laws[32] (such as Tennessee and Kentucky), preferring small and midsized towns making unionization even less likely and thus keeping wages low. Buffalo was becoming increasingly peripheral compared to the center of gravity of the U.S. auto industry. The news was not all bad. Buffalo's proximity to southern Ontario's automobile industry[33] allowed it to retain an automotive components sector but not enough to save the steel industry. The Buffalo economy continued to stagnate well into the 21st century, with no real employment growth. Jobs in the private sector declined. The biggest employers at the time of writing were in the public sector—health services, social welfare, public administration— certainly not the hallmark of a healthy economy.

The Intrusive Rentier Syndrome

Buffalo's stagnation raises the question of why the Buffalo economy did not turn around and replace lost jobs in steel with jobs in growing industries. "Creative destruction," also called Schumpeter's Gale in honor of the Austrian-American economist who coined the phrase, is one of the basic foundations of growing economies. Old jobs are constantly being destroyed to be replaced by new jobs, as we saw in New York where the apparel industry, now largely gone, has been replaced by jobs in the information economy. Why did the same thing not happen in Buffalo? Part of the answer is the distinct work culture that the steel industry helped shape.

Elsewhere, I coined the term *Intrusive Rentier Syndrome* to describe local economies caught in the grip of a dominant *rentier* industry.[34] The word *rentier* refers to industries which, because of a natural or human-made advantage, are able to earn above-average profits, or *rents* in the jargon of economists. The Intrusive Rentier Syndrome was first coined with reference to the large aluminum smelting plants and paper mills that dominate many small and midsized towns in Canada.[35] Like steel, the technologies of these industries give rise to large, highly capitalized, plants in which labor costs account for a fraction of total costs. Although often generating rapid job growth at first, such industries end up crowding out other industries unable to bear similarly high wage costs, resulting in slower long-run growth for the local economy and even decline, which is why such industries are deemed "intrusive."

The intrusive nature of *rentier* industries does not stop at the crowding out of other industries, bringing us into the realm of sociology and perceptions. In his study of Buffalo's painful decline, Goldman describes Buffalo's blue-collar mindset, which goes a long way in explaining why workers raised on an ethic of "manly work" find it difficult to adjust to the new world of service industries and IT.[36] He cites a recently laid-off worker: "I loved my job. I loved the pay, with two days off what more could one ask for. I was helping to build a good product (radiators for trucks) and I was going to give those people the best dam eight hours I could. It made me feel like a man. Sitting around the house knocks your masculinity right down the drain."[37]. I do not know what happened to this worker, but it is difficult to imagine him in an office job, shuffling paper or sitting in front of a computer.

In environments where assured contracts and high blue-collar wages have long been the norm, two negative side-effects often follow: (1) education is less valued; and (2) entrepreneurship is less valued. Why go on to university if you can make good money at the neighborhood plant with only a secondary-level education? And why go to the trouble and take the associated risks of starting your own business if union contracts assure you a good lifetime income? Also, unions are not traditionally friendly to technological change, their understandable goal being to "protect" their members and not to introduce productivity-enhancing innovations that would reduce jobs. Communities afflicted with the Intrusive Rentier Syndrome therefore tend to be less entrepreneurial, less educated,[38] and less innovative.

The word *syndrome* points to a deeply engrained affliction that is difficult to cure and that indeed is its most problematic aspect, the reason why so many Rustbelt communities have failed to bounce back well after the local plant closed. Mindsets and work cultures change slowly, and some more slowly than others. It is easy with hindsight to blame Buffalo's leaders, but I know of no case of places afflicted with the Intrusive Rentier Syndrome that have managed a rapid turnaround. The road back is always long.

The Intrusive Rentier Syndrome also often has a physical-visual side. Here again, Buffalo was not spared. The region was to be the site of one of the worst environmental disasters in U.S. history—the 1978 Love Canal tragedy—the sad legacy of the region's bygone glory as center of the chemical industry. In 1953, the Hooker Chemical Company, which had used the canal as a landfill and chemical dumpsite, covered the canal with earth and sold it to the city of Niagara Falls for one dollar.[39] About one hundred homes and a school were subsequently built on the site. Some twenty-five years later, following a heavy rainfall, noxious liquids seeped up, causing suspicion. Subsequent analysis revealed that the site contained toxic carcinogen substances linked to birth defects. Some two hundred families were affected and eventually evacuated.

The visual legacy of industrial decline did irreparable damage to the region's once flourishing tourist industry, the final gale in the perfect storm. By the 1990s, most honeymooners and tourists had abandoned the U.S. side of Niagara Falls, preferring the Canadian side. Goldman paints a particularly gruesome picture of Niagara Falls, which in his words had become one of the ugliest places in the United States: "With gap-toothed streetscapes filled with vacant lots, abandoned office buildings and half-empty hotels . . . the American side of Niagara Falls, like the Love Canal that had made it notorious twenty years earlier, was more like an open wound."[40]

The Intrusive Rentier Syndrome, however, is only half the story. To fully understand Buffalo's downfall, we need to enter the realm of politics. Buffalo's problems were compounded by an institutional straightjacket that greatly constrained the ability of Buffalo's leaders to implement change—that is, had they so wished.

Politics: Handmaidens of Buffalo's Perfect Storm

The absence of political and business leadership is a continuous refrain, constantly repeated by observers of Buffalo's decline.[41] The title of Diana Dillaway's 2006 book (*Power Failure: Politics, Patronage, and the Economic*

Future of Buffalo) says it all. The list of opportunities lost and of bad decisions made is almost endless. I am not a Buffalonian; nor of course was I there at the time bad (or good) decisions were made. Pointing fingers with hindsight is easy. It is not a sport that I wish to engage in, especially as an outsider. It is entirely normal that Buffalonians themselves should be the most critical of their leaders. I tend to take a more indulgent view. The actions of Buffalo's elites at the time need to be seen in the context of the municipal and state institutions that set the bounds of their actions. Tellingly, none of the authors cited in this chapter (all Buffalonians) question the institutions that define what Buffalo is and what it can do. It's simply not on the radar, a given in the natural order of things. Yet, as the comparison with Toronto will reveal, there is nothing natural about the manner in which "cities" are defined, almost always, as the children of senior governments.

An Institutional Straightjacket

Political structures define not only what local leaders can do or not do, but also the very perception of what their "city" is. For Buffalonians, the definition is unambiguous. Buffalo's boundaries were fixed in 1835 and have not changed since. More to the point, the New York State legislature in Albany, to which all local authorities in the state are ultimately beholden, created a system of some fifteen hundred municipal units with essentially inflexible boundaries.[42] In 1926, Buffalo attempted to annex part of the neighboring town of Tonawanda but was blocked by the state legislature. New York State law was amended in 1928, making annexation virtually impossible. The following citation from a 1950 article in the *Buffalo Evening News* couldn't be clearer: "The way the state constitution reads, there isn't any likelihood that Buffalo could annex as much as a single Town of Tonawanda hot-dog stand."[43] The *City of Buffalo* was and remains a fixed unalterable territorial unit, no matter that that unit makes little economic or demographic sense.

Boundaries fashion identities and, more importantly, political constituencies. Most metropolitan areas across the world are politically fragmented. That in itself, we know, is not an impediment to social cohesion—that is, providing a culture of cooperation and mechanisms to ensure a reasonably equal delivery of people services across the urban region. Unfortunately, Buffalo's political history points to a seemingly congenital culture of mistrust between city and suburb, pitting the city of Buffalo against Erie County and surrounding communities. Again, city–suburb tensions are not unique to Buffalo, but the degree of intermunicipal squabbling and mistrust that apparently characterizes the region visibly shackled political action at a time when it was most needed. Those critical decades saw an alphabet soup of agencies, committees, and local development corporations,[44] not to mention several commissioned studies (often highly professional and sadly prescient[45]) and lists of grandiose plans, only to flounder on a bedrock of mistrust, self-interested haggling, and lack of follow through. There were some successes, notably in the health sector, but the overall record, repeatedly lamented by all observers, was not good. Among the more comic examples cited is the downtown convention center completed in 1978 but without a nearby hotel.[46]

That era saw a number of attempts at metropolitan integration, including shifting responsibilities to the county level (i.e., public hospitals). However, initiatives to formally merge municipalities or introduce revenue-sharing were systematically blocked (recall the Tonawanda example), most often by voters in small semirural suburban communities who were understandably fearful of being absorbed by their larger neighbors. There is little use in blaming suburban voters for their lack of regional spirit. If households choose to live in the suburbs, it is precisely because they do not want to live in the central city. By the same token, asking residents of richer municipalities to share their fiscal wealth with poorer communities is rarely a vote-pleaser. Revenue (or service) sharing arrangements will, need I repeat, only happen if senior governments step in. New York State, by decreeing de facto that all such initiatives needed to be popularly approved by all local parties, in effect trapped the central city (Buffalo).

The fixed nature of Buffalo's boundaries would have been of little consequence if the city's responsibilities were limited to urban services (such as parks, sanitation, and lighting) and fiscal capacities evenly distributed across the metropolitan region. Neither was the case in Buffalo. In New York State, as in most of urban America, local authorities draw the majority of their revenues from property taxes.[47] Primary and secondary schools were (and still are) financed through the city budget, accounting for approximately half of expenditures.[48] In short, local property values largely determine the quality of the school system. Let us now add in the fiscal gap between richer and poorer municipalities—and the race factor—and the end result is a perfect recipe for an increasingly unequal and politically and socially divided city, harbinger of exactly the kind of urban disaster Jane Jacobs presciently foresaw in the 1960s.

The rest of the story will be familiar to most American readers: metropolitan areas in the grips of a seemingly irreversible divide been a decaying central city and leafy, largely white suburbs. The story does not require a long narrative. As black migrants from the South moved to the central city, drawn to Buffalo by the lure of well-paying blue-collar jobs, whites moved out. The city's population fell from five hundred eighty thousand in 1950 to some two hundred sixty thousand in 2012, with the sharpest declines taking place during the 1980s. Over the same period, whites as a percentage of the total population dropped from 94 to some 50 percent today.[49] As elsewhere, the growing divide between city and suburb was not only a matter of race, but also of social class. Beginning with the great wave of suburbanization and growing car ownership following World War II, a self-reinforcing circle, again not unique to the Buffalo area, was set in motion in which better-off households moved to suburban communities, in turn enriching their fiscal base (and concomitant quality of public services, including schools). This left the central city with an ever diminishing fiscal base and declining quality of public services, which in turn further fueled the exodus of richer households to the suburbs. The following 2014 quote from Thomas nicely sums up Buffalo's center-suburb divide.[50]

> Per capita income . . . is 34 percent lower in the city than in the rest of Erie County. . . . Suburbanites collectively earned $15 billion in 2000, while Buffalonians pulled in just $4.4 billion. Nearly half of Buffalo's residents belong to minority groups. . . . But 94 percent of suburbanites are white. . . . The resulting recipe is hardly designed to create a spirit of harmony and cooperation. Start with a long-simmering base of urban-suburban conflict. Add a large helping of economic inequality. Season with racial tension. What pops out of the oven is a casserole of suspicion and isolation.

The story is all too often further poisoned by cronyism and ethnic politics. Buffalo had a particularly bloated bureaucracy with more public workers per capita than any American city, winning the dubious distinction, according to Syracuse University's Maxwell School of Public Affairs, of being the worst run city in the land with New Orleans.[51] I am, again, ill-placed as an outsider to apportion blame, but the city of Buffalo has, it seems, had more than its share of corrupt and fiscally imprudent mayors.

The combination of costly local government and low (and declining) property values make for a volatile mix, with rarely a happy ending. Few places have seen their central city decline as precipitously as Buffalo. Downtown decline is almost always the sign of much deeper problems.

Few events were more pivotal in precipitating the fall of Buffalo's downtown than the decision to relocate its university. It is to this story that I now turn, yet another demonstration of the power of senior governments to shape cities.[52]

The University Saga, Culture Wars, and the Destruction of Downtown

Buffalo's homegrown university was the University of Buffalo (UB), located downtown on Main Street with eighteen thousand students in the early 1960s, catering mainly to white middle-class families. In 1962, the governor of New York, Nelson Rockefeller, announced that UB would soon be acquired by the state to be integrated into SUNY (State University of New York) and appropriately re-baptized SUNYAB, a key piece in Rockefeller's grand plan to create a world-class university system. Projections foresaw a university with thirty-five thousand students, with an initial state investment of $100 million, which would eventually grow to $650 million. This was a monumental project that everyone understood would shape the city's landscape for decades to come. A new campus was to be built, but where? After several studies, the choice boiled down to two sites: the Buffalo waterfront close to the core of the downtown retail district and the municipality of Amherst, 12 miles to the northeast, a growing middle-class suburb with rapidly growing retailing and office sectors.

The first major consultant's report recommended the waterfront site, pointing to the potential positive contribution of the university to the city's fiscal health and the vitality of downtown, a source not only of employment (some two thousand jobs initially) but also of intellectual ferment and street life. The University Council (an advisory group that included business leaders and state officials) also favored the downtown location. However, for reasons that are still nebulous, the SUNY Board of Trustees chose the Amherst site,[53] with their decision formally announced in June 1964,

The backlash was immediate. A coalition was formed, appropriately named CURB (Committee for an Urban University of Buffalo), comprising community groups and downtown retailing associations, actively advocating for the waterfront site. The next three years saw a seesaw battle between opposing proponents of the waterfront and Amherst sites, both vying for the support of Governor Rockefeller. In today's political language, the battle had all the trappings of a culture war between community (read left-wing) activists and establishment (read right-wing) types. For the latter (with some poetic license), the university would, they argued, best flower in a setting appropriate to academic contemplation, far from the hurly burly of the city and its problems. The subtext was lost to no one: "... far from Afro-Americans and other undesirables." Dillaway cites a banker: "We don't want those New York radicals and people of color running around downtown."[54] In addition, it was not the role of the university to solve the city's social problems—NIMBYism, I'm tempted to add, draped in academic clothing.

The other side saw things differently, going so far as to regard the transfer as part of a conscious strategy to undermine downtown. The following citation from a black community leader makes this point abundantly clear: "Some very powerful people apparently want Buffalo to die. The university goes out to a flood plain. The medical school follows. . . . Apparently some men are willing to decimate Buffalo and declare (suburban) Amherst the new center of a new city."[55] To break the deadlock, Governor Rockefeller appointed Mason Gross, the highly respected president of Rutgers University (New Jersey), an outsider and thus a priori neutral observer, to do a restudy. Gross's team set about consulting various groups. The results revealed university staff and faculty to be largely in favor of the Amherst site, which was not an entirely surprising result as many lived there.[56] Gross submitted his report in February 1967. Amherst was to be the future site of SUNYAB, a decision that was formally announced a few weeks later, thus upholding the SUNY Board of Trustees' 1964 decision. The culture war was over. It was clear which side had won. Expressing a widely held sentiment on the losing side, Goldman writes: "The university . . . by moving to Amherst had rejected the city and in the process gained a new campus while losing its soul,"[57] an appropriate epitaph for this urban saga.

The Last Straw: The Wrong State

A last piece is missing if we are to fully understand Buffalo's fall from grace. The study object of this book, let us recall, is always the urban region, the collapse of the central city simply the most visible symptom of its decline. The roots of the decline of the urban region run much deeper, equally trapped in a fiscal straightjacket. But the roots are of a different nature, a misfortune Buffalo shares with sister cities in western and upstate New York: Rochester, Syracuse, Binghamton, and so on. Very simply, New York's tax burden is high compared to that of neighboring states. Why open a plant in Buffalo, if it costs less (in local and state taxes) in neighboring Ohio or Pennsylvania? According to Tax Foundation data,[58] New York had the highest (average) combined local and state tax burden of any state. States generally have three sources of revenue: income taxes, sales taxes, and property taxes. As a rule, a state will concentrate on one and go low on the other two. New York is in the top six states for all three.

Why? Is not the state of New York shooting itself in the foot? To some extent, yes. But New York can afford to have high taxes because it has something unique to offer in return called New York City, bringing us back to buzz and agglomeration economies. Buffalo, Rochester, and Syracuse are, so to speak, trapped in the wrong state whose legislation and taxes are designed for a world-class city. The following quote nicely sums up the dilemma[59]: "Basically what you've got in New York is a state tax code and regulatory regimen written for New York City. Legislators say, 'Look, New York is a center of world commerce. Businesses have to be here. It doesn't matter how high we tax them.'" So, no matter how hard locals try, growth will remain an uphill battle as long as their cities are trapped in a state with policies not designed for them. Western New York State has been in decline over the last half-century and continues to decline with little prospect of a turnaround.[60]

The ultimate irony of this unhappy story is that Buffalo has essentially become a ward of the state: 40 percent of the city's revenues are in the form state aid.[61] The state and federal governments have certainly not failed to throw money at Buffalo. The number of urban revitalization projects is almost endless, all of them surely well intentioned, focused primarily on housing, transit, social welfare, and aid to inner-city neighborhoods.[62] But few ask why these inner-city neighborhoods came to exist in the first place, or why the region has remained chronically uncompetitive. The final paradox, which would be funny if it were not sad, is that the state of New York has in essence created its own ward, forced to throw money at an ailing patient of its own making.

Toronto: The Lucky City

Toronto's story will be shorter than Buffalo's. Success is always easier and more pleasant to recount.

Let me begin with location and Buffalo's "natural" advantage, which we discovered was not natural at all. Toronto had no evident natural advantage. Its harbor on Lake Ontario was no better than that of other Great Lakes cities. Toronto owes its initial growth to American Loyalists (so-called because they wished to remain loyal to the Crown) who fled north after the American Revolution, the majority settling in what was to become the Canadian province of Ontario. In the decades that followed (1790s–), Toronto evolved as a colonial administrative outpost, a midsized service and manufacturing center, and so it would remain for more than a century.

A Lucky Industrial Legacy (and Small Market)

Toronto, unlike Buffalo, thus came into being as a "central place," and its growth was linked to that of Ontario, its economic *hinterland*. In contrast to Buffalo, Toronto had no continental ambitions; its focus was regional. Montreal, not Toronto, was Canada's cosmopolitan metropolis, entry point for European immigrants, and also Canada's great rail hub linking east and west. A visitor to Toronto in 1900 would have found a generally well-run, if staid, provincial capital, clean and efficient yes, but not a terribly exciting place. Toronto was never meant to be a great city, notes local historian Bruce Bell,[63] and did not perceive itself as such. This picture contrasts with brash Buffalo to the south, host of the Pan American Exposition of 1901.

The paradox of Toronto's unpretentious provincial beginning is that it was thereby bequeathed an economic base that would serve it well later. Central places—regional service centers—have generally fared better since the second half of the 20th century than cities founded on manufacturing, profiting from the rise of the service economy, including high-order services. White-collar industries will understandably produce a different work culture than blue-collar industries. Although Toronto was a fairly small regional center initially (Toronto was not New York), its service industry beginnings, buttressed by its role as a provincial capital, constituted Toronto's first piece of good luck.

The contrast with Buffalo's industry mix does not end there. Manufacturing was proportionately as important in Toronto as in Buffalo up to the 1950s. Unlike Buffalo, however, its manufacturing base was largely composed of midsized firms in a diversity of industries, the result of its much smaller national (Canadian) market. The huge plants that emerged in Buffalo needed a correspondingly huge market. These huge plants with attendant scale economies in part explain why wages were (and remain) higher on average in American cities, the counterpart of their vast market. However, the downside of scale-based production is the emergence of highly specialized cities like Buffalo dominated by a few large firms. Toronto's economy also deindustrialized after the 1950s, with its share of manufacturing in total employment falling (currently, it is about 15 percent); but the transformation was gradual. This is in sharp contrast with Buffalo's traumatic plant closures with no equivalent high-order service or small-business sector to fall back on. Here then was Toronto's second piece of good luck, a diversified economic base less prone to technological shocks.

Outside Events—A Very Lucky (and Unanticipated) Boost

Then, suddenly, Toronto's growth accelerated—the take-off point was roughly in the 1960s (note the upswing in Toronto's curve in Figure 4.1). The origins of that jolt was outside the city. In contrast again to Buffalo, political events and changes in transportation technology would help rather than hinder its growth.

The growth of the automobile industry would act as a first stimulus, with politics lending a helping hand. The 1965 U.S.–Canada Auto-Pact established free trade between the two nations for the production of automobiles and automobile parts. Because of the generally lower labor costs in Canada, all major U.S. car producers (GM, Chrysler, and Ford) set up plants in Canada, soon to be followed by Japanese and Korean automakers, all in southern Ontario.[64] This was a natural choice given the proximity to the U.S. car industry. The impact on the Ontario economy was immediate. The Canadian auto industry has since been plagued by many of the same problems as its U.S. sister, but the initial impact was to bolster the Ontario economy, and with it Toronto's.

Toronto Replaces Montreal as Canada's
Central Place

The major jolt to Toronto's economy would come from two events in the neighboring province of Quebec, where Montreal is located: the coming to power of a separatist government; and the destruction of Montreal's role as an air-travel hub. I shall describe these events only briefly here and will return to them in Chapter 6 when we visit Montreal. In a nutshell, Toronto received an accidental but powerful boost thanks to its neighbor's mistakes,[65] so to speak. Toronto's luck also provides a useful reminder of three basic axioms of economic geography: (1) human capital is mobile, Toronto in this case being on the lucky receiving end; (2) a city's reach almost always has a cultural dimension (recall imperial Vienna), Toronto being the lucky heir of Montreal's loss; and (3) locational advantages are always human-made in part (Buffalo already taught us this), Toronto now becoming the lucky winner. Let's consider each in turn.

The rise of Québécois nationalism in the 1960s fueled a growing sense of unease among English-speakers in the province. The pivotal event was the election of the *Parti Québécois* in 1976, which promised separation from Canada and stringent legislative measures to promote the French language. The election triggered an exodos of Anglophones, who were generally well educated, and Anglo-controlled businesses, which was to last two decades, with Toronto the primary beneficiary. In what has since gone down in history as the emblematic event of that exodus, the CEO of Sun Life, Canada's largest insurance company, announced on January 6, 1978, that it was moving its corporate headquarters to Toronto, the ostensible reason given the new law promoting French as the language of work. The Royal Bank of Canada, Canada's largest bank, and the Bank of Montreal,[66] both founded in Montreal, moved the bulk of their head-office operations to Toronto, moves that were facilitated by federal legislation. Unlike the United States where banks are state or locally chartered, Canada's banks are federally chartered with branches across the nation. This has allowed Canada, despite its small home market, to give birth to world-class banks, but in turn it has also created a highly concentrated industry dominated by five large banks, all of which today are headquartered in Toronto. This winner-take-all game allowed Toronto, once Montreal lost the race, to become the second largest financial center[67] in North America after New York.

The fear of separation aside, the move of financial and other high-order services (consultancies, management, marketing, etc.) to Toronto was entirely predictable, that is, once English lost its status as the dominant language of business in Montreal. Toronto therefore captured Montreal's market for information-rich services outside Quebec, extending its hinterland to become Canada's primary central place

How Air Travel Helped Toronto Consolidate Its Position as Canada's Central Place

Toronto's rise to the top of the urban hierarchy was facilitated by changes in transportation technology. The arrival of air travel, replacing ships for intercontinental travel changed the rules of the game for financial centers. Bankers and their clients need to meet. Negotiations, meetings, and the renewal (or building) of trust are essential building blocks of a financial center. In the days before air travel when the steamboat was the only way of traveling between financial centers, say between London and New York, great banks and corporate headquarters would predictably locate in port cities. Because of Canada's historic link with Britain, with London its financial reference, Montreal, not Toronto, was the natural point of contact with direct ocean liner service to London. Throughout history, ports and finance have generally gone together. That relationship unraveled with the arrival of air travel. A great financial center no longer needed to be a port city. Air travel also meant that inland cities could now be gateway cities, as Toronto was to become.

Toronto would undoubtedly have emerged as Canada's principal air hub in any case. Montreal's airport blunder (see Chapter 6) simply ensured that it would happen sooner (1974 to be exact) and that the transfer would be immediate and brutal. Air Canada, the nation's main carrier, would make Toronto's Pearson Airport into its main hub airport, as it still is today, making Toronto Canada's most globally connected city, bringing a second prize. Toronto became (and still is) Canada's principal port of entry for immigrants from Europe, Asia, and elsewhere. Toronto today is one of the most cosmopolitan cities in North America, with almost half of its population foreign born.[68]

Size brought other prizes. As English-speaking Canada's largest city (and Canada's after 1970), entertainment, publishing, broadcasting, advertising, and other growing "creative" industries came to concentrate in Toronto, further fueling its growth. The city was also home to Canada's top rated university, the University of Toronto, which now outranked Montreal's McGill University. The most prestigious newspapers with national readerships came out of Toronto.[69] Toronto had acquired all of the trappings of a global metropolis, becoming Canada's New York. Torontonians today tend to compare their city to New York, somewhat exaggeratedly one is tempted to say; but it is a far cry from the days when Torontonians looked up to Buffalo.

Lucky Parents—Toronto Is in Canada

Under the heading of "luck," we must equally inscribe the U.S.-Canada border. First, had the American Revolution not divided North America into two national halves, Toronto could not have emerged as the nation's central place, its position as a financial center contingent on the existence of a separate currency. Second, the border meant that Toronto, unlike Buffalo, did not have to contend with the competition of Sunbelt cities. People and firms had no sunny and right-to-work havens. Finally, the border meant that Toronto never had to confront the issue of race. One can reasonably argue that the reason Toronto and Canadian cities in general are safer than American cities and why there are no comparable inner-city ghettos[70] simply boils down to race.[71] It's easy for Canadians to be complacent. They never had to confront the legacy of slavery. Who knows how Canadian cities would have fared had it been possible to grow cotton north of the border.

Peace, Order, and Good Government

More to the point, having Canada as its parents meant that Toronto would evolve within a political culture that was very different from that of its neighbor; on this, it can be said to have been particularly lucky. Good governance is difficult to assess objectively, but one cannot but conclude that Toronto has been generally well governed throughout most of its history. Toronto has been famously described as "the city that works"[72] and "New York run by the Swiss."[73] Torontonians are not innately more virtuous than Buffalonians, for the city has had its share of scandals and wacky mayors. On the whole, however, Toronto has the reputation of a city run by generally (if not always) competent political leaders, and it generally ranks high on various livability indices.

To understand the political culture that underpins Toronto's governance (this applies to other Canadian cities as well), we need to go back in history. The Loyalists who settled Ontario, then called Upper Canada, were, by definition, *opposed* to the American Revolution and the principles it stood for. It is no accident that among the most often cited words of Canada's 1867 founding constitution[74] are: "Peace, Order, and Good Government," conveying a very different emphasis from "Life, Liberty, and the Pursuit of Happiness" in the American Declaration of Independence. In the delicate balance between freedom and order, Canadians have in general given greater weight to order, and, by the same token, they have been more willing to accept constraints on personal freedom such as higher taxes, an (obligatory) universal health care system, the outlawing of firearms, and limited municipal autonomy. Such constraints on freedom are accepted—that is the implicit premise—in exchange for the maintenance of social peace and harmony, including the prevention of socially unacceptable levels of inequality between neighborhoods or localities.

The Canadian Constitution explicitly limits the power of municipal government, pure "creatures of the State" (the provinces)[75]:

> It (the municipality) is created at the pleasure of the legislature, and need not require the consent of the people of the affected locality. The act of incorporation is not a contact between the legislatures and the local inhabitants. The authority conferred on the corporation is not local in nature but derives from the provincial government"

Canadian municipalities thus operate within a constitutional framework that puts them almost entirely at the mercy of provincial governments. At first glance, this might seem undemocratic, and it is in part. But local powers (e.g., zoning bylaws, housing codes) can be used, we know, to further exclusion, to keep "others" out. Canada is not unique in limiting the powers of local government. However, the outcomes in terms of good or bad governance ultimately depend on voter preferences (in provincial elections in the Canadian case) and on how wisely senior governments use their powers.

Metro–The City That Works

Toronto was incorporated at about the same time as Buffalo (1834) and, barring minor early annexations, stayed within its initial boundaries until 1953. Like Buffalo, the metropolitan region had by that time outgrown the city's historical borders. In both places, the city now accounted for about half the regional urbanized population. It is at this point in history—on the eve of the great suburban wave that would engulf North America— that the stories of the two cities diverge. In 1953, the Ontario government imposed a two-tier system of government on the region federating the city of Toronto, with thirteen surrounding municipalities in turn reduced to six larger lower-tier municipalities. The new entity was called the Metropolitan Municipality of Toronto ("Metro" popularly), which was to stay basically intact for the next forty-five years. It was a bold move, the first such regional government in North America, and urban planners hailed it as a model. The flattering references cited above refer to the Toronto of that period (1953– 1998). Metro had extensive powers, including property tax assessment, urban planning, sanitation, major thoroughfares, and, indirectly, education via (a now) Metro school board. Lower-tier municipalities, including the city of Toronto, continued to have jurisdiction over local roads, garbage collection, and other matters relating directly to the built environment. .

The creation of Metro was not a haphazard decision; but rather part of conscious provincial strategy to fashion a competitive and socially sustainable urban region.[76] Three key objectives drove the province's actions: ensuring a relatively uniform quality of public services through revenue-sharing and tax-pooling; distributing public housing on a "fair-share" basis; and providing a transit choice to residents without access to an automobile. Urban planning was explicitly aimed at consolidation of the downtown core and high-density residential development, prerequisites for the efficient operation of mass transit. The North-South Yonge Street corridor was to become the transit spinal cord of the region, site of the first subway line, opened in 1954. Toronto did not dismantle its streetcar network; its streetcars have since become powerful symbols of the city's identity. Much of Metro's positive image (and popular acceptance) can be traced back to those early years. Metro's reputation for efficiency and integrity owes much to its first director general, Frederick "Big Daddy" Gardiner, an imposing figure legendary for his almost obsessive cost-consciousness and no-frills management style, which set the tone for the rest of Metro's existence. This frugal approach to city management was accompanied by what one observer calls "political egalitarianism"[77] in which traffic, sewage, water, low-rent housing, and the like were all planned in accordance with a delicate balancing act that ensured that none of the six lower-tier municipalities felt slighted.

It worked. By acting early in the urbanization process before the metropolis exploded, the Ontario government, so to speak, nipped the growing center–suburb divide in the bud. Unlike Buffalo, the population of the central city did not decline. Unlike Buffalo, too, the social divide between center and suburb never happened; no massive middle-class exodus occurred. Average incomes in the city of Toronto actually increased compared to that of the rest of Metro Toronto, bypassing the suburbs in the 1990s.[78] This was no minor achievement when compared to much of the rest of urban North America. It is worth quoting Frisken.[79]

> The redistribution of property-tax revenues for social services and public education not only helped to reduce disparities in these services, but also allowed . . . Metro's poorer municipalities to provide a higher standard of local services than they would have been able to provide otherwise. And it did so without obvious harm to the City of Toronto, which not only had the highest total assessment per capita . . . , but also witnessed an increase in that assessment base relative to other Metro municipalities."

The mention of education is no accident, a crucial factor, we know, in the creation of social divides. The brutal downhill migratory spiral, the scourge of so many American cities (richer parents moving to richer municipalities with better schools, leaving behind increasingly poor municipalities with increasingly poor quality schools), did not happen in Toronto. School quality was not (and still is not, generally) the determining factor in the decision of households to choose a neighborhood. Within Metro, teachers were not better paid in some municipalities and schools better maintained and equipped.

Governance alone does not explain Toronto's success in maintaining a strong downtown core. Luck again lent a helping hand. Toronto's ascent to global metropolis delivered a powerful stimulus to the downtown economy, greatly facilitating the task of urban planners, bringing a mix of industries, like New York, with a natural propensity to locate downtown: entertainment, corporate head offices, banks, consultancies. Public policy *and* market forces worked in tandem to produce a strong central core. In the end, we can say, looking back, that the critical ingredient in Toronto's lucky mix of outside events, markets forces, and public policy was the government of Ontario's wise use of its extensive powers, and to do so in the early stages of urban growth before the dynamics of social fragmentation were irreversibly set in motion.

Epilogue: The City That Worked

I would be remiss in my duties as an honest storyteller if I were to leave the impression that Metro was a durable solution to regional governance and that the government of Ontario was unfailingly wise in its decisions. The province abolished Metro in 1998 in an uncharacteristically heavy-handed political move in which the six lower-tier municipalities, including the City of Toronto, were amalgamated into a single city, popularly referred to as Megacity, with a combined population of some 2.6 million. The old city of Toronto disappeared from the map. Opposition to the Megacity was almost unanimous, giving rise to a particularly acrimonious debate,[80] the measure opposed by all six mayors of the targeted municipalities. Jane Jacobs, together with other urban luminaries, came out against Megacity. The six municipalities organized a referendum (not recognized by the province) in which 75 percent of voters came out against amalgamation.

The government nonetheless went ahead with amalgamation. The necessary legislation was passed in 1997, and the new Megacity of Toronto came into effect on January 1, 1998. The decision was upheld by the courts,[81] reaffirming the ultimate power of the province to determine local government structures. Unlike the creation of Metro in 1953, this time the government's primary motivation was fiscal rather than social. It saw amalgamation as an efficiency measure to reduce costs, in the process allowing the province to download functions to the new, supposedly more cost-efficient city, projecting savings for the new city on the order of $1 billion.[82] The province downloaded responsibility for social welfare on the new city and reduced its contribution for public transit.

The cost savings never materialized, which should have surprised no one, for amalgamations rarely produce cost savings.[83] To make a long story short, the city of Toronto (post–1998 borders) has since evolved in a fiscal context similar to that of other major cities faced with an imbalance between responsibilities and revenues. Although the City of Toronto's finances are generally sound, funding for the maintenance and upgrading of basic infrastructures has become problematic. Enid Slack, one of the most astute observers of the Toronto economy, made this assessment[84]:

> Toronto's fiscal condition can be likened to the health of an aging Maple Leafs defenceman: he may be a solid performer on the ice and well cared for by training staff, but he is increasingly expensive and in need of major knee surgery. In other words, the City's fiscal health is sound by most measures, but it faces cost pressures and its aging infrastructure and investment needs present a huge financial challenge.

Post–1998 Toronto remains a generally well-run region, but it is no longer a model of metropolitan governance. The urban region now essentially finds itself at the same juncture as in 1953. The now City of Toronto (former Metro) accounts for only half of metropolitan Toronto, generally referred to as the Greater Toronto Area (GTA), which has long since outgrown the frontiers of post–1953 Metro. Toronto's explosive growth exposes the Achilles' heel of almost all models of regional governance. Urban areas are not stable entities, constantly expanding; at least in most cases. What once was the appropriate territory for a regional governance structure will not necessarily remain so. The Ontario government could have chosen in 1998 to simply amend the two-tier Metro formula and extend it to the GTA. Instead it chose to amalgamate old Metro into a single city, but without creating an accompanying governance framework for the now much larger region. A regional service authority was planned, but it was short-lived.

The Toronto metropolitan area today resembles the majority of North American metropolitan areas with no effective regional governance structure. The Greater Toronto Transportation Authority, a provincial crown corporation that manages the suburban rail, is the sole exception, as in many other urban regions. There is a crucial difference, however. The absence of a formal regional governance structure matters far less in Toronto today than in cities like Buffalo. The major drivers of spatial inequality were, we saw, kept within socially acceptable bounds. Toronto continues to be a highly successful city and is among the wealthiest and most livable cities anywhere. Greater Toronto is, in a sense, a victim of its own success, having grown in size and complexity. It is unlikely that the lauded two-tier governance model (1953–1998) will ever come back. That period was unique, but it laid the groundwork for today's Toronto.

A Brief Return to the Ten Pillars of Urban Success

Before leaving this chapter, I invite the reader to go back and now view the two (diverging) metropolises through the prism of our Ten Pillars (Table I.1). Let's start with Buffalo. It would be difficult to argue that the "rules governing the legal status and powers of local government" were appropriate [Pillar 1] in Buffalo, conducive to social cohesion [Pillar 2] and the "honest" and "adequate" provision of basic urban services [Pillar 3]. Buffalo did not have a competitive wages advantage [Pillar 4] or an industry mix favoring education [Pillar 5] and entrepreneurship [Pillar 6]. We can reasonably assume that its brightest talents were quite willing to decamp elsewhere: California, New York, Texas [Pillar 6]. Buffalo lost its "natural" market access advantage [Pillar 8] and saw its downtown irremediably decline [Pillar 9]. Finally, no great leader seems to have come forward "at the right moment." Buffalo's location in New York State is a hindrance rather than a help. In Buffalo, all Ten Pillars were weak, its decline the outcome of a particularly unlucky alignment of the stars.

I now invite the reader to undertake the same exercise for Toronto. We can guess the result: a very different portrait. The diverging stories of these two great cities, initially at about the same staring point, was no accident.

5

Shaping the Local Economic Environment

Corruption, Clusters, Education, and Glue

The Toronto/Buffalo comparison presented in Chapter 4 provided a powerful demonstration of how national histories and institutions shape the social fabric of urban regions. Let us now shift gears and take a closer (and also critical) look at local attributes commonly associated with economic success—education, a local ethos of hard work and enterprise, efficient and honest local administrations—and show how these attributes are in turn shaped by national/state histories and institutions. Educated populations and integrity in government are evident positive local attributes to be encouraged. However, as we shall discover, the relationship with urban success is sometimes less clear-cut than imagined. To begin our journey, let us again go back in time, starting with the history of corruption in early urban America.

Corruption and Urban Growth—Not Necessarily a Negative Relationship

The great period of urban expansion in United States between the Civil War and World War II was also a period of endemic corruption. Major American cities came to be dominated by political machines, municipal administrations controlled by "bosses" whose power bases were built on patronage, graft, and other forms of selling favors in exchange for votes.[1] Tammany Hall in New York City was among the first of the great political machines, rising to national prominence in the 1860s and 1870s under the reign of "Boss" (William) Tweed. He is reputed to have embezzled $200 million (1870 dollars) from the city coffers during his time in power.[2]

Tammany Hall was only one in a long list of corrupt city machines, including in cities that we would today deem urban successes. Albert Alonzo "Doc" Ames held four terms between 1872 and 1902 as mayor of

Minneapolis. During his last term, Ames and the city police, operating like a crime syndicate, extorted "fines" from dubious businesses, notably prostitution; the proceeds were turned over to Ames and divided among his associates in crime. Doc Ames was indicted for corruption in 1903 but never went to jail. Let us move to the San Francisco of the early 1900s. There, "Boss" (Abe) Rueff became notorious as the true power behind the throne, ruling through a puppet mayor, Eugene Schmitz. Rueff enriched himself (and Schmitz) through the sale of monopoly rights and franchises (trolley lines, telephone connections, sporting events, etc.), bribing municipal officials to look the other way. Rueff was convicted in 1908 on charges of bribery and sentenced to fourteen years in Saint Quentin Penitentiary, but was released after a year on appeal upon posting a bail bond of $600,000 (1910 dollars).

Cities Naturally Create Opportunities for Corruption

Paradoxically, urban growth provided new foundations for graft and corruption. Waterworks, sanitation systems, electric power generation and transmission, and trolley and tram lines are all network services, natural monopolies that were often under municipal jurisdiction. Before the arrival of the automobile, the granting of permits to exploit trolley, tram, or bus lines often became objects of political exchange. They became powerful sources of illicit income for mayors and municipal officials so inclined. Modern infrastructures—which needed to be built and maintained—provided a new market for kickbacks: that is, contracts granted on condition that the lucky contractor (surreptitiously) "kick" a share of the profits back to the person or persons who so generously granted the contract. Large building projects opened the door to other forms of corruption: paying off officials to look the other way in cases of collusion between firms to overprice.

The rapid growth of urban areas also created new opportunities for insider trading—that is, using advance information on where the city might apply a new zoning ordinance or build a new road, rail line, or other municipal infrastructure. Many a city councilor in the know became rich by buying up land at the right time. That corruption flourished during the first great wave of urban growth should not surprise us. It is only as today's democratic states slowly came to terms with the new opportunities for crime that new legal frameworks were gradually put in place, hopefully containing the worst abuses. Indeed, the growth of corruption in early urban America was not all that different from the new criminal opportunities that the current wave of technological change has created. The Internet, social networking websites, and digital devices have opened new doors for illicit gain to which current legal frameworks have yet to fully adapt.

Municipal administrations are supremely suited for horse trading. Voter turnout is generally lower for local elections, reinforcing the power of party stalwarts (to be rewarded). The easy identification of the beneficiaries of public largesse (a street paved, a playground repaired, etc.) lends itself to client-oriented politics. Political relationships are naturally more personal in cities; calling the mayor or his or her staff directly to ask for a favor is not unusual; generally, one does not directly call the president, governor, or prime minster.

The great era of the political machine has passed, but political machines have not disappeared. Richard J. Daly, mayor of Chicago from 1955 to 1976, ran what is arguably the most successful political machine in recent times, unabashedly buying, selling, and fabricating votes. In Chicago's machine-controlled wards, votes cast would to no one's surprise often surpass the number eligible voters, the dead brought back to life by the magical powers of Mayor Daly. Daley could "deliver" Chicago in national elections, which also meant delivering Illinois. John F. Kennedy, it is generally accepted, owed his 1960 victory over Richard Nixon to Daley, who predictably "delivered" Chicago and Illinois to Kennedy.

Ethnically divided cities provide a particularly fertile ground for client-oriented politics. Like Boss Tweed's Tammany Hall a hundred years earlier, Daley's electoral base was predominantly Irish American, maintained by Daley looking after "his people" who returned the favor by voting massively for him. Daley's ethnic-based politics did little to improve race relations in Chicago; black–white tensions continue to plague the city to this day. In Buffalo, Jim Griffin served as mayor during the city's most difficult years (1978–1994); his electoral base was largely white Catholic. Griffin's relationship with the African American community was, to put it mildly, not overly cordial, which again did little to improve intergroup relations in an already racially charged environment. Causality goes both ways. Ethnic (or class) politics can further reinforce social divides. Local administrations seen to be favoring a given group or race can trigger the flight of the outgroup to neighboring municipalities. This factor further fuelled white flight in some U.S. central cities following the election of African American mayors.

Corruption does not magically disappear in nations because they have grown rich. In the United States, almost every year sees a new crop of scandals and mayors arrested for fraud or other criminal behavior. Trenton, New Jersey Mayor Tony Mack was sentenced to fifty-eight months in prison in 2014 for taking money in exchange for obtaining approval to develop a downtown parking garage that only existed in a federal sting. Mack was one of a long list of New Jersey mayors to face corruption charges since 2000, including the mayors of Newark, Camden, and Hoboken. The mayor of Hoboken was sentenced to twenty-four months in prison in 2009 for extortion. Charlotte, North Carolina Mayor Patrick Cannon was sentenced to forty-four months in prison in 2014 for soliciting $48,000 in cash from undercover FBI agents posing as developers. Among the most publicized cases, Mayor Kwame Kilpatrick of Detroit was sentenced to twenty-eight years in prison for extortion, bribery, and conspiracy. All these cases of corruption were investigated and prosecuted by the Federal Bureau of Investigation.

Municipal corruption is hardly a peculiarly American affliction. Montreal Mayor Michael Applebaum, whose reign would last no more than a year (2012–2013), was no paragon of virtue. A Quebec court found, him guilty of eight corruption-related charges for extorting roughly $60,000 in bribes from real estate developers. Europe, too, is no stranger to corruption in municipal politics. Jacques Chirac, mayor of Paris from 1977 to 1995 and subsequently president of the Republic, put party hacks on the city payroll, reputedly made frequent use of city-owned apartments for private purposes, and allegedly allowed associates to enjoy free gardening services from the city of Paris. A later mayor would file a complaint in court for past abuse of Paris's gardening services for private purposes at an estimated cost of 700,000 euros.[3]

Integrity and the (Relative) Importance of Good Local Governance

Tales of corrupt mayors, whether in the United States, Canada, or France, present a conundrum: Corruption does not seem to have caused irreparable harm to the cities concerned. True, the misgovernment of Buffalo (or Detroit) undoubtedly contributed to its decline. Yet, it would be difficult to argue that the presence of corrupt administrations had a lasting effect on the economic performance of New York, Montreal, or Paris. Looking at cities in the Western world, we find little evidence of a systematic relationship between clean municipal government and economic performance—which begs the question of why.

The answer is threefold. First, for all the cases cited, corruption was not persistent, corresponding to particular city administrations. The second answer sends us back to senior government. There is a fundamental difference between occasionally corrupt city administrators and endemic corrupt national and/or state governments. Whatever one may think of Washington, D.C.'s political chaos, the federal government apparatus does not have a history of endemic corruption. And the FBI has a well-deserved reputation for independence, serving as a driving force behind the prosecution of criminal public officials at all levels of government. In Montreal, the province stepped in to impose stricter internal accounting controls on the city and, more to the point, created a special anticorruption unit within the provincial police with a mandate similar to that of the FBI in the wake of a series of scandals during the Applebaum and preceding Tremblay administrations.[4] This has led to prosecutions for graft not only in Montreal but across the province, with a predictable salutary dissuasive impact on the behavior of public officials.

The third reason for the corruption–urban growth paradox returns us to the concept of cities as political units. The areas where municipal corruption may damage the broader economy are limited in most nations, a reflection, precisely, of the limited power of cities. Street repair, waterworks, and public transit are important, of course, but overall they will in most cases have only minor weight in determining the productivity of firms, notably for export-oriented industries.[5] Yes, local governance matters; but the potential for causing lasting damage (where it is bad) will as a rule be limited—that is, if senior levels of government do their job in enforcing the rule of law.

The story changes in cases where the sources of corruption and mistrust run deeper, rooted in national and/or state histories.

New Orleans—An Unhappy Confluence of Populist Politics, Rentier Elites, and Racial Mistrust

New Orleans provides an instructive story of long-term decline fueled, at least in part, by persistent mismanagement and corruption. New

Orleans was once the greatest city in the American South, but it has since been overtaken by Atlanta. Here, city and state histories are inextricably interwoven, allowing us to observe the often circular relationship between lack of trust, corruption, low education, and stunted entrepreneurship.

In the preceding recital of recent U.S. mayors indicted for corruption, I purposely left out former New Orleans Mayor Ray Nagin (2002–2010), mayor when Hurricane Katrina struck in August 2005. After leaving office, Nagin was charged with twenty-one counts of bribery, money laundering, filing false tax returns, and wire fraud and was eventually sentenced to ten years in prison. His conviction was no exception but part of an unfortunate pattern. Two additional examples[6] are William Jefferson, Democratic representative of one of the two largely black congressional districts hardest hit by Katrina. Jefferson was sentenced to thirteen years in prison for bribery in 2009, the longest sentence ever given a sitting member of Congress for corruption charges. The FBI found $90,000 worth of bribe money in Jefferson's freezer; the first member of Congress, it seems, to have his office raided by federal agents. And then there is Aaron Broussard, president of predominantly white suburban Jefferson Parish, who was convicted of stealing money from the parish, appointing his girlfriend to a high-paying position, and conspiring to commit bribery and wire fraud. Broussard resigned as parish president in 2010, was indicted in 2012, and went to prison in 2013.

Not all Louisiana politicians have been corrupt; a new generation of public officials is making laudable efforts to turn the state's reputation for misgovernment around. But the roots of that unfortunate reputation run deep. During Reconstruction, "no other Southern state suffered equally with Louisiana from the corruption of carpetbag and scalawag legislatress."[7] In his 1991 book, *Peapatch Politics: The Earl Long Era in Louisiana Politics*, William J. Dodd, former lieutenant governor of Louisiana, describes corruption as "a way of life, inherited, and made quasi-respectable and legal by the French freebooters who founded, operated, and left us as the governmental blueprint that is still Louisiana's constitutional and civil law."[8] Dodd adds that the outlaws, gamblers, and fortune hunters who came down the Mississippi in river boats serving as veritable floating casinos added flavor to the Louisiana pot. New Orleans is one of the rare American cities where prostitution was tolerated at the turn of the 20th century, with a sanctioned red light district known as Storyville established by municipal ordinance (1897–1917).

Evidence for the region's reputation for lax morals is not merely anecdotal. Data compiled by the Justice Department over a thirty-year period (1976–2010) shows that Louisiana is first among the fifty states in the number of federal public corruption convictions per capita, with the majority of convictions concentrated in Louisiana's Eastern Judicial District (New Orleans).[9] New Orleans also leads the nation in the number of wrongful incarcerations per capita.[10] This does not say much about the quality of the local justice system and, more to the point, about the quality of race relations. African Americans on average are twelve times more likely to be wrongfully convicted than white defendants.

Every Man a King, But No One Wears a Crown

The roots of Louisiana's singular political culture are to be found in a unique confluence of race, clientelism, and populism. Although comparison with Argentina may seem farfetched, an analogy can be seen between Peronism and the legacy of Huey Long ("The Kingfish"), governor of Louisiana from 1928 to 1932 and then senator until his assassination in 1935. Like Perón (but without the military-dictatorial trappings), Long became the leader and later the symbol of a populist movement, "Share the Wealth," which like the *Justicialistas* overtly aimed to address the grievances of the common man, the shirtless ones hard hit by the Great Depression. These became the loyal clienteles of the political machine that Long helped build and that his successors would continue to perfect. The official slogan of the Share the Wealth movement was "Every Man a King (But No One Wears a Crown)." In both Louisiana and Buenos Aires, an initial populist upsurge, which in principle had the noblest intentions, opened the door to a succession of corrupt administrations with only occasional interruptions.

The political movement would eventually fade, but the political machine Long built did not; it became a fixture of the state's political landscape. Officials who had campaigned with the promise to carry on Long's programs to "Share Our Wealth" instead stole the wealth, tarnishing the public's perception of the movement.[11] Nonetheless, like Evita Perón, Huey would continue to serve as a martyred symbol reverently invoked by his successors. The ticket of Richard Leche and Huey's brother, Earl Long (for lieutenant governor) won the 1936 gubernatorial election in a record breaking landslide. They campaigned entirely on Huey's martyrdom and took their oaths under a colossal portrait of the Kingfish. Governor Leche continued many of Huey Long's popular programs, building roads, bridges, hospitals, and schools, and providing free school supplies, all of which were always appropriately publicized. Earl Long, who would follow Leche as governor, is famously reputed to have remarked that his constituents "don't want good government; they want good entertainment"—and that Louisiana politicians provided in spades.

A wave of scandals swept state politics during Leche's governorship centered on the misappropriation federal New Deal public works funds by state officials. Hundreds of officials and businessmen were implicated, many indicted, and seven eventually were sent to prison. Leche, with admirable honesty, is reported to have declared: "When I took the oath of office I didn't take any vow of poverty."[12] Leche would later be convicted on corruption charges and was forced to resign. Among his other exploits, Governor Leche is reported to have colluded with state officials to sell some two hundred trucks from a firm in which he had a stake to the State Highway Department to the tune of several million dollars. His conspicuous consumption—his purchase of a yacht, a country estate, and a private hunting preserve, all this on a governor's salary—eventually attracted the attention of federal authorities. Leche was sentenced to ten years in Atlanta's federal prison in 1940, served five years, was paroled in 1945, and eventually was given a full pardon by President Truman in 1952, after which he became a lobbyist.

Upon Governor Leche's resignation, Earl Long served out his term of office, becoming a popular political figure in his own right, successfully running for governor in 1948 and 1956 and completed his last term in 1960. The machine was now well oiled and largely controlled the Louisiana Democratic Party. This was the era before civil rights, when the South was still solidly Democratic (and segregationist) and the majority of African Americans were disenfranchised. The political dynasty the Longs had built reached beyond the governor's mansion, permeating all levels of Louisiana politics. Altogether, twelve members of the Long family entered politics; most have been free of scandal. The Long dynasty produced two governors, three senators, four U.S, representatives, three state legislators, and numerous state and local officials. It must be emphasized that Huey Long's legacy was not entirely negative; much good work was done. But undeniably the machine politics of the Long era contributed little to the establishment of clean government.

The prize for the most colorful—and also arguably the most entertaining—Louisiana politician must go to Edwin Edwards, governor for three nonconsecutive terms of office (1972–1980; 1984–1988; 1992–1996). The second term corresponded roughly to the years when I worked with colleagues at the University of New Orleans. This charming rascal, despite repeated accusations of misbehavior, both financial and matrimonial, remained hugely popular. Among his more colorful remarks, Edwards is reputed to have declared that he wanted to unseat an incumbent because if he didn't "there won't be anything left to steal," and during the 1992 gubernatorial race, he famously said "that [the] only way I can lose this election is if get caught in bed with a dead girl or a live boy."[13] Edwards, despite his Anglo name, had Cajun roots.[14] He was fluent in both English and Cajun French, a skill that he played up and that helped him maintain a loyal electoral base in southwestern Louisiana.

I shall not go through the litany of scandals in which Edwards was implicated, for most of which he was never indicted. But his luck would eventually run out: in 1997, an FBI surveillance videotape captured a Louisiana congressman accepting a large amount of cash from Edwards and then stuffing it in his pockets. Edwards was subsequently fingered by an entrepreneur who allegedly gave him $845,000 in a scheme to build a private juvenile prison. Edwards was finally indicted by federal prosecutors in 1998 and found guilty on seventeen counts of racketeering, extortion, money laundering, and mail and wire fraud. He was sentenced to ten years in prison and was released in 2011. According to a poll taken after his release, 30 percent of respondents named Edwards the state's best governor since 1980, which says a lot about the man but may also say something about the political mores of Louisiana. On a kinder note, perhaps this tolerant attitude toward political misbehavior is simply part of a lifestyle in which hedonic pursuits, be they food, music, or other forms of entertainment, take precedence over more mundane aspects of life. Perhaps, too, great food, great music, a laid-back lifestyle, and efficient government are incompatible. One can have three but not all four.

Race

Populism and machine politics can go only so far in explaining the culture of mistrust that seems to pervade Louisiana politics and New Orleans in particular. How communities react in times of disaster is a good measure of trust. Hurricane Katrina was a calamity by any definition: it was the costliest such natural disaster in U.S. history, with damages estimated at $108 billion (2005 dollars), inundating more than 80 percent of the city, destroying whole neighborhoods, and causing some two thousand deaths. The story of how the city's elites behaved is not pretty. In the paragraphs that follow, I quote profusely from an excellent article by Arnold Hirsch and Lee Levert at the University of New Orleans, who tell the story far better than I can.[15] Let me thus begin with a quote that summarizes why the reconstruction of post-Katrina New Orleans proceeded so chaotically, leaving much bad blood in its wake.

> The utter lack of trust, and the inability to deal in good faith across racial lines, would short-circuit those attempts at reconstruction that challenged racial verities. Old patterns of thought and behavior—on the part of both blacks and whites—were simply inadequate.[16]

Hirsch and Levert then describe how distrust between blacks and whites was fed by rumors and conspiracy theories. The black side was agitated by the rumored malevolent destruction of the Industrial Canal levee, which protected predominantly African American neighborhoods. Meanwhile, the white side was fed consistent rumors of rape, murder, and looting by black Orleanians. Both white and black perceptions were not totally without foundation. African Americans in New Orleans could look back to other instances in history when flood protection of their neighborhoods took second place—this hurricane, though the worst, was not the first hurricane to hit the area—while whites could point to occasions of looting and pillage, though not necessarily always committed by the "other" race.

There were also moments of assistance and cooperation across the racial divide; many nurses, social workers, and other professionals remained in New Orleans, even as the gale winds and flooding spread, to help victims regardless of race. There was also the so-called Cajun Navy which floated in from the western bayous,[17] and hundreds of Cajuns (white of course) on their Pirogues were credited with rescuing thousands of stranded residents, the majority of whom were black. Tragically, these acts of kindness were the exception.

But those wisps of empathy and threads of a common humanity, though essential to the reknitting of New Orleans's society, remained subordinate to a dominant, reflexive fear and hostility. . . . in the first hours and days after the levees crumbled, the reactions of both whites and blacks were reflexive. Just as surely as a knee will jerk upward when properly struck, New Orleans twitched violently along preconditioned lines in Katrina's wake.[18]

Among the ugliest and most revealing reactions, cited by *The Wall Street Journal*, were the words of the white Baton Rouge congressman, Richard Baker, who unabashedly declared: "We finally cleaned up public housing in New Orleans. We couldn't do it, but God did."[19] The antagonism between the two races led to several violent confrontations, with whites most often attempting to block the entry of blacks into their (above-sea-level) neighborhoods. The best known of these incidents involved the attempt of several hundred people, overwhelmingly black, to leave the rapidly deteriorating conditions around the Louisiana Superdome and to cross the Crescent City Connection (the bridge linking the city's east and west banks) on foot on September 1, 2005. A small contingent emerged from the town of Gretna in mainly white Jefferson Parish at the other end of the bridge to cut them off, led by a pair of sheriff's deputies, who greeted Katrina's neediest refugees with a shotgun blast over their heads and the vow that "there would be no Superdomes" in their town.[20] Roadblocks manned by sheriffs were also set up between Jefferson Parish and neighboring Orleans Parish.

New Orleans is still rebuilding. I have not been back since Katrina and will thus refrain from comments on the Crescent City's future. However, I cannot help but reflect that a city less plagued by a centuries-old legacy of racial antagonism and mistrust would have come through the hurricane better and recovered faster.

Dessalines's Legacy

No American city is totally immune from the cancer of racial mistrust and the political culture it breeds, which as we have seen is often aggravated by municipal fragmentation. New Orleans's fragmented parish structure is as much a cause as a consequence of its racial divide. But the level of mistrust revealed by Katrina begs the question of why race looms so large in the Crescent City. As always, the answer must be found in history. The dread of slave revolts and associated massacres of whites was a recurrent fear in all the slave states of the American South before the Civil War, leaving its mark on the mindset of white populations. Louisiana was no different in this respect from the rest of the Old South.

The particular force in New Orleans of that shared fear stems, I suggest, from a specific historical event: the Haitian Revolution (1796–1801), the greatest and most successful slave revolt in the history of the Americas. The dark but predictable side of the revolt was the slaughter of white planters and other white populations by black revolutionary soldiers, culminating three years after independence in the willful massacre of the remaining white population at the orders of Jean-Jacques Dessalines, a leading figure in the Haitian Revolution. But why should the memory of these terrible events be of particular importance to New Orleans? To answer that question, I shall again tell a story.

On my first visit to New Orleans, I was immediately struck by the similarity between the architecture of the city's Old French Quarter and what I had observed a few years earlier in Port au Prince's Old Town. Here, I said to myself, is what Port au Prince would have looked like had it not suffered from decades of neglect and misgovernment. New Orleans had the feel of a Caribbean city that had been mistakenly marooned in the United States. On my first days in the city, I did what I often do: I set out with my wife to visit old cemeteries. Old monuments and tombstones can teach one a lot about a place's history. The inscriptions on the earliest tombstones, often richly decorated monuments indicating persons of wealth, were in French. For persons deceased in the mid- to later decades of the 19th century, the inscriptions on the tombstones invariably read: "*Né* (or *née* for women) *à Saint Domingue, le 12 juin 1771*" (born in St. Domingo, the 12th of June 1771) or some other date in the 18th century. Saint Domingue or St. Domingo in English was the name Haiti bore under French rule before independence. The island possession was France's most lucrative colony. Its economy was built on sugar, the oil (petrol) of its time, and spawned a fabulously wealthy slave-owning class and an accompanying subjugated black slave population. St. Domingo's slave-based society was, it seems, particularly brutal and despotic even by the shameful standards of the Caribbean at the time. We saw in Chapter 1 the terrible legacy these brutal beginnings bequeathed to the future Republic of Haiti. The whites in St. Domingo, a small minority in a sea of black, were understandably obsessed by the fear of a slave revolt, which helps explain the particular brutality of the French regime. The last census before the revolution shows a population of forty thousand *Grand-blancs* (Great whites) and four hundred fifty-two thousand black slaves, a ratio of eleven to one.

When the dreaded revolt finally erupted, fueled by the ideals of the French Revolution, those whites who were not killed fled. The massacres that accompanied the revolution made headline news in the United States and came to be known as "the horrors of St. Domingo," with a predictable impact on white public opinion in the slave-owning South. The organized slaughter in 1804 ordered by Dessalines of men, women, and children left an enduring imprint on the white collective psyche. It is estimated that between three thousand and five thousand whites were killed over a three-month period. Dessalines would later defend his actions as a necessary expedient to rid the fragile young republic of possible traitors and potential counterrevolutionaries. The majority of *Grand-blancs* who survived the "the horrors of St. Domingo" fled to New Orleans, which was then still under French rule.[21]

New Orleans was settled by the survivors of those massacres whose personal stories of rape and horror (told and retold a thousand times over to acquaintances and neighbors) would come to shape the mindset of the city's white population. I had my answer. The splendid architecture of old Port au Prince and old New Orleans was the same because both were built by the same people. Those French-Creole refugees from St. Domingo/Haiti bequeathed the city a marvelous architecture; but also a frame of mind and political culture from which it has yet to free itself completely.

The consequences of that legacy are all too evident. According to rankings by the University of Syracuse (before Katrina), the City of New Orleans had the dubious distinction of being ranked the worst-run city in the United States, together with, we saw, Buffalo.[22] The state of Louisiana ranks among the bottom five states for the percentage of the population with at least a bachelor's degree.[23] New Orleans has, to my knowledge, nurtured no major corporation, and those that were born there have long since moved their headquarters to Houston, Atlanta, or elsewhere.[24]

The depressingly systematic low level of education of Louisiana's population mirrors decades of state underinvestment in education, which is perhaps the most damaging legacy bequeathed by the old planter *rentier* aristocracy, a legacy that Louisiana shares with rest of the Old South. Slaves were of course not to be educated (indeed, education was prohibited), and the rich rents generated by cotton and other plantation crops meant that education beyond a certain level was not a prerequisite for social standing in the planter class. After the Civil War, the now freed slaves could not, understandably, pass a learning ethic on to their offspring, who generally were illiterate themselves, while the children of the old planter class remained heirs to a worldview that did not put a high premium on education and looked down on business as below its dignity.

The *rentier* mentality of New Orleans's elites did not die with slavery but rather was kept alive by the conviction that its location at the head of the Mississippi River system guaranteed its dominance. This mindset was later perpetuated by the discovery of oil off Louisiana, a typical resource rent requiring little ingenuity. So we have come back full circle to the Intrusive Rentier Syndrome (Buffalo was our first exhibit) and the reasons why some societies place a higher value on education and enterprise than others. This now allows us to take a second look at clusters, which in principle offer an economic advantage but which can also sow the seeds of their own destruction.

Good Clusters, Bad Clusters

The term *cluster*, popularized by Michael Porter and his disciples,[25] takes us back to the notion of localization economies (see Chapter 2). More than a hundred years ago, the famed British economist Alfred Marshall, observing the clustering of textile mills in and around Manchester, England, wrote that "the mysteries of the trade are . . . as it were in the air. If one starts a new idea, it is taken up by others and combined with suggestions of their own, and thus become the source of new ideas."[26] No less so than in Marshall's day, it is the cross fertilization of ideas made possible by the spatial concentration of brainpower that lies at the heart of successful clusters. Ever city understandably wants its high-tech cluster, be it in health sciences, aerospace, computer gaming, or some new industry yet to emerge. It is difficult to argue with the advantages of clustering.

How the California Gold Rush Helped Shape
Silicon Valley

Silicon Valley is undisputedly the modern posterchild of the successful cluster, an unparalleled concentration of talent and know-how in a small geographical area. The emergence of Silicon Valley in California, however, is no accident; it is a particularly cogent example of the power of legislation to shape (or not) entrepreneurial environments.[27]

Let us begin by going back to the early 1950s and to the rich orchards one hour south of San Francisco along a stretch of land in what was to become Silicon Valley. The Valley had two important advantages: (1) a superb climate and unmatched scenery that beckoned new residents as suburbanization spread down the Bay Area; and (2) a world-class institution of higher learning, Stanford University, founded in 1891, focused on science and research. The Bay Area already had an established reputation in electronics and radio technology, the legacy of the pioneering work of Lee de Forest who had moved there in 1910 and invented the triode, a critical component in the development of telephone communication, radio, television, radar, and early digital electronics. When the Stanford Industrial Park was created in 1951 on land owned by the university, there was thus good reason to believe that it would attract young researchers and firms in electronics and related technologies, as indeed it did. Among the first tenants were General Electric, Eastman Kodak, and Hewlett-Packard; the last-named still has its principal offices and laboratories there.

Similar industrial and research parks were springing up elsewhere in America, notably around Boston along its vaunted Route 128, fueled by generous federal government defense spending on research in electronics and related technologies. The Cold War was at its peak. But why did the Valley in particular rise to the top? The wild risk-taking legacy of the California Gold Rush (1848+) probably left its imprint, although it is difficult to rigorously demonstrate, imbuing the region with a particular entrepreneurial ethos plus laying the foundations for a strong venture capital culture. But the Gold Rush left another legacy which some one hundred years later would provide the legal framework for an entrepreneurial environment unlike any anywhere else in the United States. In 1872, as part of California's Civil Code, the state legislature ratified a law that declared so-called non-compete agreements (NCAs) invalid in California. The anti-NCA law was arguably (and still is) *the* principal distinguishing attribute that allowed the Stanford Industrial Park to outdistance its rivals. But before explaining why, let us take a closer look at California's peculiar anti-NCA law and why the state legislature saw fit to adopt such a measure at the time.

In a nutshell, the law declared null and void any contract between a business owner and employee if said contract in any way restricted the employee's freedom to change employers, even if that meant joining the former employer's competitors. This made any NCA-type contract that bound an employee to a particular company unenforceable. The relevant clause in the law reads as follows: "Except as provided in this chapter, every contract by which anyone is restrained from engaging in a lawful profession, trade, or business of any kind is to that extent void."[28]

The rationale for the law was to reduce the chances of violence between employers (mining claimholders) and their employees panning for gold in a work environment where violent altercations and shootouts were not uncommon. The most straightforward peaceful solution for resolving a dispute was simply to let the worker walk away from his employer and, if he so wished, to leave for surrounding gold claims and potential new employers. The 1872 provision essentially made the right to walk away from one's employer a right protected by the law.

Why did the 1872 law now make California different? In most American states to my knowledge,[29] high-tech firms and private research institutions have the right to impose NCAs on their employees that prohibit them from going to work for competitors within a defined geographic area, usually for a period of two years. The reason for NCA contracts is not difficult to understand. Why invest in an employee and allow him or her access to the firm's trade secrets if said employee can walk way, freely delivering the dearly acquired secrets to a competitor? NCA agreements are often supplemented by so-called a non-disclosure agreement (NDA), which prohibits the employee from divulging confidential information to third parties. For both NCAs and NDAs to work, employers need to be able to take the culpable employee to court and to have the contracts upheld. This is where California's law differs. Because of a law enacted more than a century ago, NCAs and NDAs are unenforceable in California. California's courts have systematically refused to recognize and enforce NCAs and NDAs that prevent tech firm employees from leaving for other firms or sharing their knowledge with others. The result is an entrepreneurial environment that encourages spin-offs and the flow of ideas, the embodiment in a word of Alfred Marshall's fabled cluster, "ideas as it were in the air."

This unique legal environment helped shape the early evolution of Stanford Industrial Park, sowing the seeds of what was to become Silicon Valley. The spark that set off the boom of Silicon start-ups was a dispute in 1957 between employees of Shockley Semiconductor, located in the research park, and the company's founder, Nobel laureate and co-inventor of the transistor, William Shockley. Following a production disagreement, eight of his employees decided to quit, forming their own firm in direct competition with Shockley. The so-called Traitorous Eight went on to found Fairchild Semiconductor with funding from a New York-based competitor. Other spin-offs would follow this first walk-away. As Fairchild grew to become a major tech actor in its own right, its founders began to leave to start companies based on their own ideas, followed in turn by their employees going on to create yet another generation of start-ups; the numerous offspring of the initial parent were appropriately dubbed Fairchildren. Two of the initial Traitorous Eight left Fairchild Semiconductor to form Intel. In all, ninety-two public companies can be traced back to Fairchild, worth some $2.1 trillion in 2013, more than the annual GDP of Canada.[30]

The rest is history as new spin-offs and start-ups progressively clustered in around the original site of Stanford Industrial Park to produce the unique environment that today is Silicon Valley. Ironically, an anachronistic state law forgotten for over a hundred years, initially intended to prevent rowdy miners from shooting each other is today the basis for the most successful high-tech cluster on the planet. But then, the ways in which legislation affects local outcomes often have little relation to the legislator's initial intent, rooted in long-gone historical events.

A Fallen Cluster (Cleveland) and a Fallen Cluster Reborn (Trois Rivières)

Every cluster has the potential of turning into a handicap. Today's high-tech cluster is tomorrow's sunset industry. Buffalo's steel cluster fell victim, we saw, to changes in the production technology of steel. Should Buffalo have refused to welcome those mighty steel mills? It's easy with 20/20 hindsight to blame Buffalo's elites, but was that even an option in an era when steel was king, the very symbol of economic progress?

Few cities better illustrate the rise and fall of clusters than Cleveland. Cleveland was the Silicon Valley of the second half of the 19th century, known for its innovative entrepreneurial class, not least in different manufacturing technologies, leading the United States in patent registration and venture capital.[31] John D. Rockefeller founded Standard Oil Company there in 1870. Steel mills flourished as in Buffalo, but Cleveland's manufacturing base was less centered on a single technology. Charles Brush pioneered electric lighting in Cleveland, and Sidney Short and fellow inventors came out with electric street cars.[32] Morris Howard's inventions in the 1920s included an "electric switch," an "apparatus for and process of making tire casings," and a "writing device." In 1911, General Electric established its lighting division headquarters in the region. Cleveland excelled in a variety of manufacturing industries well into the twentieth century, including cars, chemicals, paints and varnishes, machine tools, and electrical machinery. The number of firms with industrial research laboratories grew from five in 1920 to forty-five in 1946, which by that time was employing some eight thousand knowledge workers. Although hard hit by the Great Depression, the region continued to produce a steady stream of entrepreneurial businesses and inventors well into the mid-20th century.[33]

But its story since the 1950s is one of systematic decline. The city proper, like Buffalo, has lost more than half its population, falling from nine hundred fifteen thousand to less than four hundred thousand today. Its metro population peaked in 1970 at 2.2 million and has stagnated ever since. Like Buffalo, its downtown is a mere shadow of its former glory, its magnificent buildings reminders of what once was. The reasons for Cleveland's decline remain somewhat of a mystery. Its diversified manufacturing base and research intensity were manifestly not sufficient to defend it against eventual decline. The roots of its decline, let me suggest, were in the end not all that different from Buffalo's: a fragmented municipal landscape, unequal people services, racial division, hubris, and a general culture of political mistrust, all coming together to undermine the region's competitiveness. Cleveland is yet another example (in an already long line) that even the strongest local economies are at risk where the institutional foundations are weak.

It may also be that the largely *local* nature of entrepreneur–inventor relationships, though a priori the sign of a technologically vibrant community, may have made it more vulnerable to outside shocks. Cleveland-area companies, it seems, relied almost entirely on technologies generated in the region; locally generated patents were almost exclusively intended for local firms.[34] The lack of cross breeding with actors outside the region, not only with inventors and consumers of ideas but also with financial backers, may in the end have bred a technological and entrepreneurial conservatism that would prompt future young entrepreneurs and inventors to leave the region. Other observers have equally pointed to the closed unwelcoming character of Cleveland's business elite.[35] Here is yet another lesson: local entrepreneurship and ingenuity are crucial ingredients but will eventually dry up if not continually renewed by new blood.

Let us now move to a city I know firsthand: Trois-Rivières in the province of Quebec. Its story is one of hope, proof that the Intrusive Rentier Syndrome can be overcome. In the early 1970s, I taught a part-time course at the local university. Trois-Rivières, though fairly small (metro area population: 150,000), was at the time reputedly the largest producer of paper in the world; the *New York Times* was printed on paper made in Trois Rivières. The city had a clear geographic advantage for the production of paper located downstream on the St. Maurice River from the province's rich softwood forests at the meeting point with the St. Lawrence. Logs were floated downstream, which were then turned into lighter weight and less bulky paper, and finally shipped to New York and other U.S. markets by rail or boat. Its port also gave it direct access to overseas markets. When driving into the city, the towering paper mills were easily visible from afar and also immediately recognizable by the odors emitted by the chemicals used in the production of paper, a smell not unlike that of rotten eggs. As the locals philosophically observed, with time one no longer noticed; the smell simply became part of the décor.

The paper mills paid well, unionized, of course, and formed the bedrock for a solid blue-collar middle class. The 1991 census showed average wages in Trois Rivières to be about 95 percent of those in Montreal. Comparing educational levels shows that some 13.5 percent of Montrealers over the age of fifteen held a college degree (BA and above) in 1991 compared to 9.1 percent in Trois Rivières. Trois Rivières was, in other words, a typical example of the Intrusive Rentier Syndrome, a high-wage/low-education location. Technological change hit the city hard: the first adverse change was rapidly rising productivity (fewer workers required per ton of newsprint produced) followed, in turn, by the catastrophic impact of the Internet on the demand for newsprint. Paper mills closed and unemployment rose; Trois Rivières's unemployment rate remained well above the Canadian average for most of the 1990s and the first decade of the 21st century. The city has still not fully recovered, but its unemployment rate has progressively fallen since, going below the Canadian average at the time of writing. The city has not totally shed its blue-collar image, but the chemical smell has gone, its manufacturing base has diversified into mid-tech sectors, and a fledgling software sector is visible. Trois Rivières's once fairly dilapidated downtown has been spruced up and is now surprisingly lively for such a small city.

Trois-Rivières did not descend into a cycle of seemingly endless decline like so many Rustbelt cities did. Its labor market visibly adjusted fairly rapidly. Relative wages fell about 15 percent below those of Montreal; but the change that mattered most was in mindsets, although more difficult to measure rigorously. Smokestack chasing (the hope of a new big plant) has not totally died, but the dominant message today, whether by political leaders or others, is about nurturing start-ups and helping young entrepreneurs, including attracting immigrant entrepreneurs. A local entrepreneurial culture is taking root, breaking with the blue-collar lunch box culture of the past. It's a slow process; but it's happening. Admittedly, such changes in mindsets are easier to achieve in smaller homogeneous communities like Trois Rivières, but nonetheless will only happen if local elites and opinion-makers convey the right message and if senior government policies lend a helping hand. Both the federal and provincial governments funded local development corporations expressly aimed at nurturing start-ups and maintaining fiscal regimes generally favorable to small business. The greater Trois-Rivières urban region was amalgamated into a single city in 2002, as part of a province-imposed reform, preventing the kind of political and fiscal fragmentation that continues to plague urban regions like Cleveland and Buffalo.

How then are we to view clusters and the work cultures they engender? Clusters are necessary to reap the benefits of agglomeration and specialization; but they can also, because of the very rents they generate, price an urban economy out of the market. Can we predict beforehand if a given cluster is good or bad? I'm not sure an answer is possible. The temptation understandably is to bet on current winners, be it health sciences, software development, or something else. Ultimately, the difference between a good and a bad cluster is its potential for paving the way to new clusters, which still does not tell us how we are to know this beforehand. The Intrusive Rentier Syndrome provides a partial answer. Clusters founded on "natural" advantages, generating high resource or location rents, are always at risk and are to be viewed with a healthy sense of foreboding. On the other hand, the Cleveland story tells us that that clusters based on skills do not necessarily provide a guarantee against future decline.

Industrial legacies (whether steel, slavery, or software) can only go so far in explaining local attitudes toward education, work, and enterprise. Industries do not spring forth (or decline) in a cultural vacuum. How communities react to change sends us back to the cultural baggage (values, mores, etc.) of the local population and the nation. Cultures are embedded in people, who came from somewhere.

The Imprint of the First Settlers

The value systems and worldviews of populations, whether for nations or cities, were almost always forged, at least in part, by the culture of the populations that first settled there, whether many centuries (even millennia) ago in the Old World or more recently in the New World. Ontario was settled by refugees from the American Revolution, and Louisiana by refugees from the Haitian Revolution, giving birth, as we saw, to different political cultures. Here we come back full swing back to the institutions molded by national cultures, but with the variant here that the concept of *nation* is applied to entities within political nations. This is a reasonable transposition in federations like the United States and Canada where the states/provinces have many of the powers of (unitary) nations and were first settled (with my apologies to Native Americans and Canadians) by peoples with often very different cultural roots.

Education is of course an asset for any society. However, there is little use in investing in education if graduates later leave for greener pastures.[36] Similarly, there is little use in nurturing cohorts of entrepreneurial youth if once successful they move their firm elsewhere. New York is replete with the head offices of successful corporations initially founded in Iowa, Kansas, upstate New York, or elsewhere. An additional ingredient is needed if public investments in education are to pay off. I've called this attribute *glue* for lack of a better word. Some glues are more self-evident than others, coming close to the sociological definition of nations. In Canada, French-speaking Québécois are naturally inclined to "stick" to Montreal before considering another metropolis. In the United States, Salt Lake City probably comes closest. This spiritual and cultural center for America's Mormon community is a highly successful city in its own right with a burgeoning high-tech sector, which is all the more remarkable given the city's relatively remote location.

We shall now visit two cities, Boston and Minneapolis-St. Paul, located respectively in the states of Massachusetts and Minnesota. Both are highly successful cities, with above-average incomes (per capita) and education levels. That Massachusetts and Minnesota systematically rank among the top states for the share of public investment in education is no accident, but rather is the outcome of the historical legs bequeathed by the first (European) settlers. By the same token, it is no coincidence that Massachusetts students systematically rank highest in both science and math competence PISA scores, followed by other New England states (Vermont, New Hampshire, and Maine) and by Minnesota and neighboring North Dakota.[37]

Boston: A Happy Marriage of Learning, Glue, and Mercantile Roots

My telling of the Boston story will be brief, drawing heavily on the work of Edward Glaeser.[38] Like New York and Vienna, Boston's tale is that of a city that rebounded after a period of decline. Boston's city and metropolitan populations declined during the 1970s and 1980s, and did not start to grow again until the 1990s. Over the previous two centuries, the region would confront repeated shocks: first, the arrival of steam-powered ships that would undermine its maritime trading empire founded on sailing ships, followed by the collapse of its manufacturing base founded on immigrant labor. During a good part of the 20th century, Boston was a prime example of a slow-growth economy, a victim of deindustrialization reminiscent of today's Rustbelt cities. Why did it not go the way of Buffalo or Detroit?

Innovating, Not Fleeing

Glaeser suggests several reasons. First, he draws a distinction between, on the one hand, extractive economies, where cities arose to exploit a particular resource (be it cotton, coal or something else), and settlements that arose because people *wanted* to live there with the ideal of building a community that would mirror their beliefs and values. New England, unlike the southern states and unlike, later, the coal and iron-ore based economies of the Midwest, had no major cash crop or resource. From the beginning, the Boston area economy was based on ingenuity and commerce, and not primarily on the exploitation of a nearby resource, its fish notwithstanding. Managing a far-flung trading empire and fleets of sailing ships required a diversity of skills and know-how that set the tone early on, reinforced by the work ethic and egalitarian ethos of the first Calvinist settlers. This remarkably well-educated group for the time correspondingly put a high premium on education for all classes of society. Harvard College was founded in 1636, which would go on to become one of the world's top-ranked universities, together with its sister institution, the Massachusetts Institute of Technology (MIT), located but a few blocks away. But all that lay in the future.

Boston's first economic shock came in the mid-19th century, the result of (yet again) changes in transportation technology. Before the arrival of steamships, the Liverpool–Boston run was the least expensive crossing to America, resulting in the massive arrival of Irish immigrants, many fleeing the potato famine of the 1840s. They provided an abundant labor pool that, combined with Yankee capital, allowed Boston to rapidly industrialize. Boston's industrialization, in contrast to heavy industry manufacturing cities like Detroit, Buffalo, and Pittsburgh, was based on a marriage of *different* skills, in which its know-how in maritime services and ancillary sectors such as insurance were combined with manufacturing, marketing, and retailing activities. Iron bashing was only a minor element of Boston's manufacturing base, but as elsewhere, manufacturing was destined to decline, the city descending into a long period of relative decline. By 1980, Boston was no longer a particularly well-off city. Bostonians earned less than the residents of Atlanta.[39] Twenty years later, the Greater Boston Area would register the fourth highest per capita income among U.S. metropolitan areas. Over those twenty years, Boston succeeded in replacing its lost manufacturing base with generally high-paying, knowledge-rich jobs.

Boston's success in replacing one economic base with another has many explanations, not least the quality of its educational institutions from primary school to university. Also, unlike Buffalo, Boston was the heart of the state in which it was located, resulting in a very different relationship between state and city. Massachusetts legislators could not ignore the needs of Boston. More to the point, the policies of the state of Massachusetts continued to bear the imprint of those Puritan settlers who first landed in the Massachusetts Bay Colony, colonists who *chose* to settle for reasons other than purely material ones. Boston's citizens, in Glaeser's words, "responded to crisis by innovating, not by fleeing,"[40] which nicely sums up Boston's story but still leaves one wondering why more of its citizens did not flee during the bad years.

Boston's success is all the more remarkable because it was set in America, a highly mobile society: it was a northern city like Buffalo (and all midwestern cities) with a cold climate, though blessed with an attractive shoreline. The draw of the Sunbelt is a powerful force, which Boston manifestly succeeded in resisting, which leads me into a more subjective area: the forging of strong, quasi-national, regional identities or *glue*.

Is New England a Nation?

Boston's resurgence suggests that strong regional cultures can have foundations other than language or religion, although religion did initially play a role in forging the identity of Boston's cultural space. That identity goes well beyond those initial Puritan settlers, now a small minority, with Roman Catholics now the largest religious affiliation. I have an old friend, a retired professor and a native of Boston (of Irish Italian stock, of course), who once explained to me that he could not imagine living west of an imaginary cultural line that separates New England, or Boston States as Atlantic Canadians are wont to call it, from the rest of the continent. He could see himself living in Canada's Maritime Provinces, and he did live several years in Nova Scotia, but not, for example, in the American South or in California. My colleague was not alone in perceiving Canada's four Atlantic Provinces and six New England states as a distinct cultural space. In his 1981 book, *The Nine Nations of North America*, Joel Garneau, also a native of Boston, identified the ten jurisdictions as forming the nation of New England, with Boston as its national capital.[41]

I acknowledge that this is not terribly scientific. Yet, those who have lived or traveled in this part of North America will know that the Boston States feel different. The difference is visible in numerous ways: the distinctive architecture of its homes, its neat village squares, and the seemingly endless proliferation of colleges and libraries. You know when you're in New England and when you're not. The Boston accent is immediately recognizable. More to the point, New England's political culture is historically to the left of the American mainstream, more liberal in American parlance. Hillary Clinton carried all six states in the 2016 presidential election, as did Obama in the two preceding presidential elections. It is not entirely an accident that Bernie Sanders, the only openly socialist member of the U.S. Senate, hails from Vermont. True, there are differences between the New England states, with Massachusetts and Vermont consistently more liberal, and New Hampshire more conservative. Yet, it is difficult to deny the existence of a common political culture that manifests itself, among other traits, in generally higher state taxes and correspondingly higher spending on education and generally more environmentally stringent legislation. In sum, legislative, political, and lifestyle choices have over time produced a recognizable environment that a large proportion of the population is visibly reluctant to abandon. During the 1980s, among the worst years of New England's industrial decline, with textile mills closing everywhere, many did leave but many more stayed. This was a very different reaction from the seemingly unstoppable demographic hemorrhage of the industrial Midwest.

Minneapolis-St. Paul—Norwegian Bachelor Farmers

Let me now move to the Upper Midwest, an even colder place than Boston. The continued excellent performance of Minneapolis-St. Paul on numerous indicators (income per capita, education, corporate head offices, etc.) has long fascinated me, precisely because it is such an exception. It is difficult to think of a large American city in a more peripheral location and a more inhospitable climate. Why would anyone choose to live there?

Here again, we need to go back to the area's first European settlers: largely Scandinavian (and thus already from cold lands) with also a good dose of Germans and Slavic peoples thrown in, nations with often strong social democratic traditions. The state of Minnesota predictably developed a political culture that, compared to that of most other states, places greater emphasis on social equality and income redistribution. An exception among American states at the time,[42] Minnesota introduced a form of regional government in 1967 (Metropolitan Council) based on a cost-sharing formula for the Twin City Minneapolis-St. Paul area. This regional government coordinates infrastructure planning and major zoning, avoiding the fiscal straightjacket and sharp social divide that continues to bedevil Buffalo and so many other American cities. The city and state also have a reputation for generally honest government, Nordic propriety undoubtedly being a factor. Minnesota consistently ranks among the lowest for federal corruption convictions per capita,[43] a telling contrast with Louisiana at the other end of the Mississippi.

Minneapolis-St. Paul stands out among midwestern cities for the absence of steel-basing industries, its economic base founded largely on agriculture and food processing. Coming back to glue, we find that the mix of farming (mainly dairy farming) and Scandinavian roots produced a lifestyle and culture particular to the region, or at least perceived as such by its inhabitants, which has visibly produced a strong sense of loyalty. How else is one to explain the region's success in spawning a broad range of industries whose production facilities and head offices have remained in the region? A listing of the principal corporations headquartered in Minneapolis-St. Paul (Target, Best Buy, 3M, General Mills, Land O Lakes, among the better-known) is testimony to the region's propensity not only to produce entrepreneurs but also to hold them.

Some years ago, intrigued by this concentration of head offices in such a cold and peripheral place, I flew to the Twin Cities with the purpose of doing a survey.[44] I diligently drew up a questionnaire for corporate executives kind enough to receive me. The questionnaire listed all the standard reasons why a corporation might choose to locate its production facilities and head office in a given city: taxes; labor costs; suppliers; market access; availability of skilled and educated workers; and so on. I rapidly realized that the questionnaire was useless. I invariably got the same response: "we did not choose to locate here, we are from here." All corporations were homegrown, the founder-owner a native of either Minnesota or the neighboring Dakotas. Of the five corporations listed above, note that two are food-processing giants and two are large bargain retailers, typical of the industries one would expect to emerge in local economies dominated by family farms and agriculture.

Minnesotans (and those nearby) do visibly view themselves as different, the object of anecdotes and (requisite) self-depreciating humor. The supposed quirks of Minnesotans became a mainstay of American nighttime radio thanks to the popular show *A Prairie Home Companion* broadcast by Minnesota Public Radio, hosted by Garrison Keillor for over forty years (1974–2006). Keillor would invariably start off the show with a few words about his favorite invented characters: "Norwegian Bachelor Farmers"—stoic, upstanding, and good Lutherans all—embodiments, so the listener understood. of Prairie virtues. Fun, sun, and games were for lazy outsiders, not for true Minnesotans who understood the healing virtues of pain, cold winters, and hard work. Those who didn't agree could always drive down to Florida or Texas: and good riddance to them. The point here is not whether this obvious caricature is accurate, but rather that the region developed a sufficiently strong self-image to hold on to its young even after they succeeded.

The Boston and Minneapolis-St. Paul stories illustrate the interplay between values, institutions, geography, and historical accident; which does not easily lend itself to grand theories. I have no simple explanation of why Ohio, Indiana, Illinois, and other Rustbelt states did not succeed in generating the same degree of loyalty. As we saw in the Buffalo and Cleveland stories, these are politically and racially fractured places with industrial landscapes that do not easily invite affection. Perhaps, too, the geographic scattering of Rustbelt cities with rival urban centers (Buffalo, Cleveland, Pittsburgh, Cincinnati, Detroit, Milwaukee) precluded the early emergence of a dominant regional center that might have given the region a degree of cultural unity. Boston, Minneapolis-St. Paul, and Chicago are the undisputed central places of their respective cultural hinterlands, serving as natural magnets for the young. Chicago eventually rose to become the Midwest's primary central place and continues to act as a magnet; which perhaps indirectly weakened the glue of its less successful rivals.

Education: Can Johnny Write and Suzie Count?

We have already commented on the positive link between high human capital (often measured by the share of the workforce with a postsecondary education) and urban growth, amply documented by numerous studies, notably for U.S. cities.[45] The evidence for Europe points in the same direction.[46] Cities with highly educated populations will as a rule be richer and grow faster than others. We have seen, however, that a city need not necessarily be a top center of learning to generate a high standard of living for its citizens, Vienna being our prime exhibit. Not every city can be home to an MIT, Harvard, or Stanford. But the presence of a reasonably high-quality university (or more than one), accessible to all who wish to study, is without doubt a positive asset, certainly for large cities.

Here again, the decisions taken by senior governments can be pivotal. Had the New York State legislature chosen in 1865 to establish its only land grant college (which was to become Cornell University) in Buffalo rather than the isolated small town of Ithaca, Buffalo's history might well have evolved differently. The University of Michigan is an equally telling example. Initially founded in Detroit in 1817, the Michigan legislature chose to move the main campus to Ann Arbor in 1837. Had the legislature chosen to leave the University of Michigan, today one of the world's great universities, in Detroit, perhaps that city's history would also have developed differently.

That said; human capital is about much more than great research universities. The foundation for human capital, including highly educated cohorts, is a population with the basic skills of reading, writing, and numerical literacy. Education systems vary across nations and jurisdictions, involving everything from tuition costs (if any) and curriculum content to teacher pay and training. We saw in Chapter 2 that the generally poor ranking of Mexican students on PISA scores as well as the poor ranking of Mexican universities can in part be traced back to a particularly deficient primary school system in which teachers are hired on the basis of patronage, not competence. The low scores for Louisiana students also helps explain why New Orleans does not have a top-ranking research university.

The importance of a solid primary and secondary education (*relative* to postsecondary education) increases as we move down the urban ladder. The positive relationship between the share of the workforce with a postsecondary education and growth breaks down as one goes down the urban ladder.[47] The reason is simple: the goods and services that can be more efficiently produced in smaller places will as a rule require *relatively* less postsecondary educated labor. The production of midtechnology products, no less than high-end information-rich services, requires the presence of an educated workforce capable of understanding complex written instructions and, more to the point, capable of adapting production techniques to changing conditions and of introducing new ways of doing things. The most important productivity gains are often realized on the factory floor, the sum of accumulated small improvements over time. Economic historians have long pointed to the importance of small inventions.[48] Productive innovation, as we saw in Chapter 2, is not limited to big cities, providing (at least in technologically advanced economies) the presence of a labor force with a basic knowledge of science and associated cognitive skills.

Let us thus return to Drummondville, our small-town success story. Some 10 percent of the Drummondville population over fourteen years of age had a B.A. degree or higher, compared to 24 percent for Montreal.[49]

It is thus difficult to attribute Drummondville's economic performance to the presence of a large university-educated population. Indeed, the gap for university graduates between Drummondville and Montreal has grown in recent years.[50] That is not where the town's skill advantage lies. Once we add graduates with nonuniversity postsecondary degrees, the gap between the two cities disappears. This result can be largely attributed to Quebec's system of community colleges (*Collèges d'enseigment général et professionnel* [CEGEPs]/General and Professional/Vocational Colleges). This system was created by the province in 1968 from old Catholic colleges, replaced with secular science and arts-based curricula—a revolutionary idea at the time. CEGEPs are public with no tuition fees, an explicit policy choice, but with also a predictable impact on the public purse. A distinguishing feature of the system, notably outside large urban centers, is the design of curricula in association with the local business community, including apprenticeship programs and continuing education for employees. Drummondville's CEGEP is one of the largest in the province, offering programs, among others, in computer sciences, mechanical engineering, transport logistics, as well as accounting and business administration.

The old French-language Catholic primary and secondary school systems were also brought under state control during the 1960s, as part of a global reform of education, which will be elaborated on in Chapter 6. The province invested heavily in the new public system. According to recent data, Quebec spends proportionally more on education (public spending as a percentage of GDP) than other North American jurisdictions—twice the percentage for Louisiana. Its spending is in the same league as Scandinavian top performers such as Finland and Sweden.[51] The investment has paid off: PISA score results for recent years put Quebec's fifteen-year olds in the top ranking class for mathematical competence, just after Japan and above Switzerland.[52] In sum, an employer coming to Drummondville or starting up a business knows he or she will find a workforce where John (or Jean) can read and Suzie (Suzanne) can count, and at a lower cost than in the big city.

The reform of Drummondville's school system was part of a social transformation sweeping all of Quebec at the time, which sets the stage for our next chapter.

6

Montreal

Story of a Successful (But Costly) Social Revolution

Montreal is a generally safe city with a reasonably good quality of life.[1,2] Surveys suggest that Montrealers are on the whole satisfied with their lot, although such things are admittedly highly subjective.[3] Montreal today is an admirably "civil" place with one of the lowest crime rates in North America. Yet, Montreal could also be called a divided city, a city historically split between two linguistic groups (Francophones and Anglophones), indeed between two different peoples. As such, Montreal provides a rare and encouraging demonstration that different peoples *can* live together without slipping into violence. How did this come about? As we shall see, it was not always so.

Montreal's story is really two stories: first, that of a great metropolis that fell from greatness, only to be reborn; and second, that of a socially divided city that succeeded in overcoming its divisions but that required a social and political revolution. The two stories, we shall discover, are not unrelated. Montreal's story is unique in that the social revolution that triggered its fall also laid the foundations for its resurgence. Economic change sometimes requires social change; that is the message of Montreal's story. But social revolutions, even successful ones, rarely come without a cost.

Before the Fall—Canada's Metropolis

Montreal in the 1950s was, adjusting for size,[4] the New York of Canada, a city with which it had much in common: the nation's premier city, the most cosmopolitan in outlook, the principal point of entry for immigrants from war-torn Europe. Among Montreal's best known contributions to gastronomy was smoked meat (cured beef), the northern parent of New York's pastrami sandwich, a legacy in both places of the waves of Russian Jews who had fled the Czars' pogroms at the turn of the 20th century. Both were ports, merchant cities. Like New York, Montreal was the center of the nation's garment industry, fueled by low-paid immigrant workers and, in the case of Montreal, rural French Canadian migrants fleeing the country-side. Montreal's elites ruled the nation. Its great commercial institutions—the Canadian Pacific Railway and the Bank of Montreal—were the visual symbols of its power and were generally unloved. Like New York bashing, Montreal bashing was a national sport.

In at least one respect, Montreal was even more dominant than the Big Apple, combining the advantages of New York and Chicago. Montreal was the railhead and terminus for Canada's vast railway network stretching from the Atlantic to the Pacific. The Canadian West was settled via Montreal by thousands upon thousands of Germans, Ukrainians, and others in search of land passing through its doors on their way to the rich farmlands-to-be of the Canadian Prairies. In the opposing direction, eastbound goods (wheat, lumber, minerals, etc.) passed through Montreal on their way to European markets. Everything moved through Montreal, the nation's transport hub. Its hub function in turn gave rise to an important rolling stock industry, massive railyards and locomotive repair shops dotting its industrial landscape.

Post-World War II Montreal—Unrivaled Growth

World War II was good for the Montreal economy, the outcome of a favorable combination of geography and industrial structure. Britain needed armaments, planes, and other equipment. Canada represented the ideal location for wartime production, out of reach of the German Luftwaffe. The other choice, Toronto, further inland, would have added more costs in money and time. Halifax was closer to the European theater of war but did not have Montreal's industrial base. Employment in manufacturing catapulted from one hundred fifteen thousand to one hundred eighty thousand jobs during the first three years of the war. The need for explosives and medicine jumpstarted the chemical and pharmaceutical industries. The apparel industry also profited: an army needs uniforms and boots. Montreal's accumulated experience in rolling stock manufacturing and engineering provided the foundation for the emerging aircraft industry. The Hawker Hurricane, made famous in the Battle of Britain (1940), was designed and assembled in Montreal.

The need for war propaganda prompted the federal government to create the National Film Board (NFB), establishing its main studios in Montreal, which would become the nursery for French Canadian cinema. The postwar years also saw the advent of new communications technologies. In 1952, CBC/Radio-Canada's first televised programs appeared on the small screen. Here again, the federal government's decision to locate the main studios in Montreal set the stage for development of a lively broadcasting industry and associated sectors such as advertising, recording, and the performing arts.

The postwar years saw the rise of commercial aviation, with Montreal again the winner. Everything pointed to Montreal inheriting the same predominant position for air travel that it occupied for maritime and rail transport. The federal government chose Montreal as the nation's air hub not only because it was the largest city, but also for technical reasons. Aircraft at the time had only a limited range, and Montreal was the natural entry point for flights to and from Europe. Federal regulations required incoming carriers from Europe to land in Montreal; internal routes were reserved for national carriers. The largest national carrier, Trans Canada Airlines, later renamed Air Canada, had its head office and principal maintenance base at Montreal's Dorval Airport. Montreal, in a word, was Canada's aviation center and major North American hub. It was no accident that the International Civil Aviation Organization (ICAO), created in 1947 by fifty-two member states, established its head office in Montreal, where it remains to this day.

Trade grew exponentially during the halcyon years of postwar expansion, fueling the growth of the port of Montreal. Only one cloud lurked on the horizon: Toronto's financial sector, buoyed by the vigor of the Ontario economy, began to rival Montreal's. By the early 1960s Toronto had surpassed Montreal in retail banking and equity markets, measured by the total value of checks cleared by Toronto banks and transactions on the Toronto Stock Exchange.[5] Canada thus boasted two major financial centers of almost equal size, a rare occurrence in any country. Which city would finally prevail? The answer would come sooner than anticipated.

Montreal continued to register unrivaled growth during the postwar decades, further fueled by the high birth rate of French Canadian women and by rural populations flocking to the city. Metro Montreal's population doubled in the twenty years between 1951 and 1971, nearing the three million mark, the measure of a true metropolis. The rivalry with Toronto seemed to have been settled once and for all: Montreal was Canada's metropolis, period. Few onlookers were surprised when then Mayor Jean Drapeau, during the 1966 mayoral elections, declared: "The 1960s will be Montreal's decade. The city will become our London, our Paris, the metropolis of Canada and of North America."[6]

The Expo Years

The 1967 Montreal World's Fair (Expo 67) marked the high point of this era of unbridled optimism. Expo 67's most enduring impact was arguably psychological; it was a huge coming-of-age party, bearing witness that Montreal had finally arrived in its long journey from colonial outpost to global metropolis. It is difficult for those who did not have the good fortune of witnessing those events at first hand to understand the depth of Expo's symbolism. Everybody, but everybody, went to Expo. The various national pavilions—Japanese, U.S., French, Soviet, and so on—became the subject of daily conversation: which served the best and most exotic food? Expo 67 was a commercial success, its attendance double that predicted: some fifty million paid admissions over a 183-day period.[7] The city would name its new baseball team the Montreal Expos (*Les Expos*), a National League franchise proudly obtained in 1969, only to be lost in 2004 (to become the Washington Nationals), a harbinger of what was to come.

Expo 67 holds a lesson for us. Great events like international exhibitions or the Olympics are often maligned as wasteful public expenditures that do little for a city's economy. That judgment is generally correct. Why then was Expo 67 different? Many factors came together. Because Expo 67 coincided with the centenary celebrations of the founding of the Canadian Confederation, public infrastructure costs were shared among the three levels of government, with Ottawa taking the largest share and the City the smallest. The event was generally well managed and scandal free, and construction deadlines were met. Expo 67 came with other infrastructures, not least of which was the new metro (subway) system. La Ronde, an amusement park on the Expo site, became a favorite playground for Montrealers for years to come. But above all, Expo 67 coincided with the cultural and economic reawakening of French Canada. Montreal was French Canada's metropolis. Expo 67, simply put, became the showcase for all the world to see of Quebec's arrival as a modern, forward-looking society. The timing could not have been better. Quebecers wanted and got a party to celebrate.

The Quiet Revolution

The *Quiet Revolution*, now an accepted term in historiography, coincides roughly with the decade of the 1960s, following the defeat of the clergy-beholden *Union nationale* government that had ruled the province of Quebec on and off for thirty years or so. The 1960 election of a Liberal government changed all that, beginning a succession of secularizing and modernizing provincial administrations. The first two Liberal administrations (1960–1966) were led by a charismatic premier, Jean Lesage, surrounded by a team of young reform-minded cabinet ministers. Ownership and management of schools and hospitals was transferred from the Church to the Quebec state. The greatest achievement of the Quiet Revolution was undoubtedly the modernization of the French-language school system alluded to earlier, laying the foundation for a new generation of Québécois as Quebec's French Canadians would increasingly come to call themselves. In the space of a generation, Québécois would jump from below-average levels of education to one of the best educated populations in the Western world. The Quiet Revolution was more than a political changing of the guard. It ushered in a transformation in values and mindsets; not least of which was a change in attitudes toward business.

Montreal was the primary target—both victim and beneficiary—of the reforms introduced by the Quiet Revolution. The public institutions generated by the Quiet Revolution would be almost exclusively Montreal-based among which the *Régie d'assurance maladie* (the provincial crown corporation mandated to administer the public health insurance plan, created in 1961) and the *Caisse de Dépôt et de Placement* (the public pension fund manager, created in 1965), which today is one of the biggest investment portfolios in North America. However, the most symbolically charged addition to the city's skyline was the inauguration in 1963 of the new head office of *Hydro-Quebec*, the giant public power utility, created by the nationalization of Quebec's remaining private hydroelectric companies. Thanks to the hydroelectric potential of Quebec's many rivers, *Hydro-Quebec* would grow to become the largest public power utility of its kind in North America.

Other reforms fueled the local economy, among which was the founding in 1968 of the University of Quebec at Montreal (UQAM). Public-sector jobs more than tripled between 1960 and 1970, in turn inducing private-sector employment growth, notably in consulting engineering, a by-product of Hydro-Quebec's giant hydroelectric projects in the province's north.

Hydro-Quebec and the projects it gave rise to would act as the breeding ground for a new generation of engineers and managers, forerunners of French Quebec's rising entrepreneurial class. The initial impact of the Quiet Revolution was unequivocally positive: here was a society modernizing, throwing off the shackles of the past. Soon, however, the Quiet Revolution would become less quiet.

A Social Cauldron

Expo 67 was the last party, a joyful illusion like all carnivals. Montreal was a city of contradictions. Despite the rapid postwar expansion, its economic base had changed only little, the emergence of new industries (e.g.,aerospace and pharmaceuticals) notwithstanding. The clothing and textiles industries were still the leading sources of manufacturing employment. Montreal's industry mix was not the only thing that seemed fixed in time. The social divide separating Francophones from Anglophones seemed a permanent fixture, its roots going back to the 19th century. The city was over two-thirds Francophone (80 percent for the province); but the business community was almost exclusively Anglophone, dominated by an old Anglo-Scottish elite with basically the same families since Confederation was enacted in 1867.

The divide predictably produced a growing sense of exclusion among newly educated young Francophones, who were less and less inclined to accept the subordinate status of their forefathers. It is difficult a half-a-century later to fully understand the level of pent-up frustration Québécois youth felt at the time. The relationship was perceived (not totally incorrectly) as semicolonial. Montreal was a divided, segregated city: in the west, there were rich, leafy Anglo neighborhoods and in the east, poor working-class Francophone neighborhoods. Many young Québécois saw an analogy between their aspirations and the civil rights struggle in the United States at the time. In 1968, Pierre Vallières, a Québécois intellectual, published *Nègres blancs d'Amérique*[8] (White Niggers of America), which became a minor best-seller.

These were not simply the musings of a wild-eyed intellectual. Statistical proof of the social divide came with the 1961 census, the first to provide such data.[9] Unilingual Francophones (i.e., those who spoke French only) in Montreal earned only half the wage of unilingual Anglophones.

Equally revealing was the finding that unilingual Anglophones (those who spoke no French) earned a third more than bilingual Francophones. Not only was French visibly not a language worth learning, but being a native English-speaker was visibly a social plus. French Canadians were clearly a lesser breed, maybe not "white niggers," but certainly below those fortunate enough to be of Anglo-Scottish stock. Having grown up in New York, I had the advantage of speaking accent-free English and was thus able to view from the inside how Anglos perceived their French Canadian neighbors at the time. When on occasion, usually at some social function, I asked my Anglo friend why he or she spoke no French, the invariable answer, spokenwith an appropriate surprised look and condescending tone, was: "Why learn French? These people don't speak French; they speak a peasant patois that even the French don't understand." They were right of course. Why learn a useless, socially inferior language? The outward signs of the second-class status of French were everywhere. Most shop signs were in English; contracts and instructions were most often in English only. Going into a downtown department store in the 1960s and asking to be served in French was an act of political courage. Québécois were foreigners in their own land, or so many felt, and not without reason.

The cauldron did almost explode. The *Front de Libération du Québec* (FLQ, or Quebec Liberation Front), which today would be called a terrorist organization, began its violent actions in 1963. On May 17 of that year, bombs exploded in ten Westmount mailboxes, a wealthy Anglo neighborhood. In May 1966, a secretary in an Anglo institution was killed by a mail bomb. Monuments that evoked the British presence were regularly targeted. Queen Victoria and Admiral Nelson were knocked off their pedestals on more than one occasion. The culmination of the FLQ's terrorist reign was the so-called October Crisis of 1970 during which the British Consul in Montreal was kidnapped and a Quebec cabinet minister was savagely executed. The federal government declared the War Measures Act and, at the province's request, brought in the army. Some five hundred persons were detained or arrested. The October Crisis marked the end of the FLQ, whose leaders were either incarcerated or exiled to Cuba, putting an end to the cycle of violence.

Remarkably, the violence did not resume. What happened that allowed society to defuse the time bomb in its midst? The answer would come some years later. But before getting to the answer, we need to consider two events that would negatively affect Montreal, contributing to its coming decline.

The Airport Fiasco—How to Destroy a Hub Overnight

Montreal provides a unique laboratory test in which a city loses its hub function literally overnight. Its sudden loss in 1975 of its air hub was entirely a result of gross incompetence, a story of politics trumping common sense and technical facts.

By the late 1960s, airplanes could now bypass Montreal and fly directly to Toronto and destinations further west. But this did not necessarily mean that they *would* bypass Montreal. Canadian federal regulations continued to favor Montreal, requiring incoming carriers from Europe to land in Montreal. To understand why, after 1975, most carriers chose to avoid Montreal, a brief detour into political history is in order, not unrelated to the rise of Québécois nationalism. In April 1968, Pierre-Elliott Trudeau, one of the most charismatic and also most controversial prime ministers in recent Canadian history, was elected. He also promised a revolution, but at the federal level, in response to the grievances of his fellow Québécois and the growing separatist movement that threatened to take Quebec out of Canada. The separatist *Parti Québécois* was founded that same year with a no less charismatic leader, René Lévesque, a former provincial cabinet minister. Trudeau set out to convince Québécois that Canada was also their country. He succeeded, among other things, in transforming the federal apparatus, passing (long-overdue) legislation, making Canada formally bilingual and generally enhancing the standing of the French language across Canada. Never again would Canada have a prime minster who spoke only English.

At the same time, the Trudeau government wanted to do something tangible and visible to boost Montreal's economy, demonstrating to Québécois that the government cared. Trudeua wanted a big project that would strike the imagination. The new minister of transport, Jean Marchand, also a Québécois, delivered: he announced that Ottawa would endow Montreal with an ultramodern international airport, touted to be the biggest in the world. Here was a project worthy of a world-class metropolis. In addition, the airport would open in time for the 1976 Summer Olympics, which had recently been awared to Montreal, yet another feather in Montreal's cap.

The technical rationale for a new airport was based (1) on travel demand projections suggesting that Dorval, the current airport, would soon be saturated and (2) on the notion that the noise produced by new jetliners made urban-located Dorval undesirable. Both parts of this rationale proved to be wrong, the first in part because of the 1973 oil shock, which halted growth in demand, and the second because of improvements in aviation technology, which alleviated noise problems. Indeed, demand projections were already being questioned. At the time, I was part of a research team commissioned by the Quebec government to study the impact of the new airport on the Montreal economy.[10] I well remember informal conversations I held in the autumn of 1970 with planners at the Federal Department of Transport in Ottawa, who covertly expressed their doubts about the demand projections. But their political masters had decided: the airport would be built.

Things went badly from the very beginning. The first act in the saga was the choice of the site for new mega-airport, leading to competing studies and a tug-of-war between Ottawa and Quebec City. Ottawa preferred a site to the west of Montreal, facilitating links with Ottawa, while Quebec City pushed for a site to the east, facilitating links with Quebec City. The federal government had the last word and finally opted for a rural village some 40 kilometers northwest of Montreal with the unlikely name of Sainte-Scholastique. A contest was launched to find a classier name for the new airport. The closest town, several wags at the time noted, was Lachute, but that would not do; *la chute* in French means "the fall." Eventually, the name *Mirabel* was chosen for the newly rebaptized village, and the new mega-airport was appropriately dubbed Montreal–Mirabel International Airport or *Mirabel* for short, as it came to be popularly known.

Mirabel was located in a largely agricultural area, leading to the forcible expropriation of hundreds of family farms, much of which proved to be unnecessary later, leaving a bitter taste that lasts to this day. More to the point, Mirabel was located outside a major transport axis that would have allowed an eventual rail or highway link to be integrated into an existing corridor connecting the airport to downtown Montreal. As was soon discovered, a dedicated rail or highway link was not financially viable. Airports alone rarely generate sufficient traffic to warrant the construction of a dedicated rail link, and Mirabel was no exception, something planners at the time should have known. A planned highway was never completed and projections for a high-speed rail link never got beyond the planning stage. But poor location is only half of the story.

Construction began in June 1970, and the airport opened its doors in October 1975 at a cost of 500 million Canadian dollars, or about $2.5 billion in today's dollars; it was said to be the most technologically advanced airport in the world at the time. Montreal now had two airports: Dorval and

Mirabel. Then, almost overnight, Montreal's share of Canadian air traffic plummeted. The total number of passengers (arrivals and departures) for both Montreal airports would stagnate for the subsequent twenty years (1975–1995). Passenger traffic would more than triple in Toronto over the same period. By 1985, Montreal's share of Canadian air passenger traffic would fall to a ludicrous 10 percent. Passengers making connecting flights—the hallmark of a hub airport—all but disappeared. By 1990, connecting flights were five times as numerous at Toronto's Pearson Airport as the total for Montreal's two airports. Montreal had fallen to the status of a provincial town as far as air travel was concerned.

The reason behind this debacle was surprisingly simple. More surprising is that no one saw it coming. The presence of two airports in a small market like Montreal precluded either airport from functioning as a full-service hub. Federal regulation stupidly (there is no other word) divided the market between the two airports: Mirabel would handle overseas flights while Dorval would keep continental flights. The two airports were 30 kilometers from each other, making connections between overseas and intracontinental flights impractical. A passenger arriving from, say, London on his or her way to Cleveland needed to change airports, landing first at Mirabel and then make his or her way to Dorval for the connecting flight to Cleveland. It is easy to understand why the Londoner would choose to fly to Atlanta or Toronto instead where he or she could make the connection in the same airport. Major hubs are almost always built around a single airport with a sufficient roster of arriving and departing flights (a lesson well learned by Atlanta and Chicago as we shall see in Chapter 7).

By splitting air traffic between two half-service airports, federal regulation destroyed the chance of endowing Montreal with a single modern hub airport that would have assured its continued status as a major hub. But that (one-time) opportunity was lost forever. The wise choice at the time would have been to upgrade Dorval. Had those $2.5 billion been spent on refurbishing Dorval, the story would have been different. But Ottawa wanted to make a big splash, and that it did. Building a shiny new airport is more impressive than upgrading an old one.

The federal government now found itself in a self-inflicted quandary. Montreal had one airport too many; but closing one or the other had a political price. A strong lobby favored keeping Dorval open, arguing that it provided easy accessibility to downtown Montreal. Mirabel also had its lobby, pointing out the airport's modernity and the moneys already invested.

For the federal government, closing Mirabel was equivalent to admitting that it had made a mistake (a very expensive one), something governments are loath to do.

In the meantime, the negative impact of the two-headed airport monster on Montreal was becoming painfully evident. By a cruel twist of fate, it coincided with other events that would hasten the city's economic decline (see next sections below). The twenty-one years (1975–1996) during which Montreal had two airports coincided almost perfectly with Montreal's worst years. Convention business plummeted, and attracting international or even national head offices became well-nigh impossible. Moreover, it was not unusual for Montreal businesspeople to prefer flying through Toronto via Dorval on their way to European destinations rather than to trek out to Mirabel. That Mirabel had to go was becoming increasingly obvious. However, what political leader wished to go down in history as having mothballed a two billion dollar public investment? Public debates and tug-of-wars continued for two decades, during which the Montreal economy continued to suffer.

In 1992, the new Conservative government in Ottawa transferred the hot potato to a newly created, locally administrated airport authority (*Aéroports de Montréal* [ADM]) with responsibility for managing both airports. The decision was now for the locals to make. If ADM recommended a downgrade or full closure of one of the two airports, the federal government would comply. After numerous studies, much public discussion, and a long-overdue dose of political courage, the mayor of Montreal, supported by the Metropolitan Chamber of Commerce, came out openly in favor of closing Mirabel. In 1995, ADM announced that it would start to upgrade Dorval and thus implicitly downgrade Mirabel, which would inevitably lead to the latter's closure, although ADM could not say so openly. Ultimately, Mirabel was gradually dismantled, and its modern terminal was torn down—a monument to failure. Road signs on Montreal's highways still point to a now de-funct airport, an adventure most Montrealers would rather forget.

In 1997, Dorval was once again allowed to receive intercontinental flights. Construction to double its capacity began in 2000. All passenger flights, continental and intercontinental, were transferred back to Dorval in 2004, and Montreal finally had a "normal" airport again. But the damage was done: the opportunities lost during those fateful years could not be won back. Montreal has recaptured some of its lost market share and now has an airport appropriate to the city's size and standing. All the same, there is little chance that it will ever regain its status as Canada's gateway city and main hub for air travel.

The Olympic Disaster

Misfortune seldom strikes only once. The blame for Montreal's airport fiasco can be laid squarely at the feet of the federal government in Ottawa. Montreal's 1976 Olympic disaster, however, was almost entirely one of local doing. Surfing on the triumph of Expo 67, Mayor Drapeau in 1969 submitted the city's candidature for the upcoming Summer Olympics. In May of the following year, the International Olympic Committee announced that Montreal had been chosen to host the Games of the XXIst Olympiad, the first Canadian city to be so honored. The games were to be held between July 17 and August 1, 1976. This was to be Mayor Drapeau's crowning legacy to the city who, not averse to thinking big, announced that Montreal's Olympic Stadium (which was to be built) would become the city's signature landmark, much like the Eiffel Tower for Paris, a monument to Montreal's global stature.

Mayor Drapeau commissioned Paris-based architect, Roger Tallibert, to design and oversee the construction of the new Olympic Stadium, which came to known as the "Big O." Its design was truly monumental; it would be the largest stadium in Canada, with a retractable roof—an engineering feat—and purportedly the largest inclined tower in the world. (The tower was needed to hold the wires for the retractable roof.) A new swimming basin, Olympic Village, and velodrome were also to be built. Those who dared question the costs, which would be almost entirely borne by the city, were summarily rebuked by Mayor Drapeau in a statement that would come to haunt him. On January 29, 1973, in answer to a reporter's questions, the mayor famously declared "The Montreal Olympics can no more have a deficit, than a man can have a baby." Whatever one may think of the mayor's unfortunate analogy, it was a boon to political cartoonists who in the coming years would never miss an opportunity to portray Mayor Drapeau with child.

Things went badly from the outset. Construction work was marred by strikes, poor labor relations, bad management, and frequent delays. Although the Olympics opened on schedule—they had to—several installations were still unfinished, most shamefully the Olympic Stadium with its retractable roof still not functional. The retractable roof would never become functional—not for lack of numerous attempts to fix it—and remains the object of running gags among Montrealers. Although the Games as such were generally successful (a boycott by African states notwithstanding[11]), they turned into a financial disaster. The original cost of the Games was estimated at $120 million in 1970 and three years later, at the time of the mayor's famous statement, was upped to $310 million. And even this amount turned out to be a gross underestimate. The final cost has been estimated at some $1.6 billion, or $3 billion in today's dollars, once interest payments, maintenance costs, and roof repair costs are added in.[12]

The morning after the games, Montrealers woke up with a $1.5 billion headache, which they would spend the next thirty years paying off; the Big "O" had become the big "Owe." Far from an object of pride, the Olympic Stadium became a symbol of municipal mismanagement and hubris. The final payment on the Olympic debt was made in November 2006, financed in large part by a special tax on cigarettes. The Olympic installations, including the stadium, continue to operate at an annual deficit of about $20 million, subsidized by Montreal taxpayers. The departure of the Montreal Expos baseball team in 2004 meant that the Stadium lacks a major tenant and is chronically underused, standing empty almost half the year.

After the Olympics, the Quebec government set up a commission of inquiry to look into what went wrong, revealing an unlovely story of miscalculation, gullibility, and patronage. The Games had basically been a one-man show: Mayor Drapeau's self-assurance and authoritarian streak prevented effective independent oversight. The still lingering glory of Expo 67, only a few years earlier, may have blinded the mayor to the possibility that the Olympics could turn sour. The Olympic saga holds a number of lessons; not least of which is the obvious need for independent oversight. It also demonstrates that the costs of mega-events are generally beyond the means of a single party, the City of Montreal in this instance. The province eventually stepped in to oversee the remaining construction work but too late to prevent the coming debacle. The 1976 Olympics manifestly hurt the city's self-image, not to mention its impact on the city's finances. As misfortune would have it, the Olympic disaster coincided with other events—this time those of a political nature—that would shake the city's social fabric and economy.

The Second Revolution

The pent-up aspirations of Francophones during the 1970s continued to fuel Québécois nationalism with calls for Quebec's independence and measures to promote the French language. The turning point, as we learned in the Toronto story, came on November 15, 1976, with the surprise electoral victory of the separatist PQ (*Parti Québécois*), sending shockwaves throughout the province and Canada. Was Canada about to be torn apart? Up to now, separation—or sovereignty as its proponents preferred to call it—was considered a pipedream, and the PQ was regarded as a marginal party of dreamers and intellectuals. The PQ was in many respects a revolutionary party, certainly in the eyes of many Anglo-Montrealers and Canadians outside Quebec. Not only did the PQ threaten to take Quebec out of Canada, but it also promised to introduce draconian legislation to impose the use of French, which it promptly set out to do. After November 15, 1976, Quebec would never be the same.

The Charter of the French Language, popularly known as Bill 101, was adopted by the Quebec National Assembly on August 27, 1977, which many Québécois regard as the founding covenant of modern Quebec. Henceforth, French was to be the language of the province in all spheres of life, as well as the language of schooling of future immigrants. The reaction was as swift as it was painful for some. *The Conseil du Patronat du Québec* (a business lobby) recorded 263 head office departures, nearly all for Toronto, between January 1977 and November 1978.[13] The exodus of capital and talent reached its peak during the second half of the 1970s. In all, it is estimated that two hundred thousand Montrealers left between 1971 and 1991, of which forty-five thousand were college graduates (with a B.A. degree or higher), generally again to the benefit of Toronto.[14]

This exodus of brains and capital, visibly detrimental to Montreal, prompts two questions. What impelled Quebec voters to elect such a "revolutionary" government and, in turn, drove it to take such draconian measures in full knowledge that there would be a price to pay? The answer is language. The first half of the 1970s was a period of mounting linguistic tension; the right (never questioned before) of parents to freely choose the language of education of their children had become a core issue. Quebec had always had two public school systems—one English and one French—which were freely accessible to all.[15] It was understandably a highly emotional issue, directly affecting the lives of families. Opposing camps took to the streets with occasional clashes, the specter of open violence not far from the surface. But why did the schooling issue arise, and why now?

A new ingredient, as toxic as the social divide, had been thrown into the cauldron: demography. Among the most direct social transformations brought about by the Quiet Revolution, a visible sign of a rapidly modernizing society, was a precipitous fall in birth rates. In 1963, Québécois women gave birth on average to 3.6 children; ten years later, the rate had fallen below the replacement level to 1.8, never to rise again.[16] This fall in the birth rate destroyed the historical balance between Francophones and Anglophones which had existed for a century. Since Confederation (1867), the proportion of Francophones (mother tongue) in the province had consistently hovered around 80 percent and around 66 percent in Montreal. This entirely accidental equilibrium was the outcome of a balancing act between immigration, on the one hand, which bolstered the Anglo population, and high Francophone birth rates on the other. New immigrants overwhelmingly chose to send their children to English schools, another painful sign of the lower social standing of the French language. The now low Francophone birth rates meant that the equilibrium had broken down. If nothing was done, continued immigration would inevitably drive down the weight of Francophones. Demography was turning into a national obsession, with demographers becoming media personalities with dire predictions that the share of Francophones in Montreal would soon fall below the 50 percent mark. The social divide was now compounded by a sense of existential insecurity.[17] The very survival of the nation was at stake. For many Québécois, the only way out of this dilemma was a full break (separation). The election of the PQ in November 1976 should have surprised no one.

In the event, the new PQ government set out immediately to redress the balance. The linguistic equilibrium could only be reestablished by halting immigration, an unacceptable option, or by francizing new immigrants. The centerpiece of Bill 101—and also the most controversial—was the mandatory French schooling of the children of new immigrants. Bill 101 went even further: it abrogated the principle of freedom of choice between the two school systems. Henceforth, only parents who had themselves received their primary schooling in English *in Canada* could send their children to English schools. The measure was predictably contested in the courts but upheld by the Supreme Court of Canada.[18] This was a momentous change, altering forever what it means to be Québécois. School-age children of new immigrants would from now on go into the French school system, changing the very fabric of Québécois society, now becoming an increasingly diverse and multiracial society, similar to the rest of Canada, but with the difference that it functioned in French.

Bill 101 also changed Montreal's outward appearance. If French was to be a language of social advancement, it had to be perceived to be so. Symbols matter. Advertising and public signs now had to be in French.[19] If the linguistic message was clear, so too was the impact on commerce and business. French, the now required language of work in firms with fifty or more employees, raised the economic and social value of the French language. The growth of the public sector and the rise of a new Francophone entrepreneurial class meant that French was gradually gaining ground as a vehicle of social advancement. The 1981 census confirmed the extent of the turnaround: the wage gap between bilingual Francophones and Anglophones had disappeared, and that between unilinguals had narrowed by two-thirds.[20] Succeeding censuses would confirm that the trend continued to favor Francophones, with the eventual total disappearance of the income gap between the two linguistic groups. The social divide between the two would cease to be an issue of public debate.

The elimination of the social gap between Francophones and Anglophones in the course of a single generation was an achievement with few, if any, parallels in modern history. No less remarkable was the lifting, almost overnight, of the existential threat hanging over Francophones. In this, the separatist PQ government unwittingly undermined its own cause. The grievances that initially fueled the call for Quebec independence were now less and less relevant, a victim of its own success. Quebec would stay in Canada: the separatist option was defeated in two successive referendums in 1980 and 1995.

Decline: Paying the Price

The end of the unequal relationship between Anglophones and Francophones came at a price. The 1981 census revealed that Toronto's population now surpassed that of Montreal; the gap would widen over subsequent decades. The numbers did not lie. Toronto, and not Montreal, would be Canada's metropolis (the reasons for the shift are largely explained in Chapter 4 in the Toronto story). Montreal could not be both French and Canada's metropolis. Even without the threat of separation, the francization of Montreal made the exodus of Anglo-controlled head offices (not all thankfully, but many) inevitable, predictably followed by business service firms whose market area went beyond Quebec. In a word, Montreal's hinterland shrank, now basically limited to French-speaking Canada, with the clearest shift occurring in finance. The culmination came in 1997 when the Montreal Stock Exchange transferred all trading in ordinary shares to Toronto, although it maintained its hold for derivatives, finally merging with the Toronto Stock Exchange in 2007.

The Bad Years

The economic costs of Quebec's social revolution would become painfully evident over the next two decades. Beginning in the mid-1970s, Montreal would enter a two-decades-long period of economic underperformance. The metropolitan area systematically posted unemployment rates well above the Canadian average. For both political and business elites, it was a period of introspection and questioning. Clearly, something was wrong. Montreal's economy became the subject of numerous studies and commissions, the most well known of which was the Picard Report,[21] commissioned by the federal government. Montreal was estimated to have a structural job deficit of some two hundred thousand jobs—that is, the number of additional jobs it would have generated over the last two decades, had the region's performance equaled that of comparable North American cities. Montreal was down, and no one was terribly sure what to do. I recall all too clearly the cloud of pessimism that hung over the business community at the time, as well as the innumerable seminars and symposiums on what ailed Montreal.[22]

The fundamental cause of Montreal's economic woes was no secret. It had suffered a triple punch in which all three levels of government had played a part: the federal government (the airport fiasco); an overconfident mayor (the Olympic disaster); and, most importantly, a nationalist provincial government (Bill 101 and the threat of separation).

Rebirth

By the mid-1990s, Montreal's economy began to grow again. In the five years between 1996 and 2001, two hundred twenty thousand new jobs were added to the regional economy, a 15 percent increase. Montreal had ceased to be a sick economy. It would continue to grow. Though not a star performer, it would generally succeed in providing a reasonably good quality of life for the majority of its citizens. Montreal today—that is, the main message of the remainder of this chapter—is a reinvented city, both socially and economically. The principal causes of its fall had also laid the foundations for its subsequent rebirth, "rising again from the same ashes," to quote the title of a recent article.[23]

A New Business Elite

The social transformations brought about by the Quiet Revolution were starting to bear fruit. A Francophone business class was beginning to emerge. By 1995, the family portrait of Montreal's economic elite had completely changed. The second referendum on separation, held in 1995, did not produce the same shockwaves as the first referendum in 1980, signifying a radical change in the composition of Montreal's business community. No exodus occurred this time. Put bluntly, those Anglo-owned businesses that wanted to leave had now left. Those Anglophones (or other non-Francophones) who did not feel at ease in Montreal's new linguistic environment had also left, leaving a very different Anglo community in its place. Census data would reveal that the majority of Anglophones had now mastered French. The social barriers that traditionally separated Anglophones and Francophones were finally disappearing. In 1992, in a highly symbolic gesture, the Montreal Board of Trade, the traditional preserve of the Anglo elite, merged with the *Chambre de commerce de Montréal* to form the new, fully bilingual *Chambre de commerce de Montréal métropolitain*/Board of Trade of Metropolitan Montreal.

The merger of the two boards signaled not only the end of the social divide between the two elites, but also the coming of age of the Francophone business community. Francophones on corporate boards of directors, exotic rarities before the 1970s, were now commonplace. The expression *Quebec Inc.* entered the vocabulary; a reference to the growing network of

Quebec-based (generally, Montreal headquartered) corporations. Among the stars, often extolled in the media, were Jean-Coutu in retailing (pharmacies), Héroux-Devtek in aerospace, Quebecor in printing and entertainment, and, of course, Cascades and Bombardier whom we met earlier, both of which were now multinationals. Francophone corporations also emerged in the advanced service sector: Ubisoft and CGI in information technology, SECOR in management consulting, and SNC-Lavalin in consulting engineering. In the meantime, the office towers of Francophone financial institutions (National Bank, Caisses Desjardins, etc.) were reshaping the central business district (CBD). A simple look at those same office towers confirmed that business was no longer an Anglo preserve. To Montrealers today, this all seems natural. It is all too easy to forget that this truly was a revolution. Francophone-controlled firms, by some reports, now accounted for three times as many jobs as Anglo-controlled businesses.[24]

The exodus of Anglo capital and talent also had a positive side, facilitating the rise of a Francophone business elite and ambitious Francophone entrepreneurs eager to fill the void that had opened up. The consequences of the exodus would undoubtedly have been far worse had a new business elite not been ready to step in. The PQ government also lent a helping hand. The introduction in 1979 of a stock savings plan, facilitating the capitalization of Quebec-based firms, was explicitly aimed at boosting Québécois entrepreneurship.[25] In the event, the exodus of capital and talent facilitated the entry of newcomers, leaving the field open. The story of Toronto-controlled *Dominion Stores*, long one of the largest supermarket chains in the province (the name alone said it all), provides a highly symbolic example. In 1983, *Dominion* abandoned the Quebec market, selling its stores to a Francophone consortium which renamed the stores *Provigo*, a label that soon became synonymous with Francophone business success. The expression *État Provigo* (the Provigo State) became popular shorthand for the alliance between the Francophone business community and the Quebec government, a play on the French term for welfare state (*l'État providence*). The group subsequently bought *Steinberg's*, another large supermarket chain, integrating it into the *Provigo* label. In 1998, *Provigo* was acquired by Toronto-based Loblaws, which wisely chose to keep the *Provigo* label.

The francization of Montreal also altered the city's relationship with the rest of the province, which was overwhelmingly French. Montreal ceased to be a foreign city, or at least less so. It was now Quebec's metropolis, and that is how Montreal now proudly marketed itself: *la métropole du Québec*. Like a true metropolis, it drew in talent from its hinterland. English remains important (and always will) with a vibrant English-speaking community and proud institutions such as McGill University. But the linguistic ground rules were clear: French was the officially dominant language. Montreal became the natural magnet for nascent entrepreneurs from across French-speaking Canada and the Francophone and Francophile world. Here we have a fundamental difference with cities like Cleveland or Buffalo. A growing firm in western New York State with international ambitions would most probably look to Chicago or New York to relocate its head office, not to Buffalo or Cleveland. For aspiring Québécois entrepreneurs with international ambitions, Montreal, not Toronto, is their natural metropolis, the top spot on the urban hierarchy.

A New Hinterland

The francization of Montreal consolidated the division of Canada into two linguistically distinct markets for goods and services sensitive to language and to cultural codes. One does not market soap or soft drinks exactly the same way in Montreal as in Toronto. French Canada has its own media stars and public personalities, and consumers want to see them on the screen. The French-language market is smaller than the English-language market, but it is not insignificant: some eight million consumers, representing a market about the size of Sweden or Switzerland. By consolidating the French language in Quebec, Bill 101 assured Montreal a captive market, albeit a smaller one. Montreal lost an empire but gained a nation.[26]

Montreal's position as a central place allowed it to consolidate its service sector, including everything from wholesaling and distribution to information-rich business services, and also provide a continuing base for a healthy entertainment industry. Here we have another difference with Buffalo. Although Buffalo is a proud metropolis, it never became a major service center, the central place to which western New York State might look. Also, unlike western New York, which has been economically depressed for decades, Montreal's hinterland continued to grow, providing the foundations on which to build its service economy.

The language barrier also helped shape local service firms. The *Cirque du Soleil*, today a multinational enterprise, provides an eloquent example, inventing a circus without words. The rapid growth of Montreal's video-gaming industry, now ranked among the top in the world, is an example of an industry where language proficiency is not a major competitive factor, but rather the workforce's technical competence and creativity. Montreal-based performers have become regular features of the French entrainment scene, a rarity in France before the 1980s. Engineering firms have expanded into French-speaking Africa and Latin America. The language barrier, while a constraint, accelerated the internationalization of Montreal's economy, forcing it to look beyond North America and also undoubtedly affecting the market reach of manufacturing firms. CAE, the world's largest manufacturer of flight simulators, exports some 90 percent of its production outside Canada.

A final advantage of the language barrier, though not necessarily new, was cost. Montreal was never a high-wage economy. Before the 1960s, a plentiful, captive, rural (French Canadian) labor pool, replenished by high birth rates, allowed Montreal to keep wages low, providing the backbone of its apparel industry. That initial cost advantage has since disappeared. However, the comparative reluctance of Québécois to leave their province (what I have called "glue") has meant that Francophone workers are more willing on average to accept slightly lower wages (i.e., before considering moving elsewhere) than comparable workers in other provinces. This glue indirectly translates into two non-negligible advantages: (1) investments in education are less likely to be lost, educated youth are more likely to stay, and investments in worker training are less likely to be lost, the young nerd who just mastered a new algorithm is less likely to run off to California, a factor in Montreal's success in the video-gaming industry.[27]

Social Cohesion/Metropolitan Governance

Montreal's success in creating a generally livable and socially cohesive city also has its roots in provincial government actions aimed explicitly at preventing the emergence of social and center/suburb divides.[28]

Merger, Demerger, and Remerger

Here, the story reads in part like a repetition of the Toronto story, with senior government stepping in to impose revenue-sharing schemes and municipal amalgamations, often against the wishes of the locals. This is Canada.

The Montreal Urban Community (MUC), a weaker version of Metro Toronto, was created in 1970, grouping the twenty-seven municipalities on the Island of Montreal, a formula that worked fairly well for thirty years. As in Toronto, metropolitan growth soon outgrew the initial structure, the Island now accounting for only half the population of the region. In 2002, the PQ government forcibly merged the MUC (like Mega Toronto) into a single city. With the notable exception of the mayor of Montreal, the merger was hotly contested by all the mayors on the Island. The opposition Liberal Party promised to undo the unpopular merger if it came to power. The Liberal Party won the next election and true to its promise subsequently organized referendums. The 2004 municipal referendums on the Island of Montreal turned highly acrimonious, with language a factor (though unspoken). The strongest opposition came from wealthier, often Anglo, suburban (now-merged) municipalities. In the event, twelve municipalities voted to stay in, but fifteen opted out of the mega-city, generally wealthier, but small, largely Anglo municipalities.

The heavy-handed behavior (as in Ontario) of the Quebec government aside, the merger/demerger saga is a useful demonstration that fragmentation per se is not the problem. It's the resources being fragmented that matter. The secession of the fifteen recalcitrant municipalities increased fragmentation on paper, with now sixteen municipalities rather than a single city on the Island of Montreal. However, that refragmentation had no significant impact on welfare differences across the island; first, because people services (education, health, etc.) continued, as before, to be centrally financed via the province. Second, the province, again to the displeasure of many locals, imposed a revenue-sharing superstructure on the Island, a new entity called the *Conseil d'Agglomération* (Agglomeration Council). This organization was mandated to administer all Island services, notably public transit and police, in the end leaving the secessionist municipalities with limited responsibilities and resources: park and street maintenance; libraries; snow removal, and the like. They recovered certain urban planning prerogatives, such as building permits and zoning rights, but again within limits set by the province, a typical Canadian compromise in which communities are allowed to preserve features important for their identity (which, for example, meant that most of the fifteen municipalities retained their bilingual status) but without exacerbating social divisions.

Despite these departures, the final municipal map resulted in a much enlarged City of Montreal, almost doubling its population and now accounting for nearly half the metropolitan population, which is of some importance for regional governance. In the wake of the merger–demerger saga, the province created a new regional structure to be chaired by the mayor of Montreal, the Montreal Metropolitan Community (MMC) with loose consultative and planning powers and cover the entire metropolitan area, including the Island of Montreal. To the surprise of many who saw the MMC as no more than a talking shop, its performance has been generally positive, not least as a metropolitan-wide consensus-building forum. The MMC published a regional plan in 2015 approved by all eighty-two participating mayors—no mean achievement.

The absence of an entrenched political city/suburb divide also owes much to a unique feature of Quebec's municipal politics: the separation between national politics and local politics, very different from of the politicized U.S. and French political landscapes in which the same political parties permeate all levels of government. Parties at the municipal level in Quebec are exclusively local, created solely for that purpose, with no formal links to national political parties. Thus, the ruling party during the last city administration (2013–2017) was simply called "Team Coderre," after its leader and mayor, Denis Coderre. The intense partisan rivalry built into local politics in many other nations has no equivalent in Quebec. There is no partisan divide that prevents mayors or councilors from different municipalities from working together.

A Strong Downtown

Provincial policies have also contributed to the maintenance of a strong downtown which, together with its expanded fiscal base following from amalgamation, has allowed the City of Montreal to maintain a strong fiscal footing. Montreal never let its downtown core collapse. Its downtown, with about three hundred thousand jobs, is one of the densest in North America. Like Manhattan, but on a much smaller scale, Montreal's downtown draws much of its strength from its role as central place for a wider cultural community, high-order services naturally drawn to central locations.

In addition to the market forces that favor Montreal's downtown, public policy has pushed in the same direction. The first three subway lines, built during Expo 67, converged on the center. An equally telling example of center-oriented public action was the provincial government's decision in 1968 to locate the campus of the University of Quebec at Montreal (UQAM), the flagship of the new UQ state university system, downtown. The government chose a central neighborhood with the expressly declared objective of building an *urban* university. The neighborhood chosen had become largely derelict and was visibly in need of rejuvenation. The new campus was built with direct access to a subway (metro) station and it is worth noting, with no parking facilities. The campus has since expanded and now has about forty-five thousand students. Other campuses of the UQ system, *École de technologie supérieure* (ÉTS; a polytechnic institute), the Montreal arm of the School of Public Administration (ÉNAP), as well as my own institution (INRS-UCS), would also be located in central neighborhoods, ÉTS in a recycled industrial brewery just south of the CBD. More recently (2017), the province chose to locate the University of Montreal's new research hospital in the center, a stone's throw from UQAM. The reader will certainly not have failed to note the contrast with Buffalo's university saga.

Looking back, we find that the actions taken by the province over the years, though not always with great tact, have on the whole successfully helped avert a social and fiscal rift between center and suburb. Montreal has thus escaped the downward demographic/fiscal spiral that bedeviled so many American central cities. Average family incomes in the City of Montreal do not deviate significantly from suburban incomes, and there is no social stigma attached to living in the city compared to living in the suburbs.

A Flexible Housing Market

Other public policies have contributed to the city's good ranking on livability. Montreal has managed to keep housing prices within limits, despite a now growing economy. Montreal and its surrounding municipalities have historically adopted a fairly liberal approach to housing construction and land development with fewer urban planning restrictions. Montreal does not, for example, impact charges on builders. The costs of most basic infrastructure (sewage, water, street access, etc.) are borne by municipalities, paid through local property taxes. The result is a housing market with somewhat higher property taxes, but where market entry is easier for small builders. The result is a generally flexible housing market in which supply adjusts fairly rapidly to demand, characterized by comparatively high densities and many small and midsized units. The neatly arrayed duplexes and triplexes with their winding exterior staircases have become emblematic features of Montreal's urban landscape, with high proportions of small owners and renters.

This market flexibility has allowed Montreal to maintain a stock of relatively affordable housing. Average prices have systematically remained below those for other Canadian metropolitan areas, historically half those in Toronto and a third those in Vancouver.[29] Houston is generally cited as the arch U.S. example of a city with low housing prices, the outcome of its permissive planning bylaws and correspondingly flexible housing market. Yet, available data show that average rental prices are about 50 percent lower in Montreal than in the Houston area.[30] No less tellingly, the same source finds that average rental costs in Montreal are lower than those in Buffalo (by 9 percent), a smaller metropolitan area which, we know, does not have a particularly dynamic economy.

By delivering a comparatively affordable housing stock, Montreal's housing market indirectly contributes to social cohesion; households on average spend less of their income on housing.[31] Public housing, a shared responsibility of federal, provincial, and local governments, though accounting for only about 5 percent of the regional housing stock (but about 10 percent of the rental stock), has also been instrumental in promoting socially mixed neigborhoods The distinguishing feature of Montreal's social housing programs is the small scale and spatial dispersion of publicly subsided housing, a conscious policy choice going back to the 1960s.[32] Since its inception, publicly funded projects have been deliberately dispersed across the city, including in middle and upper class neighborhood; units are rarely more than several stories high, blending into the surrounding neighborhoods. My own upper-middle-class neighborhood contains a number of public housing projects, but they can be identified only by small plaques stating that the particular apartment was built with public funds. The buildings are of generally good quality, built with the same material as surrounding constructions. There is no apparent social stigma attached to living in these subsidized apartment buildings.

One last piece is missing in our understanding of the province's success in building a generally nonconflictual society. Canadians, we already saw in the Toronto story, are more willing than Americans to accept higher taxes and constraints on freedom in exchange for greater social harmony and equality. Within Canada, Quebecers exhibit an even stronger preference for equality, as seen in a number of policies and programs: more progressive income tax schedules than elsewhere in Canada; subsidized daycare facilities; public prescription medicine insurance; and lower college and university tuition fees. It is often said that "it's better to be rich in the US and poor in Canada . . . especially in Quebec." Humor aside, the figures do not lie: income distributions across households have systematically remained less unequal in Quebec than elsewhere in Canada.[33]

This is not to say that all is sweetness and light in Montreal. Intermunicipal rivalry continues and always will exist. The organization of transit services remains fragmented. Nor is there complete harmony between Montreal's diverse populations. Linguistic tensions do flare up from time to time and will undoubtedly never entirely disappear. Racism is a reality in Montreal as elsewhere. Homelessness, too, is a problem, most visibly among destitute Native (First Nation) populations. Montreal has neighborhoods with high proportions of minority populations but so far at least has produced nothing like the concentrated poverty of the Paris *banlieue* or the inner-city ghettos of America. It is precisely this diversity, which under other circumstances might have produced a deeply divided and conflictual city, that makes Montreal's story so remarkable.

* * *

The generally livable, socially cohesive, and prosperous city that Montreal is today, and will hopefully remain, is the outcome of a more than fifty-year journey during which the state (the province of Quebec here) was a key actor, intervening at multiple levels. Montreal teaches us that building a socially cohesive environment in an initially divided and unequal city requires not only measures that ensure a minimum level of spatial equality, but also measures that explicitly seek to redress the social imbalance between populations and also, where needed, to diffuse cultural fears that often emerge when different peoples live side by side. This is a tall order indeed. However, the Montreal story tells us that it can be done.

7

Shaping the Playing Field

Costs, Connectivity, and the Battle for Markets, Brains, and the Top Spot

Nations are economic unions in which goods, labor, and capital can move freely from place to place.[1] Within nations, cities compete not only for the resources that allow cities to create wealth, not least human capital, but also for transportation infrastructure that allows them to capture markets. The conditions that define the national playing field will not be the same everywhere. First and most basically, geographies differ across nations. Second, the institutions that define the conditions under which cities compete and how the outcomes are managed differ across nations.

Thus far, we have focused mainly on how different societies manage differences within cities, with some societies more willing to tolerate intracity social divisions than others. Some societies are also more willing than others to tolerate social differences between cities. The two are not unrelated. As with intracity divisions, the financing of people services, the organization of housing markets, and the presence (or lack) of income and/or revenue-sharing mechanisms lie at the heart of national differences.

The Fiscal Playing Field

Local taxes are rarely a major element in inter-urban competition; that is, where people services (education and health primarily) are centrally financed through taxes paid to national governments, as is the case in most European unitary states. In most, taxes collected and retained by local authorities are a minor element in the total sum of taxes paid to all levels of government. National government revenues and expenditures are implicitly redistributed across the nation, often including transfers to local levels of government on a per capita basis or other criteria, ensuring a reasonably equal delivery of major public services. In France teachers, wherever they may be working, are paid directly by the national government in Paris.

Most federal states in the developed world, including Australia, Germany, and Switzerland, have some form of equalization payments whereby tax revenues are redistributed between richer and poorer member states (states, Länder, cantons) to reduce fiscal disparities. By the same token, this reduces the need for member states to vary tax rates to ensure comparable levels of public service provision.[2] Canada has three main transfer programs (from the federal government to the provinces): the Canada Health Transfer, the Canada Social Transfer, and so-called Equalization Payments. The last-named are unconditional grants, again lessening the need for major tax differences between provinces (although tax competition exists). Within provinces, as we learned in the Toronto and Montreal stories, local authorities below the province level have limited taxing powers, generally restricted to property taxes, the counterpart of their limited powers and responsibilities. In addition, all provincial governments set limits on the ability of local authorities to vary local tax rates (i.e., property mill rates[3]), thereby reducing the risk of intermunicipal tax competition between neighboring jurisdictions. This is in addition to the propensity of Canadian provincial governments, as we have seen, to force municipalities to share revenues, even to the point of amalgamation.

The United States stands out not only in the absence of any institutionalized federal equalization scheme across states but also in the range and weight of taxes state and local authorities can collect. New York City is an extreme case at the municipal level of having its own income tax in addition to state and federal income taxes. Differences across states can and do have a major impact on the competiveness of cities. Buffalo, our prime exhibit, is trapped in a high-tax state together with its sister upstate New York cities.[4] Most American states do set limits on the range within which mill rates can vary for different types of property (residential, commercial, etc.), reducing tax competition. But American states are on the whole more willing to tolerate inter municipal tax competition, including that within metropolitan areas, Buffalo again our prime exhibit. We have so far focused on the negative consequences of intrametropolitan tax competition. From a strict cost perspective, however, such competition may be seen as a good thing, driving down taxes.

An influential school of thought generally referred to as the public choice theory harks back to the 1956 article, "A Pure Theory of Public

Expenditures," by the American economist Charles Tiebout.[5] The theory posits that intermunicipal tax competition is beneficial not only because it forces municipalities to keep their taxes low but also because it allows residents to choose between different municipalities and the service packages they offer. Populations vote, so to speak, with their feet. This school of thought, though still influential, especially in more conservative circles, is less persuasive today. I shall let the reader decide whether the posited cost benefits of intrametropolitan tax competition, which can be real, outweigh the potential negative social consequences, no less real. It very much depends on which services are financed via local taxes; the potential for negative effects is greatest where local taxes are used to finance people services.

Tiebout's reasoning can be transposed to the intercity level with similar trade-offs. Differences in taxes and public service packages are undoubtedly a factor, though they are difficult to measure, in the continued sorting of populations across American cities. The results, at least for the United States, suggest that the impact of higher taxes on the movement of people and firms can go both ways; this is part of what I call the cost paradox. Taxes voted by, hopefully, democratically elected legislatures or city councils can be reasonably assumed to reflect the values and preferences of the electorate. Minneapolis-St. Paul is a comparatively high-tax jurisdiction[6] mirroring Minnesota's above-average combined local and state tax rates. Boston and San Francisco are also located in high-tax states[7] that, like Minnesota, have historically invested heavily in education, New Orleans, at the other end of the spectrum, is located in a low-tax state with correspondingly low investments in education.

Thus, low taxes are good where they reflect more efficient and responsive government, but they are not good where they reflect below-optimal expenditures on public services, notably people services. Higher taxes (i.e., where used to proper ends) are not incompatible with urban success, which brings me to the cost paradox.

The Cost Paradox: The Two Faces of Higher Housing and Wage Costs

In most nations, the major cost difference between cities lies in land and housing prices; the two are closely linked, part of the same cost package.

Where housing costs are high, workers will expect higher wages. Low housing and wage costs are an obvious asset but somewhat of a schizoid beast for city economies. High costs, whether expressed in high wages, high real estate values, or high taxes, can be both a sign of success and a source of failure. New York is certainly not a low-cost location, but it can bear these costs and flourish because it is New York: high costs are the natural counterpart of its location rent and everything we have learned about agglomeration economies, the reason firms, and individuals are ready to pay a minor fortune to locate there. On the flip side, high housing and wage costs will hurt cities that have no compensating agglomeration advantage. Yet again, Buffalo is our prime exhibit.

Smaller places will not generate the location rent and agglomeration economies of a large city. Smaller cities must compete on other attributes, among which are costs. Trois Rivières's resurgence, we saw, required that relative wages fall and that worker expectations adjust accordingly. Every mayor, of course, wants his or her city to generate the highest possible wages and highest land rents and the potential taxes they bring. At the same time, every mayor also wants his or her city to remain competitive.

Housing: It's All about Supply

Housing markets are truly *local* and thus one of the rare policy areas over which local authorities have some control, although again almost always within the legislative framework as set by senior governments. Montreal's generally affordable housing, as we saw, was the direct outcome of a fairly liberal approach to residential construction, facilitating market entry for smaller home builders. Toronto, by contrast, has a much more regulated housing market (the flip side of its "well"-planned development), which goes a long way in explaining its higher housing prices. First, provincial policy imposes fairly steep development charges, amounting to nearly $50,000 (Canadian dollars) per housing unit.[8] Second, builders are subject to more stringent urban planning regulations. Compared to Montreal, in Toronto average approval times for building permits were longer, the percentage of building projects requiring zoning changes was higher, and the probability of community opposition was greater In other words, entry into the housing market as a builder in Toronto required not only deep pockets, but also patience, negotiating skills, and legal expertise that was generally beyond the means of smaller entrepreneurs.

The result is a market dominated by large property developers with pockets deep enough to bear such costs. It is no accident that Toronto has given birth to the largest property development companies in the world, Olympia and York being a prime example. During its glory period of the 1980s, Olympia and York built and managed the World Trade Center in New York and Canary Wharf in London. The prevalence of large property developers also explains the popularity of high-rise apartment towers in Toronto, which are more expensive to build and have longer delivery periods. The result is a less elastic housing supply and supply consistently trailing demand. While this is not the only explanation (more rapidly rising demand in Toronto also matters), it helps demonstrate why housing prices have remained higher in Toronto than in Montreal.

A corollary of the above, though not always well understood, is that policies that stimulate *demand* (i.e., making housing easier to purchase or to rent) can be counterproductive; *supply* must also follow. Policies that seek to facilitate access to home ownership or rental housing via mortgage or rent relief (whether tax deductions, lower interest rates, or direct subsidies) are obviously popular with electorates everywhere. Such policies, however well intentioned, increase *demand*. Simple economics tells us that increasing demand without an equivalent increase in supply equals higher prices. The reader will have understood the key role here of central banks and regulatory frameworks governing mortgage lending institutions. In the absence of responsive housing markets, constrained by urban planning regulations or other restrictions, policies aimed at helping potential buyers or renters will invariably further fuel housing prices.

Rent control, a traditional demand of community groups, is often suggested as a means of keeping prices under control. Most big cities have at some time or other applied some form of rent control. Here again, basic economics helps us to understand why rent control is rarely a viable solution. "Next to direct aerial bombing, the best way to destroy a city is universal rent control" is a favorite old saw among urban economists. Again, the problem is supply. Why would a private developer or investor build rental housing without the assurance that the price (rent) he or she can charge will ensure a reasonable return? Rent control, that is, freezing rents at some preestablished level, is no different from freezing the price of bread and then asking bakers to continue to bake bread despite rising labor and ingredient costs. At one point, once the controlled price falls below production costs, baking bread will simply become unprofitable. By the same token, why would a landlord invest in repairs and normal maintenance if he or she could not recoup the costs through higher rents?

Most people now understand this principle, and so "hard" rent control has gone out of fashion. Montreal has a fairly soft form of rent control in which rents are allowed to vary, subject to the oversight of a provincial housing board.[9] Even that soft approach, however, caused many builders to switch to condominiums. In any case, hard rent control is difficult to enforce. Where prices are set too low to satisfy demand, the predictable outcome is a black market that replicates real market prices. In Vienna, the apartment I stayed at during my early visits was rent-controlled, a legacy of Red Vienna. My hosts paid a pittance in official rent, but they paid informal annual maintenance fees to the owner in addition to *Schlüsselgeld* (Key Money), the price of the keys to the apartment. Any new tenant needed to pay a so-called key deposit, matching the going market value of the unit, since official rent had become meaningless. Vienna, like many other cities, has since moved away from rent control. In the end, politics was undone by the laws of supply and demand.

A more currently fashionable approach among proponents of affordable housing is to require developers to include a given percentage of low-rent units in a new building project. This practice is commonly called "inclusionary zoning" or "fair share." The authorization to implement such practices generally requires prior senior government approval (i.e., states or provinces in North America). Inclusionary zoning is popular, first, because it does not require direct governments outlays and, second, because it is an expedient political tool allowing mayors (or others) to pose in front of completed projects and announce that x number of affordable units have been put on the market thanks to the judicious actions of their administration. Whatever its merits, inclusionary zoning is in the end a form of regulatory constraint, the costs carried by the developer who will necessarily pass them on to the tenants or buyers of units that are not part of the inclusionary share.[10] The net impact on the market can sometimes be an increase in noninclusionary housing prices. Montreal, consistent with the city's generally liberal approach to housing, has no statutory inclusionary zoning. However, the current municipal administration has announced its intention to introduce a form of inclusionary zoning.

The (Impossible?) Trade-Off between Affordable Housing and Smart Growth

The preceding discussion on the negative effects of restrictions on housing supply prompts the question of why Toronto, or any other city for that matter, should choose to implement policies that manifestly diminish its cost competitiveness and possibly stunt its growth. The answer takes us back to electorates and social preferences, at least in democratic societies.

A quasi-philosophical debate on the benefits and dangers of development (urban agglomeration, in other words) for the environment is beyond the scope of this book.[11] Scientific arguments aside, humans have a natural tendency to see nature—green fields, woodlands, unspoiled forests—as purer and somehow morally superior to built-up, paved, dirty, noisy cities and towns. Every green field lost to urbanization is a loss to be bemoaned. One need not be a poet or a romantic to harbor such sentiments. I'm probably no different from the majority of humanity—at least in the developed world—in wishing to live in a city where nature is not too far away, with ample parks and green spaces. Almost all cities have protected natural areas, farmland, or parkland where building is prohibited. London, one of the earliest examples well before environmentalism became fashionable, established the statutory Metropolitan Green Belt in the 1930s. Following the London example, greater Toronto now has a green belt, voted on by the Ontario legislature in 2005. The two green belts have most probably contributed to higher housing prices, although precise impacts are difficult to measure.[12] The moral of the story remains the same: no city can escape the trade-off between environmental and/or urban planning objectives and affordable housing.

In Chapter 3, we examined the social consequences of NIMBYs, a powerful driver behind residential segregation and social and racial exclusion, notably in the United States. Richard Florida argues that NIMBYs are also the chief culprit behind restrictions on housing supply in American cities, preventing them from densifying and growing as they should.[13] On this, Florida is undoubtedly right. But why, then, are NIMBYs, decried everywhere by urbanists and urban planners, so prevalent? Let us thus take a kinder view of NIMBYs or what is sometimes called Smart Growth, NIMBY's good sister. The desire to control the built environment is entirely natural. That is why urban planning and zoning regulations exist. No one wants to live next to a warehouse, with trucks moving in and out every hour of the day, or live in the shadows of a high-rise apartment tower blocking out the afternoon sun. There are also sound economic arguments for spatial planning, including, among other arguments, to lower unit infrastructure and service costs, notably for public transit.

We are back to the trade-off between unconstrained development, including free housing markets, and urban quality of life, where the latter may translate into higher housing prices. The trade-off is difficult to rigorously quantify; it is a subject that provokes continuing heated debate, often with strong ideological overtones. The proponents of freer housing markets will regularly accuse the other side of selfish NIMBYism and obstructionism, who in turn will accuse the former (i.e., the greedy developers) of ignoring the environment and neighborhood needs, with an eye only on profits. As viewed from their standpoint, neither is totally wrong. Residents of pleasant neighborhoods will naturally seek to protect the value of their homes and the quality of their environment. The objective of developers, naturally, is to identify profitable investments; that's how markets provide housing.

I do not wish to leave the reader with the impression that advocates of smart growth are driven chiefly by veiled selfish motives. It is difficult, however, to divorce financial gains from environmental objectives. Zoning a green belt (a park, a nature reserve, and so on) around a high-demand, built-up area will drive up property values. This is a financial windfall for those already in place and is the very definition of a *rent*. The larger community may recuperate a share if property taxes are correctly adjudicated and the revenues are appropriately used to the benefit of all. But that is another matter, taking us back to questions of metropolitan governance which we addressed in earlier chapters.

Let us return to Los Angeles. The majority of the land area of the City of Los Angeles is zoned for single-family homes and that is what most residents want. It has historically been very difficult to get approval for high-rise or denser housing projects. *The Economist* cities the case of a proposed housing project near Long Beach in which the developer was eventually forced to scale down the original proposal by more than a half after neighbors protested that it would bring extra traffic. The same article also cities the case of a judge who struck down what he called a "fatally flawed" plan to build taller, denser buildings in some parts of Hollywood, after community groups sued under California's Environmental Quality Act (CEQA), complaining that the plan would "Manhattanize" Hollywood.[14]

Little wonder that housing prices in Los Angeles are also among the highest in the United States, despite the lack of geographic constraints.

The battle between pro- and antidevelopment advocates will undoubtedly never end, mirroring opposing objectives. Most recently, the battle came to a head in Los Angeles where in a citywide referendum in 2017 voters soundly rejected (by 68 percent) a proposed measure, appropriately called the Neighborhood Integrity Imitative. It would have frozen development in the city for two years on projects requiring discretionary approval by city agencies. The defeat of the initiative, strongly opposed by the city administration, business, and labor organizations, suggests that opinions can shift. Angelenos, the initiative's defeat suggests, are becoming increasingly aware—undoubtedly fueled by long commutes and recurring gridlock and traffic jams—of the need for denser development if the region is one day to develop a viable transit system.

This brings home the trade-off not only between affordable housing and controls on growth, but also between local (neighborhood) and metropolitan perspectives. Viewed at the metropolitan level, enforcing denser forms of development may indeed be desirable; but denser, higher, residential construction may run into neighborhood NIMBY resistance, in essence putting two visions of what is "smart" in opposition. Here, municipal boundaries are of some importance and, by the same token, the spatial scale at which local (NIMBY-type) popular initiatives are allowed, if at all, generally determined by state legislation. As we learned in Chapter 3, many jurisdictions have limited, if not formally abolished, the right of local populations to launch binding referendums or consultations.

Would You Rather Live in (Affordable) Houston or (Smart) San Francisco?

The United Sates with its diversity of regulatory environments provides a unique laboratory for gauging the trade-offs between freer and less freer housing markets. San Francisco and Houston, taking two often cited examples, are at the antipodes of the urban planning spectrum but are fairly comparable on other criteria, both economically successful and growing metropolitan areas. On the one hand, Houston is often touted as the arch example of an unregulated metropolis with no formal zoning bylaws and no urban spatial plan; developers can basically build where they want and what they want, with no or few design or height restrictions.[15] San Francisco, on the other hand, has the deserved reputation of being one of the best planned cities in the United States, with stringent zoning and building codes. Not least, San Francisco has an activist political tradition where community scrutiny of new projects is the rule, more often than not leading to proposed projects being refused or substantially amended. The state of California has a well-established tradition of pro-environmental legislation, which gives locals the power to challenge proposed changes in zoning, building limits, or other regulatory statutes. California's Environmental Quality Act (CEQA), which we encountered earlier, signed by Governor Ronald Reagan in 1970, has acted as a powerful facilitator of community activism, allowing slow-growth proponents to contest vertical expansion (taller buildings) on numerous occasions.[16]

The two metropolitan areas are of comparable size, but Houston has been growing somewhat faster. San Francisco is wealthier than Houston and has historically higher per capita incomes. We would thus expect San Francisco to have higher housing prices than Houston. Geography also matters. The city of San Francisco proper lies on a peninsula, constraining the land area that is available for construction. The rest of the metropolitan area, though mountainous, is less burdened by geographic constraints. Even so, the difference in housing prices between the two cities goes well beyond what geography, income, or population growth differences would predict. Housing prices in San Francisco in comparable neighborhoods were on average at least two times those of Houston. Average monthly rent in the spring of 2017 for a one-bedroom apartment cost $3470 in San Francisco (the city proper) compared to $1540 in Houston's costliest area (Memorial); the figures for a two-bedroom unit were, respectively, $ 4560 and $2160.[17] We can reasonably conclude that a significant part of the difference is attributable to the difference in regulatory environments. Housing is cheaper in Houston because builders are essentially free to build anywhere.

Is the difference worth it? Is San Francisco doing the right thing in planning its environment so strictly? The answer is necessarily subjective, at least in part. Some lucky few may be entirely happy to pay three times more to live in San Francisco because they want what it offers. The higher wages in San Francisco also means that proportionally more of its residents are able to bear the higher costs. This brings us back to the circular relationship between wages and housing and, of course, agglomeration economies, which we have met so often in this book, and the *rents* they generate. This raises a more fundamental question: Has San Francisco's highly regulated environment contributed to the creation of agglomeration economies and corresponding location rents or, on the contrary, are San Francisco's high real estate prices the outcome of a distorted market that artificially drives up prices? I'm not sure an answer is possible, not least because causal relationships go in both directions, which is why the urban planning/free market debate continues to be a subject of political discord.

The two regulatory regimes, as we would expect, have created two very different cities. Houston is more spread out, with lower densities and a more autodependent culture. Which of the two better meets the expectations of its residents? It's not an easy question to answer. The information published on a regular basis by Apartment List[18] includes the results for renter satisfaction surveys, which, though perhaps not rigorously scientific, provide a good idea of how locals view each city. The results are close to what one would expect. Both metropolitan areas are positively ranked on jobs and career opportunities (graded A and A+), mirroring their positive economic performance. But the two are almost polar opposites on other criteria. San Francisco is positively perceived on public transit and amenities and recreational facilities (an A on both), but negatively on housing affordability (F) and state and local taxes (C), while Houston comes out well on housing affordability (B+) and state and local taxes (A–). Finally, San Francisco (A–) does better on overall satisfaction than Houston (B). In short, in each city the trade-off meant that residents had to sacrifice one thing in order to get another. Residents of San Francisco had to accept higher taxes and housing costs in return for better public transit and urban amenities, while Houstonians had to accept poor public transit and fewer urban amenities in return for lower taxes and housing prices. The last grade—overall satisfaction—suggests that Houstonians are globally less happy with the trade-off than San Franciscans.

The lesson from the Houston–San Francisco comparison is simple: Where there are no geographic and regulatory constraints on building, upwards or outwards, housing prices *can* be prevented from exploding, even under conditions of rapid growth. The comparison also tells us that a less regulated environment carries a price in the form of a less "well-planned" and arguably less desirable urban environment. It is no accident that San Francisco systematically comes out first among American cities on quality-of-life rankings. Those who have had the good fortune of visiting San Francisco know what a fabulous place it is. Those who have the even greater good fortune of living there know this even better. It is an urban jewel to be cherished and to be protected, but at a price.

The Luck of Small Cities: The Other Face of the Cost Paradox

Whether high land, housing, and wage costs in large growing cities are driven by market forces (location rent created by agglomeration economies) or by administrative restrictions on supply (location rents produced by public policy) or by a combination of the two, the outcome translates into a competitive advantage for smaller cities. Costlier big cities make smaller cities more competitive, and if big cities are silly enough to impose regulations that make them even more costly, all the better. One man's loss is another man's gain.

The obvious message here is that small cities need to work at preserving their cost advantage. Much of the cost advantage is automatic (back to market forces) but not all. Small and midsized cities are, as a rule, not overburdened by urban planning restrictions. Popular pressures in favor of slow or antigrowth policies are less common in smaller places. With the notable exception of natural amenity-rich locations (mountains, beach, or lakefronts) coveted by retirees or owners of vacation homes, land is rarely an issue. Assuring affordable housing will seldom be an issue. Where smaller cities are reasonably well governed with suitable infrastructure (industrial parks, roads, etc.) and not too far from markets, they should naturally attract or spawn firms for which space and wages are major cost factors. The important datum here is the *relative* cost of labor and land; the higher the costs in big cities, the greater the impetus to produce space and labor-intensive goods elsewhere. At the risk of repetition, cities of different sizes exist for a reason.

Let me restate this idea in more technical language. As long as the drivers of agglomeration economies continue to generate high location rents in some places (read: big cities) *within nations,* production less in need of agglomeration economies—what I have called midtech goods and services—will continue to move down the urban hierarchy. This goes a long way in explaining the "mysterious" symmetry of national urban systems, to rephrase the quote from Krugman cited in the Introduction.[19] If a nation meets the necessary institutional prerequisites for the creation of wealth (back to Pillar1), individual cities don't really matter. Depending on the nation's industrial structure, firms in different industries will sort out across space, producing big and small cities in accordance with their needs, some moving up and others down the national urban hierarchy as technologies change. This view of cities (almost anti-city some might say) may seem extreme, but it is nonetheless the corollary of a city systems perspective consistent with Zipf's Rank-Size Rule or Gibrat's law, which implicitly postulate a Pareto optimum for firms and workers across alternative locations within nations.[20]

Let us leave the realm of abstract reasoning and return to the real world. The expulsion effects generated by high costs in large cities will not automatically ensure the growth of small cities. Small cities will be competing with other cities of similar size with comparable lower costs. Where big-city agglomeration economies are lacking, lower land and wage costs need to be matched by other advantages. Let us thus return once again to Drummondville. The town had the initial good fortune of a low-wage industrial legacy, textiles and clothing, thus avoiding the pitfalls of the Intrusive Rentier Syndrome. Wages, on average, have remained some 20 percent below those in Montreal, the closest big city. Senior government has also lent a helping hand. Quebec's decision, going back to the 1960s, to focus on hydroelectric rather than nuclear or fossil-based power generation has meant lower electricity bills than in neighboring Ontario and New York State. This is of some importance for much mid-tech manufacturing. No less important, we saw, was Quebec's network of community colleges, ensuring a reasonably well-educated, numerically literate labor force. Both of these attributes also benefited other small cities in the province.

Let us thus dig deeper. Drummondville's reputation as a city with a consensual political culture, generally good labor–management relations, and a business-friendly environment is not an accident. Behind every successful man (if I may be forgiven the analogy) is a women, in this case Francine Ruest-Juncas, the mayor of Drummondville (1987–2012) during the crucial years when the city changed from a one-industry town to a diversified midtech manufacturing center. During her administration, the city acquired a reputation as a generally scandal-free, efficiently-run municipality with among the lowest property taxes in the province,[21]. Drummonville was also among the first in the province to create a local development corporation expressly focused on promoting a local start-ups and business-friendly climate,[22] well before such things became fashionable.

Drummondville may be small, but looking back at our template (Table I.1), we can now say that it combines most of the essential attributes of a successful city: located in a reasonably well-run nation and province; socially cohesive; generally well administered; not far from major markets; competitive costs (taxes, land, and labor); and finally, a labor force with the requisite education and skills for the types of industries most likely to locate there. Drummondville also demonstrates that leadership can make a difference; that is, provided most of the other pillars are solid.

The Battle for Connectivity and Hinterlands

Let us now move up the urban ladder and focus on the battle for commercial hinterlands. The battle between cities for market share, whether for information-rich services or for more traditional services (wholesaling, distribution, marketing, etc.) has been at the core of intercity competition since the modern era began. The city that emerged as the busiest transport hub and captured the largest shares would also become a natural locus for the production of goods, a prize well worth fighting for.

Use of the word *battle* is no coincidence. Here, we truly are on a playing field where *capturing* the fruits of wealth is the name of the game rather than generating wealth as such, although the two are never totally independent— a typical chicken-and-egg problem. Did New York *capture* human capital from across America and around the world because of its connectivity, or was its initial rich human capital (entrepreneurial) endowment the mother of its connectivity and reach? Be that as it may, the battle for reach is in part a true zero-sum game. An increase in New York's market share—say for newspaper readership—will necessarily mean that Philadelphia's share will shrink. New York's greater reach will mean that *The New York Times* and New York-based media are able to command higher advertising rates per page or hour than competing Philadelphia media and correspondingly create more jobs.

Urban America and the Battle for Market Share

America again provides a unique natural laboratory for studying the battle for hinterlands. As the young nation was still being settled, it was by no means certain which cities would eventually come out on top. The early history of urban America is very much a story of continuing battles for market share. City fathers and mothers intuitively understood that the greater the city's market area, the greater its chance of attracting capital and industry. Centrality was not an abstract notion, although the city leaders were undoubtedly unfamiliar with the concept. In this vast linguistically homogeneous land that was America, now stretching from the Atlantic to the Pacific, the name of the game was transportation, capturing the greatest share of trade and commerce. Before the advent of railways and even for some time after, waterways were the privileged means of travel and merchandise transport. All of America's first great inland cities grew up along waterways: Cincinnati, Cleveland, Chicago, and of course Buffalo. The city that could command the largest transport hinterland would grow the fastest.

The first battles centered on the construction of canals and improvements to existing waterways (dredging, levies, etc.). The Erie Canal, which we first met in the Buffalo story, inaugurated in 1825, gave New York direct water transport access to inland markets, thus beating out Baltimore and Philadelphia. New York became the chief point of entry for goods coming from Europe to be transshipped to inland markets, laying the groundwork for the emergence of the Big Apple as a global city. The point here is not that New York won the battle for direct access to the West, but that the construction of the Erie was the outcome of a state initiative. Though hotly debated at the time,[23] the construction of the canal was underwritten by an appropriation of some $7 million (a fortune at the time) voted on by the New York State legislature. The sum was later entirely recovered through tolls.

Chicago and the Inland Empire

New York won the East Coast game; but who would win the great Inland Empire? With the arrival of railways in the mid-19th century, rail became the name of the game. The battle for the dominance of America's vast inland empire between the Appalachian and Rocky Mountains—now being rapidly settled—was now joined, interrupted only by the Civil War (1861–1865), to resume again after the war at an even faster pace. The city that would come to dominate this inland empire would emerge as America's great new metropolis, perhaps even overtaking New York. The primary contenders were

St. Louis and Chicago. St. Louis was initially favored by its midcontinent situation and strategic location on the Mississippi River, whose system of waterways commanded shipping from Minneapolis to New Orleans. Yet, Chicago eventually emerged as mid-America's metropolis, a useful antidote to geographic determinism.[24]

The story begins again with canals. The Illinois and Michigan Canal, a federal project, was opened in 1848. The canal established a direct water link between Chicago and the Mississippi and thus between the two great waterway systems—the Mississippi and the Great Lakes—with Chicago as the principal transshipment node. The Chicago business community aggressively pursued a policy of railway construction, based in large part on locally subscribed and controlled railway companies. By 1880, some 15,000 miles of railway lines had been laid reaching into northwest and upper Mississippi regions radiating from Chicago in a vast regional hub and spoke network.[25] The St. Louis business community was less aggressive, less attuned it seems to the need for investments in railways, the emerging transport mode. Perhaps the Gateway City's central location on the mighty Mississippi made its business community complacent, its nickname tellingly betraying St. Louis's self-perception, its elites comfortably ensconced in their belief, like Buffalo's some decades later, in the God-given nature of its "natural" advantage. Whatever the reason for St. Louis's inaction, the vast railway network that emerged around Chicago entrenched its position as the Inland Empire's capital.

Chicago illustrates the importance of centrality for sustained growth, even in the face of economic downturns. Chicago has largely escaped the Rustbelt curse, an exception among large midwestern cities.[26] Unlike Cleveland, Cincinnati, Detroit, Pittsburgh, Milwaukee, and Buffalo, the Chicago metropolitan area never registered a period of negative population growth, although growth slowed down in the 1970s and 1980s, only to pick up again in recent times. Chicago, like other great midwestern metropolises, had a strong manufacturing sector and was very much a city built on brawn. The Chicago urban region, like its sisters, suffered heavy job losses in manufacturing. Nor has Chicago been spared the racial tensions that continue to plague all too many Rustbelt cities and remain Chicago's Achilles heel, as witnessed by its continued above-average crime rates.

Nonetheless, Chicago has not succumbed to its sisters' infernal cycle of decline and is a generally prosperous (though racially divided) metropolis in an otherwise declining region. Its position as the Midwest's preeminent central place meant that Chicago also developed a diversified service base with a strong financial sector and a wide array of firms in marketing, retailing, and wholesaling. In a word, Chicago's connectivity and reach allowed it to fall back on a diverse constellation of growing service industries that compensated in large part for manufacturing losses and other brawn-based industries.

Centrality must be defended, however. When air started to replace rail as the dominant transport technology in the late 1950s, Chicago business and political leaders made the right decision in focusing on a *single* modern airport, eventually transferring all scheduled operations from the old municipal airport (Midway) to what was to become O'Hare International Airport, one the busiest air hubs in the world.[27] O'Hare's design was revolutionary—a system of central walkways linking semiautonomous terminals that facilitate stopovers—. The 1950s regional master plan also provided for direct highway access and included provisions for construction of a mass transit link to the Loop, the heart of Chicago's CBD. In a word, Chicago planned well, a very different story from Montreal's airport fiasco: its ill-fated Mirabel Airport was, we saw, poorly connected and was simply one airport too many.

Atlanta: Rail Terminus to Global hub

The most remarkable story of a city whose growth in recent times has been almost entirely driven by connectivity, willed and planned by its elites, is Atlanta, home to the world's busiest airport and home base for the world's largest airline, Delta.[28] Atlanta is also home base for two emblematic American global corporations, Coca-Cola and CNN, although CNN now has most of its production studios in New York and Los Angeles. Atlanta's ascent to become the world's busiest air hub is no small achievement for a place that not so long ago was essentially a regional center far removed from the global glitterati of London, Paris, and New York. Few in 1950 would have given Atlanta a second thought. Unlike Chicago, Atlanta had neither size nor a central location. It was not situated on a waterway or port. Atlanta had no natural resource base or natural advantage to speak of, and it was located in what was at the time—the mid-20th- century—America's most impoverished region. It had no particular human capital advantage, certainly not compared to the great centers of learning of Boston, New York, and Chicago.[29]

Atlanta's principal claim to fame was its position as a regional rail terminus, and so it might have remained: a regional center but little more. Here, the city's industrial legacy steps in. Drew Whitelegg, a geographer at Emory University, suggests[30] that from the very beginning Atlanta's economic raison d'être was transportation, human-made and not given by nature. This, early-on may have shaped the outlook of Atlanta's business and political elites, making them aware of the strategic role of transportation and the need to adapt to technological change. Atlanta's rise as an aviation center following World War I—aviation was a new and risky technology at the time—owes much to the triangular relationship between Delta Airlines, the city, and its business community. It is the combination of all three—a dynamic company, political leaders who believed in the future of aviation, and banks willing to back the new technology—that makes Atlanta's story unique.

First, the story is that of a small crop-dusting air service in the early 1920s operating out of Louisiana (thus the name Delta, for the Mississippi Delta), whose owners chose in 1941 to move its base of operations to Atlanta. History would have been different had they chosen New Orleans. Perhaps the owners saw that Atlanta offered a more entrepreneurial business climate than New Orleans, which despite its undoubted charms had acquired an unfortunately justified reputation for corruption and mismanagement. Delta moved to Atlanta where it has remained ever since to become a leading player in the city's business community.

Second, the story is that of a young city councilman, William B. Hartsfield, first elected in 1922, who would go on to become Atlanta's longest serving mayor (1937–1962, with one interruption). Luckily for Atlanta, Hartsfield was an aviation bug. He convinced the city to build its first airport and over the years would work ceaselessly to modernize the airport in close cooperation with Delta and the local business and political community. Hartsfield became the airport's chief booster, persuading the Federal Aviation Authority in 1929 to designate Atlanta the chief air-transfer point for the American South. The airport would eventually come to bear his name, Hartsfield International Airport, and it was later renamed Hartsfield-Jackson in honor of Atlanta's first black mayor—and that, too, is part of the story.

As Delta grew, emerging as a major national carrier after World War II, the company's and the airport's fortunes came to be increasingly identified with that of the city. Hartsfield-Jackson was Delta's airport; its success was tied to that of the airport and vice versa. Delta was rapidly acquiring a reputation as an innovative airline, pioneering in matters such as off-hours and Family Plan pricing, hub-and-spoke scheduling, credit card services, and employer–management relations. Its boldest move, however, was the switch in the 1950s from propellers to jet engines. Delta was one of the first airlines to bet on the new jet technology, tying its fortunes to a major promise of purchase of new Douglas DC-8 jetliners, a wager openly backed by Mayor Hartsfield and, more to the point, by the local banking community in the form of a revolving credit agreement.[31] The wager paid off. Delta introduced its first direct jet flight to New York in 1959 in direct competition with Eastern Airlines, which had chosen to remain with propellers. Eastern Airlines would eventually fail, finally disappearing from the scene in 1991. Delta purchased the majority of its assets, consolidating Delta's quasi-monopoly position at Hartsfield-Jackson, which now was truly Delta's airport.

To succeed, the jet wager required an airport tailored to the new technology. Construction of a new terminal began in the mid-1950s and was finally completed in 1961; it was among the first in the world constructed explicitly to accommodate jets. All this may seem self-evident with hindsight, but jets were still seen in many quarters as risky, newfangled contraptions. Crashes were not uncommon. Propellers were relatively easy to understand: they were similar to propellers on a boat, but jet propulsion? Looking back, it is difficult not to admire the foresight of Atlanta's city fathers and mothers. The construction of the new jet-age terminal, underwritten by the City of Atlanta and the city's corporate elite, was a bold gesture whose symbolic, mobilizing value was not lost on the mayor. Mayor Hartsfield understood the power of symbols. As Whitelegg states: "he wanted it tall and prominent so that the public would *know* Atlanta had an airport," and not just any airport. 'This is one of the world's seven biggest airports. It's Atlanta's' . . . *yours!*"[32]

This is also the period when the mayor coined the slogan "the city too busy to hate." The message was clear: the business of Atlanta was business, progress, not refighting the battles of the Civil War. The 1950s and 1960s were a tumultuous period not only in the South but in all of America. The battle for desegregation was in full swing, sometimes involving the deployment of federal troops. For his last term (1957–1962), Hartsfield ran against an unyielding segregationist, George Wallace, and won, an indication not only of the city's growing African American population (which would pass the 50 percent mark during the 1960s), but we can only hope also of a more tolerant electorate. Atlanta is no less segregated than other American cities, and, as elsewhere, race is a part of daily urban life. However, Atlanta has gained a reputation for being a racially more open society than most, compared to other places in the American South. Atlanta is home to a thriving black middle class and business community and to the largest historically African American university (Atlanta University Center), and, not least, it is the home of Martin Luther King (1929–1968), emblematic leader of the civil rights movement. Why Atlanta and not other southern cities such as New Orleans, Charleston, or Charlotte? I do not have a proper answer. We are back to social cohesion and glue, whose foundations are as much sociological and political as strictly economic. Perhaps Hartsfield's slogan was not entirely off the mark. Perhaps Atlanta's singleminded focus on economic achievement—and its visible success—truly acted as a partial but nonetheless effective antidote to race-based anxieties.

The story does not end here. Delta continued on its successful path to become a global carrier, with air traffic in and out of Atlanta growing correspondingly. Soon, the new terminal would no longer suffice. Few foresaw the meteoric rise of jet travel. The terminal was initially designed to service six million passengers. Within five years of its opening, the figure was already double that. The choice was clear: either expand Hartsfield-Jackson (although it was not yet called that), adding a new terminal, or build a new airport. In 1973, Maynard Jackson, at the young age of thirty-five, became the first elected African American mayor of a major southern city. Jackson initially favored the construction of a new airport to the south of the city, closer to predominantly black neighborhoods, understandably pushing for greater African American participation in any new or expanded airport. However, any new construction was unthinkable without Delta. Although the City would bear the brunt of the costs, any new construction would also require major investments by the company. Delta, in the process of consolidating its monopoly position at Hartsfield-Jackson, favored expanding the existing airport.

Delta's preferred option finally won: Hartsfield-Jackson would get a new terminal, formally inaugurated in 1980 with Maynard Jackson the presiding mayor. Although the airport and new terminal were technically owned by the City, management was entrusted to a private corporation controlled by Delta,[33] further cementing the symbiotic relationship between the City, Delta, and the airport. The point here is not that Delta got its terminal—the wise decision—but that economic logic trumped politics. The inauguration of the new terminal in 1980, with City support, had more than just ceremonial value. It signaled the importance of aviation as a cornerstone of Atlanta's prosperity, the visible expression of a regional consensus that went beyond race and municipal boundaries. Atlantans were right to be proud. The new terminal was at the time the biggest in the world. More to the point, it was the first jet-age terminal *specifically* designed as a transfer hub to ensure a smooth, seamless flow on connecting flights between arriving and departing passengers. Delta as well as the airport's planners understood that the only way a relatively small local market such as Atlanta's (which was not much bigger than Montreal's) could hope to attain global status was by providing superior service to travelers whose final destination or point of departure was *not* Atlanta, the very definition of a hub. The rest is history. Hartsfield-Jackson International went on to become the world's busiest hub airport. This was a monumental achievement for a metropolitan area that at the time was barely a tenth the size of New York.

Between 1950 and 2015, metro Atlanta's population grew sixfold, from less than one million to almost six million. Its population today is four times that of metro New Orleans, once its rival. Causation is always difficult to prove in the social sciences. Yet, it is impossible not to see a direct link between Atlanta's ascent as a global air hub and its parallel rise as a major corporate and financial center. One may well ask whether Coca-Cola would have maintained its head office in Atlanta had not the city provided it with the connectivity it needed to run a global corporation efficiently. Other major corporations have since made Atlanta their home: NCR (National Cash Register), Home Depot, and more than a dozen others listed in *Fortune 500*. Perhaps the most emblematic move was that of UPS (United Parcel Service), reputed to be the world's largest package delivery service, which in 1991 chose to transfer its corporate head office from Greenwich, Connecticut, to Atlanta.

In the end, what makes Atlanta's story so extraordinary is that its success is almost wholly a local story. This is a rare exception in this book in which I have continually drawn attention to the limits of local action. But then again, local action worked *because it could*. Had the United States, like most nations, decided to initially back a state-owned national carrier (like

Air France and Air Canada[34]), Delta might never have seen the light of day. It is highly unlikely that Washington's political elites at the time would have picked Atlanta as the hub city for the nation's flagship airline.

Chasing Brains

We now come to the main prize in the battle for centrality. During the 19th century and much of the 20th, the battle was chiefly about transportation, a necessary foundation also for manufacturing. With the rise since of the service economy, the focus has shifted to brains. The name of the game now is attracting young skilled individuals, a primary objective, of local economic development agencies around the world. The emblematic book behind this change in perspective among urban activists and scholars was undisputedly Richard Florida's *The Rise of the Creative Class*.[35] Florida's insight was simple: if cities could only attract the "creative class," success was assured.

Florida's book came at the right time and in the right place. Thinking had changed. It was now generally accepted, and not just by economists, that human, not physical, capital was the primary driver of sustained increases in productivity and economic growth, and this was no less true for cities. The work by Edward Glaeser and other urban economists on the role of human capital in urban growth and the writings of Florida and his disciples[36] on the creative class are basically two sides of the same coin. Since human capital (whether we call it the "creative class" or not does not really matter) is the key, then the recipe for success is making cities magnets for the creative class. Here, the battle is less about capturing the fruits of wealth (i.e., markets) than about capturing the creators of wealth (or so it is hoped).

The Hunt for the Creative Class

I do not wish to embark on a discussion of the definition of the "creative class." Although an object of continued academic debate, it is not really central to the issue at hand. The concept is intuitively easy to comprehend: it is a handy label for the young, well-educated, ambitious, and "creative" individuals who drive the modern knowledge economy, a variation ultimately on the concept of human capital. The precise contours of this lucky class may vary, but we again intuitively know that we are not talking about truck drivers, janitors, or waitresses. The prefix "creative" is pleasing to the ear, less mercenary than human capital, which surely helps explain its success. The term has since taken on a life of its own, with cities around the world boasting about their lot of creative districts and creative industries.

The real source of success of the creative class label among urban advocates, however, was Florida's recipe for attracting this privileged class. Young, educated, creatively inclined individuals are attracted, he argued, to particular urban environments, a point on which he was not totally wrong, recalling our earlier discussion on central neighborhoods. In a nutshell, young, educated, creative individuals are disproportionally attracted to central, lively, walkable, cosmopolitan, and socially diverse neighborhoods, which Florida summarizes by way of his Bohemian Index.[37] The reader will undoubtedly have recognized the kinship with the walkable neighborhoods much beloved by Jane Jacobs.

The arts community (actors, musicians, and designers) jumped on the concept and for good reason. A Bohemian lifestyle, creativity, and the arts are closely associated in the popular mind. It is thus not surprising that the creative class paradigm extolling the virtues of this lucky class was enthusiastically embraced by the arts community, proof of its hitherto underappreciated role as prime contributors to urban growth and economic development. A minor cottage industry of writings emerged on culture and the arts as essential drivers of modern urban economies.[38] In a nutshell: a vibrant cultural scene and artistic community—great museums, world-class symphony orchestras, and an active theater life—were essential ingredients for attracting and holding the creative class. It was now clear what cities had to do to attract and to hold human capital.

Don't get me wrong, I'm not against the arts, sidewalk cafés, or bicycle paths. My own Montreal neighborhood would probably rank fairly high on Florida's Bohemian Index. Where I disagree is on the arts as drivers of economic development,[39] the arts and other cultural industries seen as more deserving of public funds than, say, an industrial park or social housing. The implicit message, which some rightly interpret as elitist, is that the tastes of a particular group—the consumers of culture—are now the beacons for measuring a city's success. A particular kind of city becomes the model. By making the urban lifestyle preferences of a particular class the focus of the hunt for human capital, some cities will necessarily be left behind. Not all are equally equipped to play this game. Buffalo has its "creative" enclaves, but it's simply not in the same league with New York or San Francisco.

Thus seen, creative class-based strategies end up sowing the seeds of their own ineffectiveness, to paraphrase a well-worn cliché. Where all are vying for the favors of the same class of individuals, all will end up doing the same thing, which in the end does little to alter the *relative* competitiveness of competing cities. Building bicycle paths, converting abandoned warehouses, or promoting arts festivals is not necessarily a bad thing, but every city is most probably doing the same. Almost every city and town worth its salt, not just those in North America, endeavors to position itself as a center of culture and creativity. And every city has its "creative" community, if only a few coffee houses and art galleries, to show the passing visitor.

Viewed from the perspective of national systems of cities, the competition for human capital inevitably has a flip side. Barring foreign immigration, highly educated populations are finite in number at any given point in time. Someone must lose. We are back to zero-sum games; one city's gain is another's loss. Unlike the focus on nurturing creators of wealth (recall our discussions on education), here the game is capturing them; snatching might be the more appropriate word. On the other hand, the movement of individuals between cities in order to improve their lot is entirely normal and indeed desirable from the point of view of both the individual and the nation; that is, where workers are moving to locations where they will be more productive, thus increasing the national pie. This should not be a cause for concern, and it is not in most nations. In Australia, Canada, and most Western European nations, England being a notable exception,[40] the internal migration of human capital has not produced a seemingly irreparable gulf between successful and unsuccessful cities. Taking Canada as a point of reference, its six metropolitan areas with populations over one million have followed different growth paths, but it is difficult to argue that this has produced deep divides between them in levels of welfare and livability.[41]

Diverging Concentrations of Brainpower: Market or Policy-Driven?

The preceding sections bring us face to face with a central question: what is the weight of public policy and institutions compared to geography and market forces in explaining observed urban differences *within nations* in livability and wealth? As the reader will certainly have surmised, no easy answer exists. Whatever the nation considered, the playing field on which cities compete is not a blank sheet; outcomes are always a mix of market forces and public policy. The evidence suggests[42] that highly educated populations continue to disproportionality migrate to large urban areas with above-average educated populations, not only in the United States but also in other nations. Deep-seated market forces are visibly at play, not least the force of human capital-based agglomeration economies in today's knowledge-driven economies. The best (human capital-rich) jobs are increasingly concentrated in select cities.[43]

It is difficult, however, to conclude, given everything we have learned so far about the impact of institutions, that the differences in economic fortunes across urban America are solely the outcome of market forces. America's playing field is unique in many respects. Its size and highly mobile population have allowed it to create super concentrations of brainpower— Boston and the San Francisco Bay Area being prime exhibits—evidence of the power of modern agglomeration economies. Yet, one could argue that the spatial sorting of American workers is as much a cause as a consequence of inter-urban differences in livability, incentives to move, the product in part of institutional choices rooted in the nation's history. I shall return to America's institutional legacy in the Conclusion, but for the moment let us consider the possible link with *intra*-urban population movements.

We have observed on numerous occasions how public policy has shaped social divides within cities, many central cities becoming mere shadows of their former selves. Should not the relative social cohesion of cities also affect migratory choices? Socially divided cities will, one would reasonably expect, be less attractive to the creative class. Florida recognizes as much in his latest book, *The New Urban Crisis*, diagnosing by the same token the darker side of the creative class, a change in perspective for which he is to be commended.[44] True, he notes, the rise of the creative class was behind the resurgence of many cities and neighborhoods in recent decades, but it also left others behind, producing what Florida calls "winner-take-all urbanism," NIMBYs often not far behind, which goes beyond within-city disparities, also pitting city against city.

To illustrate the possible relationship between the two, we need look no further than Buffalo, our chosen suffering American city. Greater Buffalo continues to be one of America's most socially fractured cities and also, we may reasonably assume, a net exporter of brains. Buffalo's exiled creative class has undoubtedly contributed, we may equally assume, to San Francisco's success, many now ensconced in the city's best neighborhoods and perhaps now among the most ardent defenders of "smart" zoning. The cost to Buffalo is compounded by the absence of compensatory (federal) fiscal mechanisms and local financing of primary and secondary education. The taxpayers of Buffalo in essence are subsidizing the enrichment of San Francisco.

A Brief Excursion to Singapore

It is impossible to write a book on the wealth of cities without mentioning Singapore, however briefly. Its rise to riches is miraculous. The figures speak for themselves. At the time of independence in 1965, Singapore's real income per capita was a mere seventh that of New York; it was a Third World city and about ten times smaller than New York City. Today, Singapore's income per capita is above that of New York, one of the world's wealthiest cities.[45] Singapore is a global powerhouse, systematically ranked among the top global financial centers, in the same league with New York, London, and Tokyo.[46]

Singapore provides a unique laboratory for at least two reasons. First, Singapore is its own parent, to use the anthropomorphic vocabulary of our template (Table I.1), whose wisdom is the only one that counts, with no tension between nation and city—a unique test of how a city might work if it had all powers. Second, those powers were largely held and used by a single individual, Lee Kuan Yew, father of Singapore's independence and its de facto ruler for almost half a century.[47] Lee could instead have used those powers unwisely.

Singapore's success was not a foregone conclusion. Who in 1965 would have predicted a bright future for this impoverished island state without resources, an abandoned outpost of a declining British Empire, stranded in a region plagued by civil strife? Being its own nation, Singapore had no captive hinterland to fall back on. The resources, human or otherwise, for creating wealth had to be nurtured locally, and any markets to be captured would be foreign—a pure example so to speak of wealth creation from within without contributing outside help. Lee set out to create a new Singapore with a singlemindedness that has few equivalents in recent history. It's almost as

if Lee had read this book and taken the Ten Pillars as his guide. He explicitly pursued policies to promote social cohesion, administratively allocating
housing to foster ethnic and social mixing. He also eschewed fiscal municipal decentralization, an institutional choice, and imposed strong punitive
measures to fight corruption. Lee's approach to maintaining a strong center
was no less draconian: he imposed punitive taxes on the purchase of private automobiles, ensuring continued demand for transit even in the face
of rising incomes. If we now add these typically urban policies to national
government polices—liberal trade rules, sound macroeconomic management, a stable currency, and not least massive investment in education (its
students systematically among the top in PISA rankings)—the result is a
powerful mix for fostering economic growth. Visibly, Lee Kuan Yew's recipe
worked.

The feature that sets Lee's recipe apart is the connection (which he obviously saw) between social cohesion and the pursuit of economic success.
He seems to have perfectly grasped the dynamics of central place competition in a region of divergent cultures and business practices. When
Singapore separated from Malaysia to become independent, Lee could
have chosen to take Singapore along the same route as its neighbors, focusing on low-wage manufacturing exports (clothing, electronics, etc.).
Instead, Lee set out explicitly to make Singapore Southeast Asia's high-
order service center and transport hub. Singapore made modernization of its transport infrastructures a state priority. The state-controlled
Port of Singapore Authority acted on various fronts: on the technological front, Singapore became the first port in Southeast Asia to introduce
containerization in the early 1970s; and on the governance front, strict
organizational controls were imposed to ensure cost efficiency and an environment free of merchandise theft and bribable customs officials (an endemic problem in the region). Depending on the year, Singapore today
ranks as East Asia's busiest or second busiest port, the primary logistics
hub for much of the region.

Singapore's approach to air travel was no less aggressive. I shall not go
into a detailed account of the history of Changi International Airport or of
Singapore Airlines, both of which are state-controlled the latter via a mixed
holding company. What matters are results. Singapore today is one of Asia's
principal air hubs, with Changi systematically ranked as one of the world's
best airports. Singapore Airlines is also ranked among the world's best, according to passenger satisfaction surveys.[48] But connectivity—transporting

goods and people—is only half the story, which brings us back to social cohesion.

Following independence, Lee's policy choices on schooling and language were crucial ingredients in establishing its centrality. In a multination region like Southeast Asia, its central place needed a language perceived as both neutral and possessing reach that went beyond its borders. Lee's choice to impose English as the island state's official language and language of schooling may have been his most momentous decision. He could have chosen to keep Malay, the language of Malaysia from which Singapore had seceded, or like Switzerland he might have chosen to make the three most frequently used languages (Mandarin, Malay, and Tamil) the official languages, with three parallel school systems. Fortunately for Singapore, he did not. The choice of English also had the non-negligible advantage of cutting across the city's ethnic groups, favoring none and facilitating the creation of a common national identity. Lee also encouraged the teaching of local languages as second languages. Ethnic Chinese students would not only learn English, but also the language of their ancestors. Thus, a Chinese, Malaysian, or Indonesian[49] businessman could come to Singapore with the assurance that he would be able to deal with persons who understood his language and cultural codes. And, of course, Singapore also spoke the global language with all the trappings of a modern state.

Singapore, its undeniable economic success notwithstanding, raises a number of troubling questions. Lee's Singapore is not a model democracy; the press is kept in check, and labor relations are tightly controlled. Lee's relentless pursuit of social cohesion and glue with the stated goal of enforcing a common national ethos (in which filial respect, propriety, and hard work remain key values) and building a unified national identity has led the Singaporean state into areas of private life incompatible with Western notions of freedom. Lee argued, as he often did, that his directive mode of governance, which he was wont to describe as reflecting "Asian values," was necessary for maintaining a well-ordered society.[50] It is impossible to say whether Singapore could have achieved a similar level of cohesion and prosperity with a less authoritarian leader, no matter how benevolent, sending us back to the trade-off between freedom and (necessary?) coercion in ethnically and culturally divided societies. To this question, I have no readymade answer. Singapore would probably not rank high on Florida's Bohemian Index; it is neither very tolerant nor terribly "cool," yet it systematically comes out on top (or near) on various city rankings for innovation and start-ups.[51] One may well ask whether Lee would have succeeded as he did in the absence of the Confucian-Buddhist heritage of the island's majority group.[52] Finally, from a strict urban economics perspective, one may also well ask what Singapore's success has to do with agglomeration; it just so happens that the nation was also a city, and not a very big one at that.

8

Paris

Greatness Threatened

Paris is a city I know well and love,[1,2] a truly great city. Unlike Buenos Aires's short span of greatness, brutally brought to an end by national mismanagement and folly, Paris's greatness is rooted in centuries of institution building and human genius, difficult to undo. Yet, its greatness is under threat. I have chosen Paris as my last city story because few cities better illustrate the power of national destinies and national governments to shape cities. Also, I can think of no better example of the often schizophrenic relationship between the nation and its largest city: Paris, the nation's prized urban jewel to be proudly displayed; Paris, the urban monster to be contained, at odds with the values of *La France profonde* (true France).[3] In this respect, France is no different from other urbanized nations where political divides have come to mirror spatial divides, whether between city and suburb or between metropolis and small town.

The French state has over the years showered its capital with grand monuments and impressive infrastructure; indeed, no other capital can match its architectural grandeur. Yet, the state has not always been kind to Paris. Greater Paris remains an administrative nightmare, a fragmented metropolis. The French state's regional planning strategy after World War II, what the French call *Aménagement du territoire* (for which there is no English translation), explicitly sought to promote the growth of cities outside Paris, ranging from subsidies to firms to move their activities far from Paris to the mandatory relocation of public institutions. Explicitly anti-Paris policies have been largely abandoned in recent years as a result of globalization, France's membership in the EU, and the growing realization that Paris finds itself in direct competition with other great cities.

Paris's underperformance has several roots: France's legacy of centralized economic governance; the region's deep social divides; the weakening economic potential of central Paris; the decline of French and French culture on the world stage. The first three are directly linked to actions by the

French state; the fourth requires that we go back in time, briefly examining the history of France and of its language as well.

Shrinking Reach

Paris's decline as a great city[4]—true or perceived—has become something of an obsession in French political and intellectual circles, almost to the point of existential angst. Whether on TV talk shows, the Internet, or op-ed pieces, Paris has become a favored subject of soul searching. Every pundit has his or her diagnosis and proffered solution. For readers who speak French, a recent example of the genre is the semifictional novel *Le Grand Paris*,[5] which traces the efforts of a newly elected president of the French Republic intent on restoring Paris to its glory, the centerpiece a futuristic transport system that would once again make Paris a worthy competitor of London and New York. Whatever the truth behind these existential fears, a sober look at Paris today reveals that it punches below its weight.

Paris is the largest city in continental Europe. With a metropolitan population of some twelve million, Paris is twice the size of Madrid and Berlin, the next runners up, and more than three times the size of Amsterdam, Brussels, and Greater Frankfurt.[6] Only London matches it in size, but London is not located on the Continent and is more peripheral despite the Chunnel. The laws of economic geography would predict that Paris would be continental Europe's preeminent central place, its corporate and financial capital, its great center of learning and science. But it is not. Paris is indisputably one of Europe's great cities, unrivaled in its beauty for a city its size. No city in the world attracts more tourists. Yet, Paris today resembles a giant unsure of his weight. Paris is home to several excellent institutions of higher learning, but it does not stand out among the cities of Europe as a center of academic excellence.[7] Paris is home to several large corporations and large banks, almost all exclusively French, but here again Paris does not stand out in Europe. London aside, American and Asian-controlled global corporations generally prefer cities such as Amsterdam and Zurich as locations for their European head office. Nor is it an accident that Frankfurt inherited the European Central Bank, proof if need be of Paris's secondary status as a financial center. Yet, Paris was continental Europe's leading financial center on the eve of World War I.

Paris is a warning that connectivity does not ensure commercial reach. Its underperformance has little to do with loss of connectivity. Paris is extraordinarily well connected; its principal airport (CDG: Charles De Gaulle) is one of the busiest in the world and a major hub. Nor can one attribute Paris's underperformance to a lack of investments in transportation infrastructure. Starting in the 1970s, the French state embarked on one of the most ambitious infrastructure programs in recent history, endowing France with among the first high-speed rail networks in the world, the first TGV,[8] inaugurated in September 1981 linking Lyon, France's second city, with (of course) Paris. Eventually, all of France's major cities were linked to the capital in a hub-and-spoke of high rail lines centered on Paris. Its centrality within France remains unchallenged. Subsequent high-speed rail links have also consolidated its position within Europe with connections to Brussels, Geneva, and other cities, not forgetting the cross-channel Eurostar to London, which opened in 1994.

To understand Paris's shrinking reach, we need to go back to 18th-century Europe when Paris came to be known as the "The City of Light,"[9] an epithet born during the Age of Enlightenment. Paris emerged as the West's great intellectual metropolis, the place where new ideas were born, trendsetter for the fashions of the day, and center for the great writers and thinkers whose works were read across the civilized world. Students from across Europe flocked to Paris to learn its ways, language, and ideas. Why Paris?

The answer, as is so often the case, is demography and political power. We know that New York is New York in part because the United States is a nation of over three hundred million people as well as the most powerful nation on earth. From the Middle-Ages until the 19th century, France was the most populated nation in Europe, more than twice the size of Britain and, more importantly, a unified nation with a strong central government. Germany and Italy were patchworks of small and midsized principalities. France was the dominant power in Europe, a position it maintained for several centuries. It took the combined armies of England, Austria, Russia, and Prussia to finally defeat the armies of Napoleon in June 1815 at the Battle of Waterloo. The French royal court was *the* dominant court in Europe, the model to copy for local princes, dukes, and kings across Europe. When Louis XIV, the so-called *Roi-Soleil* (Sun King), ordered the construction of the Chateau of Versailles on the outskirts of Paris—his sumptuous palace and vast landscaped gardens, which was completed in 1715—the royal courts of Vienna, St. Petersburg, and Berlin duly followed with their own imitations, but none matched the splendor of Versailles.

I have highlighted the role of language as a central element of reach on several occasions (recall the Vienna, Montreal, and Singapore stories). Recall also the battle for market shares, although language was not an issue here, between Philadelphia and New York. The same reasoning can be transposed to the fight for customers (readers) between Paris and London. The British weekly, *The Economist*, employs thousands of workers at its London offices. According to the most recent circulation figures (paper and digital), close to 90 percent of its readership is outside Britain, a service export industry. It is doubtful that any Paris-based publication, even a prestigious newspaper like *Le Monde*, has more than 20 percent of its readership outside France. Its market is essentially local, with correspondingly less potential for adverting revenues and jobs. Extrapolating this example to other language-dependent sectors of the economy—publishing, advertising, management consultancy, the arts, and so on—gives us a measure of the impact on market reach, income, and jobs.

The Rise and Fall of French

The story of the evolution of the French language in the world over the last three centuries provides a particularly telling illustration of the power of language to shape urban destinies. It was only natural that the capital city of Europe's largest and most powerful nation would emerge as a magnet for talent across the continent, trendsetter for everything from architecture and high fashion to the culinary arts. La Sorbonne, its ancient university in the historic heart of the city, became a byword for scholarship and academic excellence; it was the Harvard of its day, and so it remained well into modern times.

The most consequential legacy, however, was language. The language of the court of Versailles was French, and thus also, *noblesse oblige*, for any nobleman across Europe worthy of his title. He might speak the local language (be it Russian, Polish, German, or whatever) to the help; but the true language *entre nobles* was French. Beginning roughly in the 16th century and lasting well into the 20th century, French replaced Latin as the lingua franca of Europe's scholars and elites, the preferred language of intellectual discourse and of diplomacy. Austria's unfortunate ultimatum to Serbia in July 1914, which unleashed World War I, was delivered—of course—in French. The operating language of the League of Nations (1919–1939), forerunner of today's United Nations, was—naturally—French. A basic mastery of French is still *de rigueur* today in European aristocratic circles, a sign of taste and good unspringing. This is the sole stratum of society where French has managed to hold on to a portion of its former glory, but one can only wonder for how long

The reason for its decline is well known: the inexorable rise of English. Whether for commerce, science, politics, or tourism, English is today Europe's common language. The decline of French in the second half of the 20th century as the natural second language of Europe's elites happened very rapidly, creating a cultural earthquake from which the French have not yet fully recovered. The evidence for English's clean sweep is overwhelming, even in traditional francophile nations. In a recent study by the European Commission in which parents (in non-English-speaking nations) were asked which second language they wanted their children to learn, 90 percent answered English, including parents in Latin nations such as Spain and Portugal.[10] I have had the privilege of visiting a number of European cities: whether Lisbon, Prague, Warsaw, or The Hague, and everywhere the second language in hotels, shops, and offices is English, where before it might have been French or perhaps German. English is today the common language of Europe's youth. Adding insult to injury, to the horror of many French intellectuals, even French pop singers and rock bands have taken to singing in English. English has also penetrated academia; courses taught in English are no longer exceptional. Also, writing in English is a prerequisite for any French scholar seeking an international career. He or she, sitting in Paris or Lyon, knows that a paper written in French will not be read outside the French-speaking world. Thus, French, though still a major world language, has ceased to be *the* natural language of international discourse and exchange.

When we examine the causes for the rapid decline of French, again we find that the reasons lie in demography and politics. First, starting in the 19th century, French fertility rates fell below those of other European nations for reasons demographers have still not fully explained. France ceased to be Europe's most populous nation; it was soon equaled by Britain and bypassed by Russia and then, after 1870, a unified Germany. For a brief period, ending with the calamity of Hitler and World War II, it seemed that German might challenge French as Europe's dominant language. Second,

France lost the battle for colonial dominance outside Europe. In a ruinous sequence of colonial wars in the 18th century, France lost its foothold in India, allowing Britain to become the dominant power on the subcontinent, and in turn lost it Canada, leaving Britain and its descendants to colonize North America. The linguistic fate of the continent was finally settled in 1803 by Napoleon's sale of the vast Louisiana Territory to the young American Republic. Britain's descendants settled Australia, New Zealand, and South Africa, with the last-named taken from the Dutch during the Napoleonic Wars. Let me stop here. The point, simply, is that English emerged in the 20th century as the dominant *Lingua Franca* for much of the planet. Lee Kuan Yew knew what he was doing when he imposed English as Singapore's official language. English today is the acknowledged common language of East and South Asia, the language Koreans, Japanese, Chinese, Indonesians, Indians, Vietnamese, and others spontaneously use to communicate with one another.

The Last Gasp: The Left Bank, de Gaulle, and the EU

The rise of America as the planet's dominant power notwithstanding, Parisians could until very recently be forgiven for feeling that theirs was still a true world language, a worthy rival to English. As in other city stories, let us take the 1950s as our starting point. World War II was over; the feared Germans defeated once and for all, their culture no longer a threat. Europe was divided—the East under Soviet control and the West in the American camp. In the West, the draw of French culture remained strong, despite the presence of American power and the lure of the American dream. The 1950s was the heyday of Existentialism, a philosophical school sweeping intellectual circles on both sides of the Atlantic. Any self-proclaimed intellectual worth his salt read Jean-Paul Sartre and Albert Camus. The 1950s was also a golden age for French avant-garde cinema, reborn after the war; it became all the craze among the New York literati. French was chic, the Paris café the ultimate symbol of cosmopolitan sophistication. New York had no sidewalk cafés at the time (they were prohibited by city ordinances) and seemed almost provincial in comparison. Greenwich Village, an exotic expectation, was the closest New York came to Paris's fabled Latin Quarter. The English-speaking world might hold the lead in technology and raw power, but French was the language of "high culture," of the arts and sophistication. Students entering high school in Manhattan in the late 1950s still made French their first choice as a foreign language, although Spanish was moving up fast. French and Spanish were the only two choices at the time.

Yet, no language—no matter how culturally sophisticated—can long prevail without the prerequisite demographic and political foundations. No one understood this better than Charles de Gaulle, France's wartime leader[11] and postwar president (1944–1946; 1958–1969). He also understood the importance of language—he was a prolific writer himself—for Paris's reach and France's position as a world power. Few leaders possessed de Gaulle's grasp of geopolitics; he saw quite clearly[12] that America's overwhelming might combined with Britain's' global linguistic legacy meant that the French language was under threat and with it France would lose its place in the world. de Gaulle's strategy, galling to many in the English-speaking world, was clear. The fall of Germany presented a window of opportunity, a rare chance to entrench French cultural dominance in Europe (outside the Soviet sphere). The recipe: keep the insufferable Anglo-Saxons (read: the United States and the United Kingdom) out of continental Europe or, at least, keep their influence to a minimum. The cornerstone of de Gaulle's strategy was French-German reconciliation and what was to become the European Economic Community (EEC) and later the EU. The EEC, created in 1957, built around the new French-German partnership, had just six members: the three small Benelux states, Italy, West Germany, and France. French would be the dominant language. The Germans were too ashamed to push their language, and the Italians, also a defeated power, were not really in the running. The strategy worked: the three capitals of the EEC were French-speaking cities: Luxembourg (European Court), Strasbourg (Parliament), and Brussels, the last-named emerging as the de facto capital of the union. The EEC functioned in French, the language any self-respecting politician or civil servant with European ambitions needed to master. During his reign, de Gaulle systematically vetoed the entry of Britain and other northern nations into the EEC, thus ensuring that France remained the dominant power in the six-nation union.

With de Gaulle's departure from power in 1969, that wall began to crumble. In 1973, Britain, Denmark, and Ireland joined the EEC, diluting its Frenchness. But a more important wall crumbled in 1989: the Berlin Wall. Then, in 1991, the Soviet Union disintegrated, leading Germany to reunite, again making Germany Western Europe's most powerful state and also allowing new members, formerly blocked by Cold War geopolitics,[13] to join the EEC, which would eventually grow to twenty-seven states. The linguistic dynamics of Europe had changed forever, and English rapidly moved in as the common language of this diverse mix of peoples. The irony would escape no one that the EEC (now rebaptized EU), once a rampart of French, had morphed into an instrument of Anglicization. *The Economist*, in a 2003 article, "The Galling Rise of English," quotes a former high-ranking Brussels civil servant: "When I left Brussels in 1995, 70% of the documents coming across my desk were in French; today 70% are in English."[14] The percentage has undoubtedly risen even further since. The common language of the Brussels bureaucracy today is English, as it is for other European institutions. Brexit—Britain's exit from the EU—will not change this dynamic. The language of Paris is no longer the language of Europe.

Language is much more than a means of communication. Language is the vessel (*Kulturträger*) by which mores, values, and ideas are transmitted. Each German, Spaniard, or Pole who today accesses *The Economist*'s website rather than *Le Monde*'s is exposed to *The Economist*'s "Anglo-Saxon" worldview. Stated differently, the decline of French has meant that the French way of thinking, including in matters of business, is no longer the norm. It is this transformation, more than anything else, that has caused Paris's light to fade, at the core of Parisians' sense of loss. Not only the English language but also the Anglo-American way of doing things has become the implicit world norm. French society is still in the process of adapting to this cultural shift, not without predictable resistance and pain.

The Jacobin Legacy

France remains in many ways a cultural exception in Europe, not least in its political institutions. "How can one possibly govern a nation that has two hundred and forty-six varieties of cheese?" General de Gaulle is famously said to have exclaimed, undoubtedly on a day when even he felt overwhelmed by the challenge of reforming France.

France's Jacobin[15] tradition of centralized and bureaucratic governance, a legacy of the French Revolution (1789), stands out as somewhat of an anomaly in today's market-driven world. France's labor market has a deserved reputation for being overly rigid, hiring and firing rules are legislated at the national level, and collective agreements for industry groups are negotiated at the national level with national labor unions. In education, the school system, from primary school to university, is centrally administered from Paris. University job openings are posted at the national level and exams are administered nationally. This top-down rigidity also extends to the local level. The City of Paris didn't even have a mayor until 1977[16]; it was centrally administered like any French *Département* by a *Préfet* appointed by the national government. The kind of business-civic partnership we witnessed in Atlanta is unimaginable in Paris. Without central government approval, very little happens, except for strictly local matters like parks and traffic management.

While France remains a technologically advanced nation with an enviable quality of life, it is important to emphasize that all advantages are relative. Compared to many other European cities, Paris offers a less congenial business climate, less in tune with the prevailing global ethos. France's Jacobin legacy also has historically meant higher taxes; its high payroll taxation, compared notably to that of Britain, puts Paris at a disadvantage in the battle for highly paid talent.[17] Aside from such fiscal considerations, the typical American or Japanese company will generally feel more at home in London, Amsterdam, or Frankfurt, cities more attuned to the new international norms of doing business. Such things are difficult to quantify. The American sociologist Saskia Sassen, a student of global cities, proposes a distinction between quality-of-life indicators and more strictly business attributes.[18] Paris generally ranks well on quality of life : it is a prime tourist destination and a favored venue for conferences, colloquia, and meetings of all kinds. People like coming to Paris. However, once other criteria are factored in, the picture is less rosy. It does not do very well on Sassen's "ease of doing business" indicator, which includes matters such as the hiring and firing of workers, regulations governing business start-ups and closures, and contract enforcement. In a word, Paris is a great place to visit but not necessarily a good choice to start up or run a global business.

Regional Governance—An Unfinished (and Not Always Happy) Story

An indirect consequence of France's Jacobin legacy is the surprising reluctance of the French state to alter or suppress communal (municipal) boundaries. Bureaucracy breeds conservatism. Municipal boundaries have remained basically frozen since the French Revolution. The City of Paris (Paris *intramuros,* the city proper) with its 2.2 million inhabitants remains trapped in its historical borders, less than a fifth of the metropolitan total of some twelve million. France counts some thirty-five thousand communes, more than the combined total for Germany, Italy, and the UK. Each commune has its urban planning prerogatives: an extreme case of municipal fragmentation.

After the war, this legacy of fragmented urban governance, overlain by some ninety *Départements* at the national level (the equivalent of U.S. counties), appeared less and less appropriate to the needs of a modern metropolis. In 1961, Paul Delouvrier, who would become the father of postwar regional planning, was named administrator (*Délégué général*) of what was then called the District of the Paris Region, by President de Gaulle, who while flying over Paris in a helicopter is reputed to have said to his new appointee: "get this mess cleaned up."[19] The story of Greater Paris since then has been the story of the hunt for a Parisian model of regional governance, to which I shall return shortly. But before that, we need to tell the story of Seine-Saint-Denis, unfortunate child of France's ongoing quest for a suitable model of metropolitan governance—proof yet again that good intentions sometimes produce bad results.

Seine-Saint-Denis. A Story of Exclusion

On October 27, 2005, in the suburban commune of Clichy-sous-Bois, northeast of Paris, two French youths fleeing police, Zyed Benna and Bouna Traoré, the first of North African and the second of African descent, accidentally electrocuted themselves when trying to hide in an electricity substation, in turn causing a blackout. The event set off demonstrations in the surrounding neighborhood. Three days later, police threw tear gas into the crowd at a nearby mosque. The two events unleashed a succession of riots beyond anything France or Europe had seen thus far. The urban violence, which would last three weeks, rapidly spread to neighboring communes, soon making horror scenes of cars, buses, and buildings burning a daily diet on national television. It is estimated that some eight thousand cars were burned, and hundreds of people were injured and hospitalized, victims of Molotov cocktails (the rioter's weapon of choice) and stray police bullets.

The French government declared a state of emergency on November 8, 2005, and three thousand individuals were either arrested or detained. Ten days later, French police declared that the situation had returned to normal, lifting the state of emergency.

More urban riots were to follow, however. The malaise had deep roots, the outcome of a history of distrust between the local population, generally of nonwhite immigrant stock, and the police. There is little evidence that the situation has improved since. On February 8, 2017, French news media released footage of a black youth (known only as Théo; his family name was not revealed) being brutally beaten by police in the commune of Aulnay-sous-Bois. The event unleashed a new wave of rioting, both in Aulnay and in neighboring communes. The important message here is not the persistence of urban violence, although that matters of course, but its geography. Both Clichy-sous-Bois and Aulnay-sous-Bois are located in the *Département* of Seine-Saint-Denis, a suburb of Paris. To understand how things got to this point, we need to understand the history of Seine-Saint-Denis, a political creation of the French state.

The story begins in the halcyon years of rapid growth following World War II. The *Département* of Seine-Saint-Denis did not exist yet; Seine-Saint-Denis was part of the *Département* of Seine (number 75[20]), which included both the City of Paris (Paris intramuros) and what were to become its suburbs as the urban region expanded. As immigrants flooded in, both from the countryside and former colonies, affordable housing became a major issue. The historic City of Paris had little room for new residents and was in addition constrained by urban planning regulations that limited building heights. The answer of the French state was to construct vast social housing estates targeting middle- and lower-income households. The majority were located in the northern and eastern suburbs, Paris's industrial belt and center of the burgeoning automobile industry. Before the war, the northeastern communes, located just beyond the confines Paris intramuros, had acquired the sobriquet "Red Belt" (*ceinture rouge*): these were blue-collar neighborhoods and the historic strongholds of the French Communist Party. That political geography remained largely unchanged after the war. The expanding northeastern blue-collar suburbs would be red and remain so.

Over time, the populations of those housing estates changed. The initial impetus behind the housing estates was entirely noble and made planning sense: bring affordable housing where the jobs were, whether automobile or other plants. Architecture in the 1960s was greatly influenced by what can only be called gigantism (often, the architects were close to the Communist Party) where bigger was better and was perceived as more modern. Unfortunately, the end result was a sequence of Soviet-style horrors, culminating in an urban landscape of concrete towers and not much else. The story of *Rose-des-Vents* in Aulnay-sous-Bois, the housing estate Théo called home, is all too typical. It was built in 1969 on former agricultural land next to a new Citroën plant. Its poetic name—Rose of the Wind—mirrors the urbanistic idealism that inspired its authors. Rose of the Wind would be big and feature all the modern facilities (refrigerator, running water, etc.). Some three thousand apartment units would house sixteen thousand residents, and it would be a veritable *Cité* (city). The word *Cité* has since become synonymous in France with such monster housing projects.

The first occupants were mainly French working-class families with a mix of Italians, Spaniards, and the occasional North African. All that changed in the 1980s as Citroën and other plants laid off workers or simply closed shop. At the same time, as native French families moved up the social ladder, many chose to move to better housing and were progressively replaced by poorer immigrant families from North Africa and sub-Saharan Africa. Clientelism accelerated the process (at least those were the rumors going around), and housing space was now assigned on the basis of ethnic connections and political support. In the event, the predictable outcome after two decades of demographic change, plant closures, and physical neglect was an urban environment much like the inner-city ghettos of urban America, with the major difference being that the French ghettos are suburban while the American are central. Contrary to the U.S. system where the word *suburb* is associated with the middle and upper classes, *banlieue* in France conjures up images of urban violence and poverty—proof if need be that outcomes are contingent on context and public policy. Poverty and violence in the center are no more natural than poverty and violence in the suburbs.

The analogy with America's inner-city ghettos is not gratuitous. What I saw in France reminded me of what I had witnessed in New York and Philadelphia, no-go zones beyond the rule of law where firefighters and local police feared to tread.[21] The same self-reinforcing spiral of poverty and violence was at work. In both nations, numerous programs with school as the primary focus have been applied in attempts to extradite the young from the circle of poverty, but none to my knowledge has been totally successful. Community policing and physical upgrading help, but the core problem in both nations remains the spatial concentration of poverty and race. The French *cités* must confront an added problem: the rise of radical Islam. Aulnay-sous-Bois counted five mosques in 2005, and there are probably more now. The disillusioned youth in places like Aulnay are easy prey for the predictors of hate. The French census contains no information on race, ethnicity, or religion,[22] but unofficial estimates for the overall *Département* of Seine-Saint-Denis (population 1.5 million in 2016) put the Muslim proportion at over one-third. The count is undoubtedly higher in communes like Aulnay and Clichy-sous-Bois.

The creation of Seine-Saint-Denis as a distinct *Département* in 1968 marks a pivotal moment in this unhappy story of ghettoization. Before that date, its forty-odd communes, together with Paris and the remaining ninety suburban communes, were all part of the Seine *Département* with a common *Préfet* (senior administrator) named by the state. The weight of left-leaning Red Belt communes meant that the Departmental Council often ended up being controlled by Communists or Socialist-Communist coalitions. The French Communist Party at the time was a powerful political force, often garnering a quarter of the national vote. It was the natural majority in places like Aulnay and Clichy-sous-Bois. In 1964, the National Assembly voted to split Seine into four parts: Paris proper, which would keep the coveted 75 code and three newly minted *Départements* with the codes 91, 92, and 93, the last assigned to newly created Seine-Saint-Denis. The most solidly left-wing and poorest communes were quarantined, so to speak, in the new *Département,* which came to be popularly known as *le 93,* now a synonym for poverty and exclusion.

Whether or not this administrative separation was truly willful, I do not know, but the consequences were more than political and subsequently reinforced by the construction of the *Périphérique* elevated highway, which physically cut off 93 from Paris intramuros. Although again built with the best of intentions (a ring-road allowing traffic to avoid Paris intramuros), the *Périphérique* developed de facto into a social barrier, notably at the city's northern edges. One lives either on the right side or on the wrong side. The symbolism of Seine-Saint-Denis's spatial separation, both physical and administrative, remains powerful, despite the best efforts of the French state.

Seine-Saint-Denis's spatial separation holds an important warning. The boiling anger of the Parisian *banlieue* tells us that a functioning social safety net, although a prerequisite, is not enough to ensure social cohesion. Health, education, and most other people services are centrally financed in France, and its welfare state is no less generous than, say, Quebec's. The schools and clinics of the *banlieue* in places like Aulnay-sous-Bois do not necessarily lack resources. The French state continues to pour significant funds into the *banlieue*. The problem is not money but the *spatial* concentration of "excluded" populations and subsequent self-reinforcing cultures of poverty, compounded in Paris's angry *Cités* by race and the soulless outsized scale of many public housing projects.[23] Paris intramuros's inflexible housing stock and consequent sky-high prices make it unattainable for most people. In the surrounding *banlieue*, public housing often accounts for more than 50 percent of the housing stock in the poorest communes. Little wonder that the 2005 urban insurrection and those that followed exploded in 93.

Le Grand Paris—A Reform in Waiting

In 2007, Nicolas Sarkozy was elected president of France on a platform of law and order. The centerpiece of his presidency was to be the reunification of Paris into a great world-class urban region, by the same token repairing the deep gash that separated Paris intramuros from its rebellious northeastern suburbs. Sarkozy failed in his endeavor to give the Greater Paris region (*Le Grand Paris*) a proper model of metropolitan governance. His successor, François Hollande (2012–2017), was only slightly more successful, and the jury is still out on the current president, Emmanuel Macron. Numerous reforms have been introduced in recent times, the favored solution being to add new layers of administration and, unfortunately, new layers of confusion. The French state is seemingly unwilling to step on any toes in the constant tug-of-war between rival political actors. France's history of distrust between political parties—mayors and councilors are elected on national party tickets—remains a powerful barrier to regional cooperation.[24] The outcome so far appears to please no one.

Thus, at the time of writing, the region presents an extraordinarily complex governance structure[25] that few appear to fully comprehend. In the simplest possible terms, the citizens of Greater Paris are beholden to (1) the national government; (2) the regional government of Île-de-France;

(3) the *Département*; and (4) the commune, which would be the City of Paris for Paris intramuros. To this complex structure, the government has added (5) a layer of intercommunal agglomerations linked through fifty-one service-sharing agreements called, alternatively, *Plaines communes*, *Communautés d'agglomérations* (CA), or *Communautés de communes* CC). In addition (6), the region counts over six hundred specialty intercommunal "syndicates": 46 *Syndicats intercommunaux à vocation multiple* (SIVOM), 464 *Syndicats intercommunaux à vocation unique* (SIVU), and 160 *Syndicats mixtes fermés* (SMF).[26]

After ten years of political haggling, the Hollande government finally adopted a law in 2016 creating the *Métropole du Grand Paris,* a new government layer that in principle brings together the 131 communes and four *Département*s of the former Seine *Département*, which have now been reorganized around the various *Plaines communes,* but without eliminating any of the other six layers or reducing their powers. At the time of writing, it was by no means clear how this new layer of governance would work in practice. Its first voted budget, a paltry 65 million euros, amounted to less than 2 percent of the combined communal budgets.[27] Most pundits do not see a bright future for this new political creature, given the unwillingness of elected officials to give up power. The borders of the one hundred and thirty suburban communes have remained intact, as have those of Paris intramuros. The social barrier between the two remains as strong as ever. The current mayor of Paris is understandably unenthusiastic about yielding power up to this new regional entity, and the president of the Île-de-France regional government is no less enthusiastic about ceding powers. Only time will tell whether this new entity will eventually morph into a useful mechanism of metropolitan governance.

I do not wish to give the wrong impression. Paris remains a reasonably well-functioning and safe metropolis, certainly no less so than New York or London. Paris intramuros, the only Paris tourists generally see, is well managed, orderly, and of course an architectural marvel. There is another Paris, though, and that was what the previous paragraphs are all about. The sad *Cités* surrounding Paris intramuros do not diminish its beauty but remain a wound that must one day be healed if Paris is to provide a good quality of life for the majority of is citizens, not just visitors. But even glorious Paris intramuros is under threat—that is, as an engine of economic growth—the direct result of the actions of the French state, to which we now turn.

A Threatened Center—Is Paris Squandering Its
Most Valuable Asset?

No city has more walkable, lively, and beautiful neighborhoods than Paris. It is in Paris that the notion of "bohemian" was born, long before New York, Boston, or San Francisco saw their first sidewalk café. Puccini's 19th-century opera *La Bohème* (The Bohemian) was set in Paris, of course. Le *Café Flore* in *Saint-Germain-des-Près* and *Le Dôme Café* in Montparnasse, once obligatory watering holes of the world's literati, hold a mystique that endures to this day. Paris's Left Bank is by all appearances as lively today as it was a century ago, its fabled Boulevards Saint-Germain and Saint-Michel—the heart of the Latin Quarter—lined with sidewalk cafés, bookstores, and produce markets of every kind and populated with seemingly endless crowds. Paris's neighborhoods have lost none of their architectural charm. And not least, Paris has a superb public transit system, no less efficient than those of New York and London.

Yet, Paris has not given birth to a digital start-up scene comparable to that of New York or London. An embryonic techno cluster has emerged just north of what used to be *Les Halles* central food market (now demolished), but it remains a pale copy of its rivals.[28] The City of Paris recently announced the inauguration of incubators and state-of-the-art IT workplaces to help start-ups. However, the Paris start-up scene remains almost exclusively French. I do not have any hard figures, but, I doubt that many American, Korean, or German budding entrepreneurs have actually *moved to* Paris to start a business, while French computer engineers are a common sight in Silicon Valley and Silicon Alley. Part of the answer, alluded to earlier, lies in the legendary rigidity of France's labor market, high taxes, and heavy-handed bureaucracy. Paris's strict urban planning regulations with the a priori laudable objective of protecting its architectural heritage introduce an additional hurdle. The conversion and retooling of buildings, which is at the core of the emergence of Manhattan's Silicon Alley, is more difficult in Paris. But that is only part of the answer.

A Modern Maginot Line

Over the last few decades, the French state has made a number of spatial planning decisions that have weakened the role of central Paris as a center of learning and intellectual ferment; and the worst, I fear, is yet to come. It's as if the French state consciously set out to destroy central Paris's economic centrality. The culprits, we shall see, are state actors who are prisoners of obsolete concepts. Let me use a military analogy. There's an old military proverb that says that generals are always fighting the last war. French military history provides one of the best-known examples: the Maginot Line, a line of tunneled fortifications built along the German border after World War I to prevent foreign invasion. That war was a war of attrition, with armies moving slowly and opposing forces dug in in trenches in vast connecting systems of tunnels. The idea that the next war (World War II) would be one of movement, dictated by planes and armored tanks, was simply not entertained by France's genera staff, who were still fighting World War I. Thus, the Maginot Line was built, a replicate of the tunneled systems of the "Last War," but which we know did nothing to stop the German panzers from overrunning France in May 1940.

The bureaucrats and others in charge of planning France's highly centralized university system are, in a word, "fighting the last war"; the prisoners of concepts that have long since gone out of fashion in North America. The meteoric rise of the great American universities (Harvard, Berkeley, Stanford, etc.) after World War II stunned the French educational elite, adding to their sense of cultural loss. What was America's secret? The concept of a university campus, a self-contained landscaped city of learning often located at some distance from the center, was unfamiliar to the French. Its great universities were resolutely urban. *Ergo*, if France was to meet the American challenge, it would need to copy the American model: build suburban campuses and the bigger the better. There is, of course, nothing inherently wrong with building suburban campuses, providing they are well designed and an *addition* to the urban economy, not built at the expense of the center.

In North America, the golden age of suburban campus construction is now past, with the focus often now shifting to strengthening urban campuses and/or attracting institutions to the urban core. In Montreal, we saw that the *École de technologie supérieure* (graduate engineering school) was housed in a recycled beer brewery on the edge of the CBD; this was a conscious planning decision. The area around the school has since emerged as a start-up cluster. New York provides an even more powerful example. Mayor Michael Bloomberg (2001–2013) declared in 2011 that the city would provide city-owned land plus $100 million toward the creation of a world-class applied sciences university campus downtown. Bloomberg's initiative led to the creation of Cornell Tech, a joint venture between Cornell University and the Technion-Israel Institute of Technology. A first campus was opened in Chelsea in 2012 in the very heart of Silicon Alley, and an ultramodern campus, at the cost of some $2 billion, built on Roosevelt Island, one subway stop from central Manhattan, was completed in 2017. New York is betting on the synergies that only central neighborhoods can provide to ensure its continued success in the digital age. Perhaps the construction of Cornell Tech will mark the moment New York started to overtake Silicon Valley—an "Erie Canal Moment" to quote the head of the city's Economic Development Corporation.[29]

Let us return to Paris where decision makers appear intent on constructing new suburban campuses. I've worked on one of those campuses, *La Cité Descartes*, a fairly recent construction that is still not totally finished, located in the new town of Marne-la-Vallée a thirty-minute train ride east of Paris. Its buildings are modern and generally functional but also sterile: the campus is totally devoid of the creative chaos needed for intellectual ferment. I found no active student life or anything resembling a café life. After classes, students and faculty simply take the train or car home. But that criticism can be hurled at many new campuses, not just those in France. The core problem lies elsewhere. *La Cité Descartes*, like most other suburban campuses around Paris, was largely built on transfers from central Paris. Since 1967, the campus has been home for the *École des Ponts*, France's largest civil engineering faculty, which formerly was located in the heart of the Latin Quarter where it was founded two centuries ago. The *École des Ponts* is not the only example. Since the 1960s, the French state has been systematically transferring university faculties and research institutes from central Paris to outlying locations.

The biggest transfer is yet to come: a planned project of pharaonic proportions. I am not aware of anything equivalent in Europe or North America. A vast techno campus is currently under construction 26 kilometers southwest of Paris near the small suburban commune of Saclay. The project, formally approved by the French state in 2010 and planned for completion in 2020, calls for the transfer of six major university faculties from central Paris. The *École Polytechnique*, another major engineering school, was transferred there some time ago. The promoters of Saclay are entirely clear about their intentions: it is openly modeled on Stanford University and Silicon Valley, or what they hope will become France's

Silicon Valley.[30] Only time will tell if they were right. Unfortunately, however, I cannot escape the feeling that Saclay will become France's modern Maginot Line

The Business of Paris Is Culture, Not Business

Paris is in danger of squandering its greatest asset in today's knowledge-led economy. This is not the time to "unclog" central Paris—often an argument for the transfers—but to strengthen it. The economic weakening of central Paris has a second dimension: France's (or at least its leaders') fixation on signature cultural monuments and heritage protection. The need to protect Paris's unique architectural heritage is indisputable; it is an objective I share. However, the example of other European cities, not least London, demonstrates that heritage protection and modernization, including higher building limits in designated zones, are not incompatible.

The strict adherence to existing densities and building heights[31] has meant, most notably, the creation—again state planned—of an alternative CBD on the western edge of Paris intramuros, the first office towers constructed in the 1970s and since expanded. The mini skyline of *La Défense,* as this planned CBD is called, is visible from Paris's western neighborhoods. In addition to its cold utilitarian look with no real street life, *La Défense* is too far from central Paris to produce the spontaneous interaction between start-ups and the financial district possible in New York or London. Again, it's almost as if the French state consciously chose (and perhaps it was a conscious decision) to exile its CBD to the periphery.[32] The message is clear: The business of Paris was culture, not business. How different, for example, from Shanghai's Pudong district, also a centrally planned CBD, whose majestic towers loom over the Bund waterfront promenade across the river (the heart of the old CBD) sending a clear message to the onlooker: Pudong is the heart of the new Shanghai. Pudong's Oriental Pearl Tower has since become the city's emblematic structure, pictured on postcards, like the Eiffel Tower. Few postcards, if any, picture *La Défense,* lost and unloved in its suburban exile.

Paris is replete with opportunities missed. When *Les Halles* wholesale market was torn down in 1971, here was a superb opportunity to densify the CBD with, possibly, a new office complex or a university faculty. Instead, a shopping mall was built, one of the few truly ugly structures in Paris, under reconstruction for the nth time at the time of writing, still in search of a mission. The *Centre Beaubourg*, almost as ugly, located a few blocks away, was bestowed to Paris in 1977 by then outgoing president Georges Pompidou. It is in my opinion entirely useless, another museum in a city that certainly does not lack museums, dedicated to the plastic arts and design. Here again was a missed opportunity to welcome a university faculty in search of space or, alternatively, to build new office space. But no, the president wanted to bequeath a cultural monument, a museum that would bear his name.[33] When the *Gare d'Orsay* railway station on the left bank of the Seine, on the edge of the Latin Quarter, finally ceased to operate in the early 1970s, here was a unique opportunity to strengthen Paris's intellectual heart. This beautiful 19th-century structure was the perfect showcase for a prestigious institute of higher learning or research. In 1986, the French state finally decided that the building would be used as a museum, *le Musée d'Orsay*, which now houses French Impressionist and post-Impressionist art.

Again, I do not wish to exaggerate. Paris will not fall into a black hole and hollow out like some midwestern Rustbelt city. Despite all the mistakes made, Paris intramuros remains the urban region's undisputed heart. One cannot easily undo centuries of investment in physical and human capital, and, yes, all the little things that make a city work and make it an enjoyable place to live. Like New York, Paris's City administration has done many things to make the city more livable: community policing; bicycle-friendly streets; landscaping the banks of the Seine; pocket parks—Paris has all that. But its economic heart is weaker than it could be and should be. When I visit New York, walking the familiar streets of Manhattan, I sense that I am at the center of things: a crazy energy—a buzz—difficult to pin down but no less real. This is of course highly subjective. I do not get the same feeling walking the boulevards of Paris. My reference to museums was not gratuitous. My fear for Paris is that people will increasingly go there to see and to admire, not to make things.

* * *

Paris will remain a great city. Its unrivaled position as *the* central place of a technologically advanced nation of some sixty-five million people and the cultural light for some one hundred million (perhaps more) French-speakers around the world mean that it will never sink to the level of a secondary metropolis. Its center will remain a glorious monument to human creativity. That said, Paris in recent times has underperformed on the global stage as a source of economic opportunity and intellectual ferment. The reasons took us back to well-known grievances against the rigid bureaucratic management of the French state and economy. But the role the French state as a direct intervener in the city in matters of urban planning and administrative organization was, we saw, no less important. The French state shaped Paris. In highly centralized nations, the state will have the means to produce great wonders (Versailles, Baron Haussmann's magnificent Boulevards, the *TGV*), but the means also to make big mistakes.

Conclusion

Why Cities Fail (Mainly, But Not Solely,
an American Story)

"For every complex problem there is a solution that is simple, neat, and wrong."

—Attributed to H. L. Mencken[1]

The core message of this book can be summed up in a single sentence: If the nation doesn't work, cities won't. Cities don't fail by themselves, no more than they succeed by themselves. Cities fail because societies fail. Most of the prescriptive literature on cities understandably focuses on the ingredients for success, not failure. Cities should be beacons of hope and opportunity. Why then dwell on failure in this concluding chapter? Failures force us to look at what needs to be fixed and also in turn to gauge the realism of the needed changes. The changes needed, the reader will certainly have understood by now, will almost always involve changes at multiple levels of society, from nation to neighborhood to borrow the subtitle of our template (see Table I.1).

I shall focus on American cities, no strangers to failure. Why America? Because the United States should have no failures or at least very few, and they should be of limited scale. America is a rich and democratic nation, wealthier than any the world has known. It is relatively easy, and disheartening, to explain how Port-au-Prince failed. We now know that cities (agglomerations, to use the preferred term of economic geographers) do not spontaneously generate wealth, or not enough, which is the lot of most Third World cities. Where they do not, we now know that the changes required will go well beyond the cities themselves.

But, why failures in the world's richest nation? Why stagnant metropolitan economies, gutted central cities, and ghetto neighborhoods locked into seemingly irreversible cycles of poverty? Urban failures like Buffalo and Detroit should never have been allowed to happen. America's urban successes—unparalleled centers of learning and creativity—are no less real. But that is precisely what makes the American experience so troubling: the contrasting fortunes of America's great cities bring home the all-too-easily ignored relationship between urban success and failure, a warning that success and failure are not incompatible.

The United States is, of course, not alone among rich nations in having engendered urban failures, the *banlieue* of Paris (sadly reproduced in many other French cities) being prime exhibits. But the reasons behind France's *banlieue* are fairly straightforward; they are unintended consequences of initially well-intentioned policies (public housing for France's rapidly expanding postwar urban middle and working class). And unlike America's urban failures, France's are of recent vintage, largely the product of recent migratory movements. The explanations for America's urban failures are more complex, taking us back to the nation's founding and the institutions that have shaped the nation since.

America's Five Institutional Legacies

Why then were America's urban failures allowed to happen? The answer requires that we go back and take a second look at the origins of America's singular institutional landscape and how over time it came to shape the nation's cities in the 20th and 21st centuries, undoubtedly very different from what the early fathers (and mothers) of the Republic intended. I have grouped America's institutional landscape under five headings: 1) Suspicion of the State and Bottom-up Democracy; 2) Local Financing of People Services; 3) A (Reluctant) Union of "Sovereign" States; 4) Freedom Above Order and Equality; 5) The Freedom to Settle.

Suspicion of the State and Bottom-up Democracy

America's deep-rooted localism is the natural partner of America's equally deep-seated tradition of mistrust of higher levels of government, Washington, D.C., being the prime target. Most recently, Donald Trump astutely played on that mistrust to build the political base that carried him to the presidency. The American Republic, harking back to the ideals of the American Revolution, engendered a model of urban governance—as we saw most clearly in the comparison between Buffalo and Toronto—that entrenched the principle of local autonomy, limiting the ability (and the will) of state governments to intervene from above. This is very different from Canada where municipalities are mere creatures of the (provincial) state. Historically, American local authorities (municipalities, townships, etc.) were mostly created from the bottom up, incorporated by state legislatures at their request.

With rare exceptions, American states have been loath to force municipalities to share revenues or to merge with neighboring municipalities. This is consistent with a political philosophy (entirely laudable in principle) that respects the wishes of local electorates, whose wishes as such cannot to be overridden by royal edicts from above. The Canadian political tradition sees the Crown (the state) as having an obligation to intervene in order to maintain social order, allowing it override the wishes of local electorates, as we saw in the Toronto and Montreal stories. The autonomy and difficult-to-alter boundaries of American municipalities would be of little concern if their responsibilities were limited to the provision of basic urban services (sewage systems, roads and traffic, sanitation, parks, lighting, local policing).

Local Financing of People Services

An accompanying feature of America's urban institutional landscape is the local financing in part or in whole of people services. In most Western nations, cities/municipalities have limited social responsibilities and, by the same token, also limited financial resources. The public services that underpin social cohesion, what I have dubbed people services (education; child care; health; etc.), are as a rule a centrally financed and/or administered, costs implicitly shared across the region or nation. This matters because access to people services plays a key role in allowing less favored individuals to move up the social ladder. In the United States, though differing across the fifty states, primary and secondary public education are, as a rule, in whole or in part financed through local property taxes.[2] Individual moving to another municipality (school district) take the tax base with them. Moves between places thus become more than a transfer of human capital; they also become a transfer of resources to finance people services, the quality of schools tied to the wealth of the local population.

The impact of the local financing of people services is most directly felt in fragmented metropolitan areas, fueling the sorting of populations across municipalities and fiscal competition between neighboring municipalities. Richer municipalities are able to offer the same level of services with lower property taxes, further fueling the sorting of populations by class and/or race (a polite word for segregation). This sorting process has generally been at the expense of the central city (municipality).

A (Reluctant) Union of "Sovereign" States

The United States is unique among federal states in the rich world in not having explicit transfer programs among member states/provinces, funneled through the federal government, to ensure a minimal level of equality in the provision of people services. This absence is the corollary, at least in part, of America's localist tradition, transposed to the state level. The Republic was founded as a loose federation of "sovereign" states (at least, many perceived it as such) which did not tolerate interference from above, no matter how benevolent. It took a civil war to finally solidify the union. Here again, the difference with Canada is telling where government-to-government transfers can account for a significant share of revenue for poorer provinces, allowing them to maintain a higher level of services and/ or lower taxes.[3] The impact on the sorting of populations on fiscal competition is analogous to that for municipalities, but now for states and ultimately also for metropolitan areas.

America's institutional landscape contains no mechanisms, implicit or otherwise, for compensating jurisdictions for exported human capital. This is of some importance where the costs of education are borne locally, exporting states or municipalities subsidizing the winners.

Freedom Above Order and Equality

It is impossible not to admire the sentiments behind "Life, Liberty, and the Pursuit of Happiness," arguably the best-known lines in the American Declaration of Independence. They betray a political philosophy in which personal freedom comes first, a very different philosophy from that behind the slogan of its sister revolution in France a few years later:

"*Liberté, Égalité, Fraternité*" (Liberty, Equality, Brotherhood). The American Revolution engendered no similar appeal to social solidarity and the importance of reciprocal obligations. How different the American slogan is, too, from Canada's "Peace, Order, and Good Government." Again, the American Revolution engendered no counsel on the need to maintain social order. Perhaps nothing better illustrates the contrasting political philosophies of North America's two nations than the United States' Second Amendment— the right to bear arms—the ultimate symbol of the rights of the individual over those of the state.

The weight of "freedom" has also meant that Americans are, as a rule, more averse to paying taxes. This is the ultimate test of the willingness to share, resulting predictably in both lower taxes and, compared to most other advanced nations, in less progressive personal income tax tables. That universal health care is still an object of debate is an equally good bellwether of the relative reluctance of Americans to share. The consequences do not really require a long commentary. No matter how bravely mayors fight against the forces driving inequality, their actions will have only limited effect if the federal tax code, to take the most obvious example, does not become more, not less, progressive.

The Freedom to Settle and Its Historical Antecedents

Finally, but not least, geography and history converged to give a special meaning to "freedom" in America. It is often forgotten that one of the motivations behind the American Revolution was to "free" America's westward-moving settlers from the constraints the Crown placed on westward expansion into Indian territory and previously French-held lands, embodied most notoriously in the infamous Quebec Act of 1774. This law reaffirmed the rights of the Catholic Church and the French language in the newly conquered interior, which many colonists saw as a direct attack on their God-given right to settle where they pleased. Adding insult to injury, the Act further strengthened the controls the Crown placed on settlement in Indian lands.

In a word, among the freedoms those first Americans sought was the freedom to settle where and when they pleased, unencumbered by the state. As usual, the contrast with Canada is instructive. The symbol of Canada's western settlement was the red-coated Mountie[4] overseeing what was a comparatively orderly affair (although many Native Canadians might not agree); at least when compared to America's appropriately named Wild West where the authority of the state was often weak, if present at all, and law enforcement a haphazard affair.

Enter geography. Things might have taken a different turn had not history also graciously provided the new American republic with a geography that allowed "freedom" to run free, so to speak. Had the new republic remained constrained within the borders of the original thirteen colonies, the perception of what "freedom" meant might have evolved quite differently. In the event, the lucky colonists inherited an entire continent in which they were free to roam and in which mobility was not only a right but also a virtue.[5] Luck and geography bequeathed their descendants a land blessed with a full range of climates and landscapes ranging from the Mediterranean climes of California, the tropical splendor of Florida, and the fertile plains of America's vast interior to the rugged Atlantic coast of New England. I mention these landscapes to bring home the singular economic space—immense and varied—within which America's cities would compete. All nations have varied geographies, but few on the scale of the United States, certainly not in the Western world.[6]

Geography also produced an evil legacy: plantation crops could be grown in the South, which meant that the new republic inherited a slave population with consequences for future relations between the races. The New Orleans story provided a vivid illustration of how mistrust between the races feeds urban failure. The combination of America's singular institutional legacies and its unparalleled diverse geography would produce the conditions that many decades later would allow all too many American cities to fail, the story to which we now turn,

Enter Industrialization and Urbanization

All the aforementioned legacies might have been of little consequence had the young nation continued to evolve as an agrarian Jeffersonian republic. Things started to turn sour when America's five institutional legacies collided with the twin transformation of industrialization and urbanization. The mix of fragmented metropolitan areas, locally financed people services, weak social welfare net, and not least race, produced a volatile cocktail. That cocktail would explode in the early 20th century as poor southern African Americans started to migrate to the industrializing cities of the North in need of labor. The movement slowed down during the Great Depression, only to take off at an even faster rate during the halcyon years of exploding urban growth following World War II. African Americans and poor immigrant populations tended to settle in central cities.

It is at this point that other policies kicked in, further spicing the cocktail: federally financed *intra*-urban highways, tax-deductible mortgage interest, and a generally car-friendly approach to urban transport, expressed in historically lower gas (petrol) prices, with crippled public transit the predictable end result. Central cities (municipalities) across America, Buffalo being but one example, sank into vicious self-reinforcing cycles of decline as better-off predominantly white populations fled to the suburbs taking their tax base with them. Another spice was thrown into the cocktail when manufacturing collapsed beginning in the 1980s. Blue-collar and black workers were the hardest hit, with only a rudimentary safety net. Those who could, generally the better educated, fled to friendlier climes and better opportunities, again taking their tax base and human capital with them, leaving impoverished cities behind. The rest of the story is well known and needs no further comment.

That populations chose to flee the failing cities is entirely normal. Workers moving from less to more productive cities is not necessarily a bad thing, but in America's institutional landscape, the freedom to move—both within and between cites—takes on a different meaning. Few Canadian or European cities, if any, find themselves in the unenviable position of a Buffalo or a similarly failing U.S. city. Consider, first, the lot of the central city (the City of Buffalo). Not only must it compete with places with more pleasant climates, but it must also compete with suburban municipalities. The town of Amherst, an example we met in Chapter 4, has better public services, better schooling, and perhaps also lower taxes. The urban region as a whole is in turn paying the price of a declining central city and downtown, foregoing the potential location rent centrality brings. If, in addition, the region has a cost disadvantage, as was the case in Buffalo, a legacy of its rusty industrial past, the challenge becomes almost insurmountable.

Great Failures, the Handmaiden
of Great Successes

The corollary of the exodus of tax resources, brains, and entrepreneurial talent from America's various Buffalos is their concentration in America's successful cities. We know the winners. Talent goes where talent is, for all the reasons subsumed under the heading of agglomeration economies. No other nation in the 20th and 21st centuries has engendered equivalent super concentrations of brains and talent. These unparalleled concentrations of brains, talent, and entrepreneurial flair—New York, San Francisco, and others—are in part the outcome not only of America's size, but also of an institutional environment that is admirably open to business, innovation, and the accumulation of wealth, the positive face of America's institutional legacy. America's singular virtues are no less real.

But it is the flipside of America's great urban achievement that interests us here. I am not the first person to comment on America's urban contradictions. In the introduction, we met Enrico Moretti, who uses the term *great divergence* to describe the increasing concentration of the best jobs in a select number of cities, and Richard Florida and his term *winner-take-all urbanism* to describe the dynamics behind America's urban divides.[7] I do not wish to return to a discussion of NIMBYs—Florida is correct in pointing to NIMBYism as a major culprit—if only to remind the reader that the prevention of NIMBYs necessarily means placing restrictions on bottom-up democracy.[8] However, fighting NIMBYism is only one part of the story.

It should be clear by now that the crux of America's urban dilemma is not the freedom to live where one chooses or even next to whom one chooses; but the powers and resources movers take with them and are willing or unwilling to share with others. The reforms required go beyond housing and restrictions on the freedom to block new construction, although these matter—which brings me to what I call the local temptation, the predictable sister of America's localist legacy.

The Local Temptation

Much of the prescriptive literature on what ails urban America points to *local* success stories: the success of such and such a city in providing affordable housing, improving community relations, introducing environmentally friendly transit or any number of worthy initiatives. I am full of admiration for, and humbled by, the commitment of community leaders, giving of their time and energy. I've been involved in community action myself (although not in the United States), working with mayors, local officials, and local activists. The Web is replete with sites that describe case studies on almost every imaginable issue.[9] These sites are inexhaustible wellsprings of ideas for everything from the design of safe bicycle paths to better methods of rubbish collection. All of this is necessary, and should certainly not be belittled.

Yet, as we have seen in city story after city story, the critical policies that allow citizens to live together productively and peacefully come from above. Only the state can redistribute income between the rich and the poor, that is, if the electorate so wishes. Only the state can ensure equal access to education and health across jurisdictions, financed by all taxpayers, again, if the electorate so wishes. Only the state can compel municipalities to share revenues or amalgamate, be it against the wishes of locals as we have seen. The mayor of New York, no matter how caring, will not out of the goodness of his heart voluntarily transfer a share of his rich tax pickings to neighboring Newark or to Jackson, Mississippi; that is, unless Washington forces him to do so.

True to America's localist roots, much of the current political discourse—both on the right and the left—points in the opposite direction, with calls for empowering communities. This recurrent theme among urban activists and scholars[10] is understandably popular with mayors and other elected officials. Moreover, "empowerment" and "community" have such a wonderfully positive ring that it is difficult not to be in favor. But more power, unless part of a meaningless slogan, also means more power to restrict and to exclude. Limits on the power to exclude can only come from above, which is the opposite of empowerment. An argument also sometimes invoked, more so since Donald Trump's election, is that more powers should be given cities because Washington is such a mess.[11] It is true that Washington in recent times has not presented a pretty picture, and that indeed is part of the problem. Similar reasoning is also sometimes heard in international development circles, a recurrent theme in the corridors of the World Bank when I worked there. The devolution of powers to cities was seen as an antidote to corrupt and venal Third World governments. As the reader will have understood by now, this is a happy illusion. If the top doesn't work, the rest won't work either.

Fixing Urban Failures

The inner-city ghettos, primarily but not solely African American, remain the most visible manifestations of America's urban failures. The prevention and/or elimination of ghettos requires a range of actions that go well beyond community action. A good safety net is a base condition, but it does not directly address the formation of ghettos. The story of Paris's Seine-Saint-Denis taught us that a generous welfare state and progressive income tax system are not *in themselves* sufficient conditions for preventing the emergence of ethnic-based ghettos. In Seine-Saint-Denis, the state made the mistake of allowing North Africans and black Africans to concentrate in specific neighborhoods, the soulless architecture of public housing projects an added punishment.

The challenge in a nutshell (a very large nutshell) before us is how to break up race-based concentrations of poverty, be it in East Side Buffalo, South Chicago, or any of the hundreds of inner-city ghettos across urban America. It may already be too late. Once ghettos are formed, turning back is almost impossible. Singapore and Vienna never let it happen, each by directly intervening in housing choices, Singapore is the most radical example. Had Singapore allowed poor Malay enclaves to develop, the history of that city-state would undoubtedly have been less peaceful. A Singapore-style policy of directing African Americans to majority-white neighborhoods is unthinkable in the United States and would in any case have only limited effect since publicly subsidized housing accounts for only a fraction of the housing market, not to mention the political costs of NIMBY opposition. Along similar lines, I sincerely doubt that a system of federally funded housing vouchers or housing tax credits targeting African Americans wishing to buy or rent in majority-white neighborhoods (or, alternatively, whites choosing to live in majority-African American neighborhoods) stands even a small chance of being considered, let alone enacted. Measures of this nature are at present simply not on the radar. The desegregation of American cities, if it is ever to come, will not be done tomorrow.

Let us consider another policy: a federally initiated political agenda to bring African American education and income levels up to that of the majority. A lesson from the Montreal story was that social peace will remain fragile unless the initially disadvantaged group is brought up to the level of the privileged group, all of which entails public investments in education and the promotion of job opportunities for the less favored group. Quebec's language laws openly discriminated in favor of French, with the avowed aim of bringing the initially socially devalued language up to the level of English. The good news is that it worked: the income disparity between the two language groups has been erased. True, one cannot compare the initial lower social status of Quebec's Francophones to that of African Americans; which simply tells us that any equivalent U.S. federal initiative would need to be even more far reaching. The message is nonetheless crystal clear. Bringing a historically underprivileged population up to the level of the majority means taxation from above and a transfer of resources.

Paths Not Traveled (Opportunities Lost)

Let me now propose a little exercise in historical science fiction to illustrate the consequences of national leadership or its lack. Let us imagine that in the years following the American Civil War President Andrew Johnson and his successors, rather than opting for reconciliation with the South and accommodation with the defeated white Southern elites, had proposed a great national crusade to uplift and integrate the ex-slaves into the national fabric. The two cornerstones of this great crusade were: (1) massive investments in the education of Negro youth to bring them up to the level of the white majority; and (2) the resettlement of America's newly acquired citizens across the nation from Maine to California. The second part of the crusade would be predictably unpopular outside the South. But the president explained that resettlement was essential not only to incorporate our new citizens into the nation, but also to address the fears of Southern whites in states like South Carolina and Mississippi, which at the time had black majorities. In the new integrated America, African Americans would be present across the land, ideally in proportions close to the national average, with each (non-southern) state taking its share. As urbanization accelerated in the late 19th century, successive federal governments would also encourage states and local governments to adopt housing and zoning policies that ensured a balanced spatial distribution of black Americans in America's growing cities, a philosophy Washington would continue to enforce well into the

20th century. Subsequent presidents would also introduce a Canadian-style equalization program to ensure a reasonably equal delivery of people services across the fifty states.

Let me come back down to earth. The above scenario of course never happened; and that precisely is the point. Looking at America's political landscape in this first quarter of the 21st century, nothing of this nature appears likely. I see little evidence that the fundamental drivers of inequality in urban America—both within and between cities—are about to disappear. The spatial sorting of the American population will continue; which now brings me to the political face of urban failure. The direction of causality goes both ways.

Urban Failure Feeds Political Polarization
(and the Other Way Around)

National policies and institutions are in the end beholden to national electorates, at least in democratic societies. Voter perceptions, fears, and preferences do not spring up in a vacuum. The ideological polarization of American politics is no accident. Spatial divides beget political divides. The results of the November 2016 presidential election for the state of New York provide a harsh illustration. The county with the highest share of votes (72 percent) for Donald J. Trump was the suburban Buffalo county of Wyoming, compared to 9.7 percent in New York County (Manhattan). It is difficult to imagine a shaper political divide.

It is difficult not to conclude that such observed spatial and political divides are in part self-reinforcing, each driving the other. I cannot help but ponder that a different urban America would have produced a different political landscape. The economic failure, administrative dysfunction, and social divisions of Greater Buffalo and similar urban regions across the land were not inevitable.

Leadership

All of this discussion of opportunities lost or opportunities not seized inevitably sends us back to the subject of leadership, which is the most volatile attribute of all. The role of national leaders in shaping the destiny of cities goes beyond budgets and legislation. National leaders set the tone of political discourse. A charismatic leader can change the course of the nation. The discourse heard from above, and not only by the president (or prime minster in other settings), molds the national mood, defining what is acceptable and what is not.

As the reader will surely have guessed, my thoughts on the impact of leadership inevitably lead to Donald J. Trump and the possible consequences of his presidency for urban America. It's not so much his persona that matters, although it is impossible to ignore, as are the political doors he is opening and closing. I do not wish to exaggerate the impact of a single man; perhaps Trump's presidency will be no more than a momentary bump in America's history. Yet, it is difficult to discount the power of the signals he and his administration are sending.

Two examples among many will suffice for our purposes here: (1) the compressive tax bill passed by Congress in December 2017, which was the most sweeping tax legislation in recent decades—greater income equality was manifestly not its objective; and (2) new directives by the Department of Justice reducing its role in overseeing municipal government and enforcing civil rights legislation—greater racial harmony was manifestly not the objective. [12] I could also mention the president's restrictive immigration regulations, his protectionist proclivities, and his evident displeasure with the independence of the Federal Reserve Bank. Over the long run, if maintained, the consequences for the ability of America's cities to create wealth and provide livable urban environments is not difficult to divine. Buenos Aires provided a sad lesson in this regard. It took four decades of nationalist economic mismanaging to bring that great metropolis down to the level of a Third World city. A similar fate for New York City is unlikely. But, Buenos Aires is no less a reminder of national governments' potential for damage. And then there is trust, the glue that allows democracies to function. Port au Prince provided an extreme example of what happens when trust breaks down. I'm certainly not suggesting that a similar fate awaits America; I only seek to point out that confidence in institutions cannot be compartmentalized. If trust is lacking at the top, the effects will inevitably trickle down. A socially cohesive city in a divided nation is an oxymoron.

Let me go down one notch to state governments. I see no movement to tear down municipal walls. What is the probability that the State of New York will take the Canadian route and impose a revenue-sharing regime on the Greater Buffalo area? Probably not good in a political universe in which suburban electorates continue to weigh heavily in state and national elections. Greater Portland and Minneapolis-St. Paul are likely to remain noble exceptions in a sea of fragmented metropolitan areas.

How then should we view the future? Barring a revolution in values, America's urban journey will continue to be a tale with two faces, stories of both unparalleled achievement and dismal failure. The great cities of America will continue to draw in talent from around the nation and hopefully from around the world. New York's Upper East Side will continue to be the overpriced reserve of the rich and famous. Manhattan's archipelago of cool neighborhoods will continue to attract techno geeks and budding artists. Rich bankers will continue to flock to Wall Street. At the other end of the continent, Santa Monica and West Hollywood will continue to give Manhattan's cool neighborhoods a run for their money; San Francisco's Ashbury Heights will continue to be one the most coveted and priciest neighborhoods on the planet. This supremely successful urban America is the America most tourists will see. The majority of Americans will continue to live in generally pleasant places and neighborhoods with a standard of living befitting that of rich developed nation. Most will never see an inner-city ghetto.

Yet, the forces driving the darker side of America's urban successes will remain just as real. Less fortunate Americans, many of them black but not only blacks, will continue to be trapped in poverty-perpetuating neighborhoods, and many central cities will continue to be trapped in fiscal/political straightjackets. The sorting of the American population and electorate will continue unabated, both between cities and between neighborhoods,

I hope I'm wrong. As we have seen elsewhere in this book, societies can and do change. There is nothing inevitable about this projected outcome.

* * *

The lessons for other nations from the American experience do not require a long explanation. Where the appropriate institutions are in place to promote economic growth, cities can become powerful engines of wealth. In this regard, America has been supremely successful. Cities are also real places where different people must learn to live together and choose, at least in free societies, to use the wealth thus created wisely to build livable cities for all. In this, America has lamentably failed in all too many places. Managing the two was never going to be easy. America's missed opportunities are a warning to the wealthy urbanizing societies of tomorrow. If the appropriate institutions are not put in place to ensure that the wealth created in cities benefits all, then cities will fail in their mission to provide a decent quality of life for all or at least for the great majority.

Notes

Acknowledgments

1. *Institut National de la Recherche Scientifique,* a graduate school and research institute, part of the University of Quebec system.

Introduction

1. The classic reference is Jane Jacobs, *Cities and the Wealth of Nations: Principles of Economic Life* (1984). Jacobs is arguably the godmother of popular urban economics. She was a city planner, not an economist. Her work remains controversial among professional economists.
2. As we shall discover, technological change is often a prime culprit in explaining why some cities have fallen on bad times.
3. The subject of social cohesion has long interested me. In 2000, I coedited a book, *The Social Sustainability of Cities,* the product of a UNESCO-funded project covering ten cities in four continents (Polèse and Stren 2000).
4. The field of inquiry in which I work has several labels: urban and regional economics; economic geography; regional science; urban planning; urban and regional studies. My degrees, in that order, are, respectively, in economics, regional science, and city planning.
5. Polèse (2009a).
6. A recent overview of the scholarly literature on urban growth by Gilles Duranton and Diego Puga, though excellent, is almost entirely devoted to American cities (Duranton and Puga 2014). A rare exception is Ketterer and Rodriguez-Pose (2018), which looks at European urban regions and includes institutional variables.
7. The recent book by Moretti (2013) is another example, but again for U.S. urban regions.
8. See, for example, Dubé and Polèse (2015) and Shearmur and Polèse (2007).
9. Duranton and Puga (2014).
10. It is perhaps no coincidence that America's two great urban gurus, Jane Jacobs and Richard Florida, both moved to Canada from the United States—to Toronto—looking in from the outside so to speak. This undoubtedly influenced their later thinking. I must admit to a similar bias, though I moved to Montreal.
11. During my career, I have had the privilege of acting as an adviser to two Montreal mayors and working with numerous local officials across Canada.
12. The classic example of the genre is Sir Peter Hall's magnificent opus, *Cities in Civilization,* which moves from ancient Athens to Hollywood (Hall 1999). A more

recent book is Michael Storper's *Keys to the City*, which looks at institutions but focuses almost exclusively on great cities such as New York, Paris, London, and Los Angeles (Storper 2013).

13. Agglomeration economies in the simplest terms refer to the benefits for firms of locating in cities—the greater the concentration the better. This is a central concept in urban economics, about which more will be said in Chapter 2.

14. Krugman (1996).

15. Black and Henderson (1999, 327).

16. See, for example, Eeckhout (2004) and Gabaix (1999).

17. Books cited earlier (Hall 1999, Jacobs 1984, and Storper 2013) are all examples of titles where the word *city* is employed generically.

18. Glaeser (2011); Hall (1999).

19. Duranton and Puga (2014).

20. A rapid glance at the Bibliography should convince the reader. Glaeser, alone or with others, is referenced more than a dozen times, starting with Glaeser, Scheinkman, and Shleifer (1995), his seminal study. This work first established the strong statistical link between initial human capital endowments and subsequent growth.

Chapter 1

1. American poet, writer, and creator/host of the popular public radio show "A Prairie Home Companion." Cited in: https://www.nytimes.com/2016/07/04/arts/garrison-keillor-turns-out-the-lights-on-lake-wobegon.html?smprod=nytcore-iphone&smid=nytcore-iphone-share&_r=2.

2. We shall meet Aunt Sylvia again in Chapter 3 when we visit Los Angeles. Sylvia would move to Los Angeles in the 1960s, changing husbands again.

3. My telling of New York's resurgence will be brief for the story has been well told elsewhere: see Glaeser (2005, 2011) and Glaeser and Ponzetto (2010).

4. According to 2010 U.S. Census figures, the City of New York had a population of 8.2 million, accounting for some 43 percent of the metropolitan area. The equivalent figures for the next two largest metro areas are 3.8 million and 30 percent (Los Angeles) and 2.7 million and 29 percent (Chicago).

5. How New York established its position as the nation's primary central place is discussed in Chapter 7 where we tell the story of the Erie Canal.

6. Because of the dual nature of the Hapsburg Empire, the situation was in reality less straightforward; tax revenues were split between Vienna (Imperial Austria) and Budapest (Hungary).

7. The United States was one of the victorious powers, but de facto only a minor player at the ensuing peace treaties, in part because of President Wilson's infirmity and Congress's reluctance to follow his lead.

8. In terms of geopolitics, Germany's annexation of Austria became possible when Mussolini's Italy became Hitler's ally, thus abandoning Italy's role as Austria's erstwhile protector.

9. Why the Soviets allowed the re-creation of a unified Austria is a subject of some debate among historians. The Soviet leadership, it is reasonable to assume, saw the creation of a neutral buffer state in the middle of Europe as being in its interest. Austrian politicians nonetheless cleverly seized the opportunity, following Stalin's death, to open negotiations with the Soviets.

10. The fact that Figl had spent a good part of the war in a Nazi concentration camp helped, giving him the necessary moral authority in the eyes of his Soviet counterparts.

11. Source: History of Jews in Vienna: http://en.wikipedia.org/wiki/History_of_the_ Jews_in_Vienna

12. Source: *The Medical School of Vienna: http://en.m.wikipedia.org/wiki/Medical_ University_of_Vienna*

13. Source: Vienna: http://en.m.wikipedia.org/wiki/Vienna

14. Estimates taking cost of living into account put Vienna's GDP per capita at between 80 and 90 percent of the New York average. Comparative GDP results vary from year to year due to fluctuations in the value of the U.S. dollar and the euro. Estimates also vary by source.

15. Goldstein et al. (2013) find a weak ecosystem in Vienna for supporting start-ups, among which is a conservative university ethos that discourages entrepreneurship.

16. Berlin is also a low-cost city, for the same reason. But Berlin, which was almost totally destroyed in World War II, cannot offer the same imperial architecture. Source: 2015 Cost of Living Rankings: http://www.mercer.com/newsroom/cost-of-living-survey.html

17. Age group 25–64, data for 2014. Source: European Union Open Data Portal: http:// open-data.europa.eu/data/dataset/ICx9d4O6LSBwNm63BiZg

18. University rankings are notoriously fickle. The source used here is the Shanghai academic ranking, generally recognized as among the most rigorous, emphasizing research excellence. Source: Academic Ranking of World Universities: https://www. google.ca/?gws_rd=ssl#q=university+rankings+shanghai

19. Source: Mayerhofer et al. (2010).

20. I owe a debt of thanks to Peter Mayerhofer of the Austrian Institute of Economic Research (WIFO) for many of the insights presented here.

21. Precise figures have little meaning because of the inherent unreliability of data for very poor nations like Haiti. My calculations from different sources suggest that GDP per capita in Port au Prince (2015 data) was around $1000, compared to $50,000 for Vienna. However, when cost of living is factored in (purchasing power parity: PPP), Port au Prince's GPP per capita increases to $1500, which is still a ratio of thirty to one.

22. I am not the first to point to "trust" as one of the fundamental underpinnings of prosperous societies. See Fukuyama (1995). The concept of social capital is part of the same family of explanations.

23. I recognize the controversial nature of what I am about to write. A white person should not comment on conflicts within the black community. My alma mater, City College in New York, is located on the fringes of Harlem. One day, walking back

from class, I witnessed two black men arguing vehemently. The words exchanged were an education in self-hatred for which I was unprepared: "you f . . . nigger, you blacker than me." This altercation helped me later recognize the terrible internal hatreds dividing Haitian society. Like many naïve outsiders, I thought that all Haitians were brothers bound by a common suffering and racial solidarity: wrong. This proud nation, the first to defeat slavery, is also among the most racist I know, a sad irony.

24. *Banlieue* is the French term for suburb. It has come to take on a negative connotation in France where the poorest and most violent neighborhoods tend to be concentrated in the suburbs in high-rise housing projects (*Cités*), which are discussed at length in chapter 8.

25. The military dictatorship of General Jorge Rafael Videla (1976–1983) waged a relentless campaign against left-wing urban guerrillas and camp followers resulting in thirty thousand deaths through disappearance and torture. To this day, mothers still demonstrate in front of the presidential palace asking for information on their disappeared sons and daughters.

26. My father was a partner in a Vienna-based travel agency with offices in both cities. My father ran the Paris office. The agency's most lucrative contract was with the American Medical Association. It accompanied American physicians across Europe with required stopovers in Paris (of course) and Vienna, which was still Europe's leading center for medical research. The agency went bankrupt during the Great Depression.

27. Precise figures for cities are difficult to come by. Using country data as substitutes and taking Argentina as the benchmark (Argentina = 100), we find that the equivalent GDP per capita index in 1929 was 85 for Austria, 108 for France, and 158 for the United States. Source: Maddison (2015).

28. Uruguay, also overwhelmingly settled by Europeans, is an exception. But Uruguay, with all due respect for its people, is culturally an extension of Argentina. Montevideo, its capital, lies across the river from B.A. with a tango scene just as vibrant, and some would argue even more so.

29. Again, using country data as a substitute, Mexico's GDP per capita was less than half that of Argentina's in 1929.

30. Source: http://en.wikipedia.org/wiki/List_of_countries_by_GDP_(nominal)_per_capita

31. Source: https://www.numbeo.com/crime/rankings.jsp

32. Source: The 250 Top Universities in Latin America 2015: http://www.topuniversities.com/latin-american-rankings

33. According to transparency international (2015 data), Chile is the least corrupt nation in the region: 5.3 percent of those surveyed said they had been victims of corruption compared to 16.8 percent in Argentina. The figure is 6.7 percent for neighboring Uruguay, the second least corrupt nation. Source: https://www.transparency.org/country/

34. An image sticks in my mind: Cristina, dressed in black, in B.A.'s metropolitan cathedral methodically thumping her chest as tearful crowds by the thousands waited in

line outside for hours, even days. President Néstor Kirchner was obviously popular, but the outbursts of emotion witnessed during those days seemed, to me at least, excessive and theatrical. But then, I'm not Argentinian.

35. For a romanticized view of Eva Perón's life, the 1996 film *Evita*, starring Madonna, is a good place to start. The words of the title song "Don't cry for me Argentina" nicely convey the epic drama of the Perón saga. Evita died of cancer at the age of thirty-three in front, literally, of her adoring followers.

36. This is not entirely correct. Similar populist left-wing rhetoric has held sway from time to time in other Latin American nations, with often an added anti-American touch. Evo Morales's Bolivia and Hugo Chávez's Venezuela are examples. However, in no nation has the movement taken on the quasi-religious fervor of Peronism and been able to keep it alive over more than half a century.

37. The Global Financial Centres Index (2014) ranks Johannesburg in thirty-second place and Mexico City in fifty-sixth place. Buenos Aires fails to make the list. Source: http://en.wikipedia.org/wiki/Global_Financial_Centres_Index

38. The same ranking puts Zurich in sixth place, following Tokyo.

39. *Economist* (2015).

40. A classic of the genre is Eduardo Galeano's *Open Veins of Latin America: Five Centuries of the Pillage of a Continent*, first published in 1971.

41. Campante and Glaeser (2009) compare Buenos Aires to Chicago. However, Chicago in the 1920s was a considerably richer city than either Montreal or Buenos Aires. Campante and Glaeser (2009) put great emphasis on Buenos Aires' lower initial endowment of human capital compared to Chicago, as measured by schooling and literacy rates. Although precise data are not available, Montreal's educational level in the 1920s was most probably closer to that of Buenos Aires due to the historically lower educational level of French Canadians.

42. Using national data as substitutes, Argentina's GDP per capita in 1929 was close to 90 percent that of Canada's. Source: Maddison (2015).

43. Emblematic corporations of the time were the Hudson's Bay Company, Canadian Pacific Railways, and the Bank of Montreal, the first two initially chartered in London. All three were heavily involved in the colonization of the Canadian West.

44. The Argentine railways system, until nationalized by Perón in the 1950s, was largely British financed and controlled.

45. A classic document of that period is the so-called Watkins Report, *Foreign Ownership and the Structure of Canadian Industry*, tabled in the House of Commons in 1968, which would eventually lead to the creation of the Foreign Investment Review Agency (FIRA) in 1974.

46. Source: Maddison (2015).

47. No Argentine company appears on the 2015 Fortune Global 500 list. Ten Canadian companies are listed, four of which are headquartered in Montreal. Source: http://fortune.com/global500/royal-dutch-shell-2

48. Donald Trump, although he may not realize it, has been surprisingly true to the populist playbook. In October 2018, President Trump expressed his displeasure at the Federal Reserve's decision to raise interest rates. Trump obviously would

have preferred a less independent central bank. As for the president's protectionist agenda and visible tolerance of budget deficits, I shall let readers draw their own conclusions.

Chapter 2

1. Gross domestic product.
2. "Real" in economics or finance refers to increases adjusted for inflation. Thus, if prices also double when GDP per capita doubles, the real increase in GDP per capita is zero.
3. Glaeser (2011).
4. Jacobs (1984).
5. Ibid., 151–154. The complete quote is given below under the heading "What Jane Jacobs Missed."
6. Sir Peter Hall's magnificent opus remains the most exhaustive investigation of the role of cities as fountainheads of culture, innovation, and technological progress (Hall 1999).
7. For readers wishing more technical references, I suggest Fujita and Thisse (2013) and Glaeser (2010). For a less technical explanation of agglomeration economies, see Polèse (2009).
8. Porter (1998).
9. Fujita and Thisse (2013), Glaeser (2010), Rosenthal and Strange (2001).
10. Source for city GDP data: https://en.m.wikipedia.org/wiki/List_of_cities_by_GDP. The advantage of this source is that it gives several GDP estimates for each metropolitan area. In each case, I have taken the average. Population data are drawn from standard sources.
11. The ratio of average GDP per capita for the nation's largest city to that of the nation, invariably above 1.0, is a fairly stable relationship. See Polèse (2009: Table 2.1) for a more complete listing of cities and nations.
12. Freire and Polèse (2003). The other three cities surveyed were San José, Costa Rica; San Salvador, El Salvador; and Belo Horizonte, Brazil. For an extensive presentation (in Spanish) of each city case study, see Freire et al. (2004).
13. *Secuestros* in Spanish—a constant fear among wealthy businessmen or anyone else suspected of having money, including return migrants from the United States and Canada.
14. Cabral et al. (2016) specifically note the impact of violence on public expenditures in Mexico.
15. Source: https://en.wikipedia.org/wiki/Programme_for_International_Student_Assessment#Results
16. *Universidad Nacional Autónoma de México*
17. Source: http://www.shanghairanking.com
18. Source: https://en.wikipedia.org/wiki/List_of_countries_by_tax_revenue_as_percentage_of_GDP

19. Among the authors who have influenced my thinking on the subject are Barro and Sala-i-Martin (1995), Denison (1985), Easterly (2002), Fukuyama (1995), Landes (1998), and Kuznets (1968).

20. A good simple source, accessible on the Web, is Montagna (1981).

21. The lesson is not only historical. Bessen (2015), looking at the modern textile industry, notes the slow cumulative process, often on the factory floor, of building up knowledge and raising productivity.

22. Montagna (1981).

23. First published in German in 1905; the first English translation came out in 1930 (Weber 1930).

24. France and Belgium also rapidly industrialized after England. Both were largely Catholic, which would tend to belie Weber's thesis, not to mention northern Italy and the Catholic regions of Germany. However, the Reformation also left its imprint on Catholic Europe, most notably societies geographically and culturally closest to those that converted to Protestantism.

25. Various economic historians such as David Landes (1998) and Angus Maddison (2015) have attempted to measure long-term increases in production since the Industrial Revolution. The results are necessarily estimates.

26. See Polèse (2005); Brülhart and Sbergami (2009); Fay and Opal (2000).

27. This is how Denison (1985) measures the contribution of urbanization to U.S. income growth. Depending on the time period, Denison attributes between 5 and 10 percent of U.S. income growth to the reallocation of labor from the land to cities.

28. Both Henderson (2003) and Duranton and Puga (2014) agree: the evidence for *dynamic* agglomeration economies is weak. Camagni et al. (2016) argue that certain agglomeration attributes have dynamic effects in European cities, but nonetheless confirm yet again the absence of a positive relationship between initial size and growth.

29. Jacobs (1984, 154–155).

30. Falk (2006).

31. This is a version of the OECD Oslo Manual definition of innovation. http://www.oecd.org/science/inno/2367580.pdf

32. The invention of the telephone is a long story that involves numerous actors. However, Bell, who immigrated to Canada from Scotland, succeeded in obtaining the first U.S. patent for this new contraption.

33. For an excellent overview of the debate on cities and innovation, see Shearmur (2012). Many of the arguments in the following paragraphs are drawn from Shearmur's work. See also Shearmur (2011a, 2011b, 2012) and Shearmur and Bonnet (2011).

34. Bettencourt et al. (2007), Sedgley and Elmslie (2011).

35. Duranton and Puga (2001) present powerful arguments to support their hypothesis, empirically supported by French data. However, their analysis does not directly look at innovation but rather at industries.

36. Shearmur (2012).

37. MacPherson (1997).

38. The concept of economic base refers to industries (goods or services) whose products are exported outside the region, allowing the region to earn income. The percentages cited here are based on the author's calculations using Statistics Canada data on employment by industry.

39. For an excellent explication of the economic rationale for different-sized cities, see Henderson (1997).

Chapter 3

1. See https://en.m.wikipedia.org/wiki/Home_mortgage_interest_deduction

2. The tax reform bill passed by Congress in 2017 reduced the value of the Mortgage Interest Tax Deduction. The main change is the maximum value of mortgage debt for which interest can be deducted, lowered from one million to 750,000 dollars.

3. Paris was a notable exception for a time, with a submerged highway along the banks of the Seine leading into the inner city. It has since been closed, replaced in some parts by a walkable embankment.

4. Jaffe (2013).

5. Schrag (2017).

6. Actually, the first pro-transit legislation was passed in 1964 (the Urban Mass Transportation Act), but this called for a fifty–fifty sharing of capital costs, beyond the means of many local authorities.

7. Glaeser (2007) and https://en.wikipedia.org/wiki/Buffalo_Metro_Rail

8. Exact comparisons of modal shares are difficult to come by, in part due to definitional problems. Data sometimes refer to cities (municipalities) and sometimes to urban regions, without necessarily being clearly stated. The reader may wish to consult the following sites: http://www.uitp.org/MCD; http://www.epomm.eu/tems/cities.phtml; https://en.wikipedia.org/wiki/Modal_share#Cities_with_over_1.2C000.2C000_inhabitants

9. I shall not give any figures because results differ for median and average income (or using GDP per capita). The point is this: the Boston and San Francisco urban areas are systematically among the top on different measures of wealth.

10. Fee and Hartley (2012). The study was for the years 1980–2010.

11. Cushman & Wakefield publishes yearly data on local office markets around the world. The data cited here are for 2016 (http://www.cushmanwakefield.ca). The CBD/Suburb ratios are similar in Los Angeles and Montreal.

12. This statement applies to local governments that draw a significant share of their revenues from property taxes, which is the case in most of North America.

13. Jacobs (1961).

14. Jane Jacobs's hometown was actually Scranton, Pennsylvania. Jacobs moved to Greenwich Village in 1935 at the age of nineteen.

15. For more on Manhattan's Silicon Alley, see Indergaard (2003, 2009) and Wortham (2010).

16. For references on London's Silicon Roundabout and New Economy districts in Canada and elsewhere, see Biddulph (2012), Duvivier and Polèse (2018), Foord (2013), Hutton (2004), and Wainright (2012). Hutton (2016) provides an excellent overview of the rise of New Economy districts in several cities.

17. Inner London = former London County, the historical core. Central Montreal = the Borough of Ville-Marie.

18. Ehrenhalt (2012).

19. Glaeser and Gottlieb (2006).

20. Katz and Wagner (2014).

21. Duvivier and Polèse (2018).

22. Indergaard (2013).

23. SoMa, abbreviation for South of Market Street, recalling Manhattan's alphabet soup of neighborhoods. For references on San Francisco's challenge to Silicon Valley, see also Cortright (2016) and Weinberg (2015).

24. On Google Buses, see De Konnick (2014), Nieva (2014), and Opillard (2015).

25. That falling communication costs facilitate spatial concentration is a basic axiom of urban economics.

26. Construction costs were estimated in the 1990s at $250 per mile, for a total cost close to $5 billion, about double in today's dollars.

27. Source: http://www.citymetric.com/transport/los-angeles-metro-great-so-why-aren-t-people-using-it-2742

28. Other sources put the ratio even higher. Measuring subway ridership is not an exact science because properly counting transfers is a major problem. Wikipedia puts New York's subway ridership, calculated on an annual basis, at thirty-five times that of Los Angeles. https://en.wikipedia.org/wiki/List_of_metro_systems#List

29. Cushman & Wakefield defines this area as West Los Angeles: http://www.cushmanwakefield.com/~/media/marketbeat/2017/01/Greater_LA_Americas_MarketBeat_Office_Q42016.pdf?_ga=1.188040107.220406630.1487429156

30. University of California at Los Angeles.

31. For maps of New Economy start-ups in Los Angeles, see: http://m.builtinla.com/2016/08/08/highest-funded-startup-neighborhoods-la; http://represent.la/

32. Elsewhere, my colleague Richard Stren and I coined the term *social sustainability*, which essentially captures the same notion (Polèse and Stren 2000).

33. Acs et al. (2017) and Glaeser et al. (2008).

34. Glaeser et al. (2008).

35. Acs et al. (2017) and Glaeser et al. (2008).

36. Mercer's Quality of Living Index is not without its failings, as are all such ranking exercises, but it is among the most rigorous, comprising thirty-nine indicators, including crime statistics: https://en.wikipedia.org/wiki/Mercer_Quality_of_Living_Survey

37. Glaeser et al. (2008).

38. Thus, the Quebec City urban region (population seven hundred fifty thousand) has a more equal income distribution across households than the Toronto urban region (population: six million).
39. The heart of the German neighborhood, also known as Yorkville, was East 86th Street called (*Der Deutsche Broadway*: The German Broadway), replete with German-language movie theaters, book shops, and restaurants.
40. Source: *Economist* (2013).
41. In authoritarian regimes, one could add the politically privileged, party members, and other friends of the regime.
42. Cheng (2017).
43. For my comments on Singapore, I am grateful to Professor Sarah Moser, Geography Department, McGill University, a recognized authority on the history of interethnic relations in the island state.
44. The bloodiest massacres occurred in 1965–1966 on the island of Java. Estimates put the total deaths between half a million and a million. Later, in May 1998, anti-ethnic Chinese riots broke out in several Indonesian cities.
45. Not In My Backyard.
46. Florida (2017).
47. Eligon et al. (2017).
48. Ibid.
49. Ibid.
50. I do not know what finally happened to the proposed legislation.
51. Einstein et al. (2018). The authors analyze planning and zoning board meetings in the Boston area, finding that participants, more often than not, tended to oppose new construction.
52. Vogel and Imbroscio (2013).
53. See Kantor et al. (2012) for a description of the regional governance structures of New York, London, Paris, and Tokyo.
54. Kauder (2015).
55. The recently published interactive *Opportunity Atlas* allows the reader to visualize the social divides for America's major metropolitan areas: https://opportunityatlas.org
56. Vienna underwent various boundary changes after World War I, notably during the Nazi period (1938–1945), but the boundaries that define Vienna are not very different today from those of a century ago.
57. For an in-depth description of the Austrian system of housing finance, see Amman and Mundt (2017). For housing prices, see Wolf (2013).
58. For a detailed analysis of Vienna's policy on immigration, see Eurofound (2009).
59. I do not wish to resurrect old ghosts, but it is sobering to recall that it was "mongrel" pre-World War I Vienna, a city where true Germans were forced to live with Slavs, Magyars, Jews, and other lesser peoples, that so shocked a youth from the provincial town of Braunau, setting him on his course to found a political movement dedicated to cleansing Vienna of its mongrel elements. In this, we sadly know, that the young Hitler would be successful.

Chapter 4

1. The Buffalo story, though admittedly not a joyous one, is dedicated to my good friend Keith Crandall, a true Buffalonian, who died at the much too young age of sixty-one on December 5, 2005. Besides great fun, Keith was an entrepreneur: he was founder and CEO of a machine manufacturing company that made equipment for securely filling industrial containers.
2. Urban area definitions: Metropolitan Statistical Area (MSA) for Buffalo and Census Metropolitan Area (CMA) for Toronto. Official Census sources in both cases.
3. Sources: Crandall (2002) for Buffalo; Canadian Census for 1951 Toronto.
4. For a blow-by-blow account of Buffalo's rise and fall, I highly recommend Goldman (1984).
5. Officially called the Buffalo Fiscal Stability Authority (BFSA) established in 2003 by the New York State Legislature. For additional information, see ONYSC (2014).
6. Erie County is part of the Buffalo-Niagara Falls MSA, which also includes Niagara County. The 2010 census gave its population as 919,040 out of 1,135,509 for the MSA.
7. Thomas (2014): Turning point 3.
8. *Britannica* (1911).
9. *Britannica* (1960: Vol. 4, 341).
10. For an excellent portrait of Buffalo at the turn of the 20th century, at the height of its glory, I recommend Lauren Belfer's historical novel *The City of Light* (Belfer 2000).
11. Cited by Thomas (2014): Turning point 3.
12. Crandall (2002).
13. Thomas (2014): Turning Point 2: Work of Art.
14. Goldman (2007, 270).
15. For much that follows, my main sources are Dillaway (2006), Goldman (1983, 2007), and Thomas (2014). To avoid overcrowding the text with footnotes, references are limited to specifically attributed statements.
16. Goldman (1983, 216 ff.).
17. Goldman (1983, 218), it is worthwhile noting, explicitly uses the word *centrality*.
18. As consultant for the Quebec government in the 1970s, I did a study on the economic consequences of the St. Lawrence Seaway. I have also drawn on Macfarlane (2010), who gives a blow-by-blow account of the creation of the Seaway.
19. Thomas (2014): Turning point 3.
20. The lack of foresight and planning of Buffalo's economic elites at the time is a recurrent theme in Dillaway (2006), Goldman (1983), and Thomas (2014).
21. Thomas (2014): Turning point 3.
22. Crandall (2002).
23. Dillaway (2006, 35).
24. For the year 1997, the average hourly manufacturing wage was $17.48 in Buffalo compared, respectively, to $13.90 and $13.99 for New York State and the United States. Crandall (2002, Table 9).
25. Crandall (2002).
26. Dillaway (2006, 33).

27. To Bethlehem Steel's credit, most retired with full pensions.
28. Dillaway (2006, 116).
29. Crandall (2002, Table 3).
30. Ibid. (Table 8).
31. Dillaway (2006, 115).
32. So-called right-to-work laws refer to legislation that restricts the use of union–employer agreements that impose obligatory union membership and payment of union dues as conditions of employment (often called "closed shops").
33. The relationship with southern Ontario was much helped by the 1965 U.S.–Canada auto pact, followed some years later by the North American Free Trade Agreement (NAFTA), signed in 1989 between the United States and Canada, and three years later by Mexico.
34. Polèse (2009, 18–23).
35. Polèse and Shearmur (2006).
36. Goldman (1984, 275 ff.; 2007, 310 ff.).
37. Goldman (2007, 311).
38. Taking 1990 as a benchmark, we see that census data put the Buffalo metropolitan area (MSA) in thirty-third place among the forty largest MSAs (population over one million) for the share of the population with a college degree. Detroit, Cleveland, Pittsburgh, Milwaukee, and St. Louis also exhibit below-average shares. Source: 1990 U.S. Census.
39. Eckhart (1979).
40. Goldman (2007, 352).
41. See, notably, Dillaway (2006), Goldman (1984, 2007), and Thomas (2014).
42. Thomas and Smith (2009, 111).
43. Thomas (2014): Turning Point 4.
44. Two examples: The Greater Buffalo Development Corporation of the 1960s and 1970s, a nonprofit organization; 1980s Western New York State Economic Development Corporation, a state-sponsored initiative.
45. Dillaway (2006, 108–111) cites the 1972 study "A Growth Strategy for the Erie-Niagara Area," in which the authors employ all the tools of economic analysis of the time, including an input–output table of the regional economy.
46. Dillaway (2006, 65).
47. In New York, a share of local sales taxes (value-added taxes: VAT) also enters into local revenues. New York City is special in having an income tax.
48. Source: ONYSC (2014).
49. Sources: U.S. Census Bureau (2016) and Buffalo Demographics (2016). The non-white total includes Hispanics.
50. Thomas (2014a).
51. Goldman (2007, 363).
52. My telling of the University of Buffalo saga draws heavily on Goldman (1984) and Dillaway (2006), respectively, pages 248–252 and 66–72. Any factual errors are of course my own.
53. Dillaway (2006, 70).

54. Ibid. (69).
55. Ibid. (98).
56. Goldman (1983, 251).
57. Ibid. (251–252).
58. Cited in Thomas and Smith (2009, 25).
59. Tucker (2015), citing Joseph Henchman of the Tax Foundation.
60. For an in- depth analysis of western New York State's plight, see Thomas and Smith (2009).
61. ONYSC (2014) refers to the 2012 city budget.
62. For a critical assessment of state and federal programs, see Glaeser (2007) and Renn (2015).
63. Quoted in Winsa (2014).
64. A GM plant near Montreal is an exception, but it has since closed.
65. Most French Quebecers would, of course, argue that the new government's policies to promote French were not mistakes. As we shall see in Chapter 6, those policies also had positive consequences.
66. In the eventuality of Quebec's separation from Canada, the Bank of Montreal was already toying with a name change to *First Canadian*. The office tower housing the Bank of Montreal's offices in Toronto was appropriately called First Canadian Place. Although now a Toronto-based bank, it has kept its original name.
67. Depending on the criteria used and source consulted, Chicago sometimes comes ahead of Toronto.
68. The 2011 Canadian reported that foreign-born accounted 46 percent of metropolitan Toronto's population.
69. *The Globe and Mail* and *National Post* are two examples.
70. This is not entirely true. Vancouver's Downtown Eastside and Winnipeg's North End neighborhood have sometimes been compared to ghettos. Both, it should be noted, have above-average proportions of Aboriginal (Native Canadian) populations.
71. Hackworth (2016) squarely points the finger at race as the chief explanation why Canadian Rustbelt cities (Windsor, Hamilton, etc.) did not develop U.S.-style ghettos.
72. "A city that works," cover article in the December 1974 issue of *Harper's* magazine.
73. Quote attributed to British actor Peter Ustinov upon visiting the city in early 1980s; cited in Relph (2014, 168).
74. The formal name was the British North America Act, a law passed by the British Parliament. The Constitution was Canadianized (repatriated) in 1982, including a number of amendments among which was a Charter of Rights and Freedoms.
75. Source: Tindal and Tindal (2000, 9).
76. Frisken et al. (2000, 73).
77. Relph (2014, 50).
78. Citing Canadian census figures, Frisken et al. (2000, 74) find that average household incomes in the city of Toronto grew from 91 to 108 percent of the Metro average between 1971 and 1991.
79. Frisken et al. (2000, 83).

80. For a blow-by-blow account of the amalgamation saga, see Hawaleshka and Chidley (2016).
81. The Municipality of North York contested Bill 103; its challenge was struck down by the courts.
82. Schwartz (2010).
83. For an in-depth analysis both of the Toronto experience and why amalgamations in general rarely produce cost savings, see Slack and Bird (2013).
84. Slack and Côté (2014, 19). See also Schwartz (2010). The important distinction here is between the operating budget, which must be in balance by law, and the capital budget.

Chapter 5

1. Menes (2003) provides a particularly useful description of that era, some of whose ideas I have borrowed.
2. Menes (2003).
3. Girod-Boos (2017).
4. *Unité permanente anticorruption* (UPC: Permanent Anticorruption unit), a Quebec government agency, was created in 2011 with some three hundred employees and an annual operating budget of $30 million (2015).
5. Menes (2003) makes the same point.
6. The Nagin case as well as the other cases cited are taken from Fuller (2014).
7. *Encyclopedia Britannica* (1960a).
8. Source: https://en.wikipedia.org/wiki/Politics_of_Louisiana
9. Source: Simpson (2012). See notably Tables 1–6.
10. Data and source cited in Mock (2017).
11. Much of my discussion of Huey Long and the period of corruption that followed his assassination is taken from Grossman (2008), a font of information for those interested in the history of corruption in America.
12. Cited in Fuller (2014).
13. Cited in ibid. Much of my information on Edwards's wrongdoing and legal tribulations also come from Grossman (2008).
14. Edwards's roots were in fact French Creole, not Cajun, but playing up the Cajun angle was electorally advantageous. Few people still identify with the old Creole elite, which is now largely extinct.
15. Hirsch and Levert (2009). For other articles on the subject, see Burns and Thomas (2014) and Lang and Danielson (2006).
16. Hirsch and Levert (2009, 208).
17. I especially liked the story of the Cajun Navy. During my years working with colleagues at the University of New Orleans, I frequently had occasion to travel to Cajun country where I came to admire those hardy descendants of the Acadians expelled from Canada more than two centuries ago. The word *Cajun* is a contraction of Acadian.
18. Hirsch and Levert (2009, 211).

19. Ibid. (212).

20. Hirsch and Levert (2009, 213).

21. For much of that period, New Orleans was actually under Spanish rule, although it was de facto French-administered.

22. Goldman (2007, 363).

23. U.S. Census Bureau: 2010 American Community Survey. Table S. 1501. https://factfinder.census.gov/faces/tableservices/

24. Jackson (2013).

25. Porter (1998).

26. Marshal (1890): cited in Polèse (2009, 38).

27. Much of what follows is taken from Gromov (2013) to whom I am greatly indebted. Any incorrect statements are of course entirely my own.

28. Excerpt from California Code—Section 16600, also known as CAL. BPC. CODE § 16600, cited in Gromov (2013).

29. Legislation on NCAs varies across states and is constantly evolving; but California's anti-NCA laws are the most extensive and go back the farthest in time.

30. Much of this paragraph is taken from Gromov (2013), to whom I again express my gratitude.

31. Lamoreaux and Levenstein (2008).

32. *Economist* (2016).

33. Lamoreaux and Levenstein (2008).

34. Lamoreaux and Levenstein (2008) suggest that the local nature of Cleveland's technology base, notably the reliance on local financial institutions, in part explains the inability of local firms to recover from the Great Depression.

35. Bartimole (2011).

36. Moretti (2012) makes much the same point, noting that the mobility of highly educated individuals greatly constrains the leeway of American states with respect to education.

37. Brochu et al. (2013) and NCES (2013).

38. The paragraphs that follow owe much to Glaeser's excellent account of Boston's economic history (Glaeser 2005a).

39. Glaeser (2005a: 147).

40. Ibid. (151).

41. Garreau (1981). The one exception was the Connecticut suburbs of New York, which Garreau put in the nation of *The Foundry*, America's industrial heartland.

42. The only other state, to my knowledge, that has since introduced a form of regional government is Oregon, which established Metro, a directly elected regional government for the greater Portland area, in 1979.

43. Simpson (2012). See notably Tables 1–6.

44. I also told this story in Polèse (2009); but it is worth repeating here. The study was financed by the Quebec government, which at the time was concerned about the flight of head offices from Montreal.

45. Glaeser et al. (1995, 2014); Glaeser and Saiz (2004); Simon (1998); and Simon and Nardinelli (2002).

46. Cheshire and Magrini (2009).
47. Glaeser el al. (2014) find for U.S. cities that the relationship is no longer significant below urban populations of fifty thousand for some time periods and regions. For Canada, our own results show no relationship, explained in large part by the weight of small cities in our universe (Shearmur and Polèse 2007).
48. See for example, Bessen (2015), a very readable presentation of the role of "small" inventions.
49. 2011 census figures.
50. The growing education gap between large and small cities is a general trend, observed in the United States, Canada, and other advanced economies.
51. NCES (2013).
52. Brochu et al. (2013).

Chapter 6

1. Given my first-hand knowledge of many of the events recounted, I have kept references to a minimum. Much of the data cited are drawn from Polèse (2017), which contains numerous tables and graphs on the Montreal economy since the 1930s.
2. Montreal ranked twenty-first in 2018 on Mercer's Quality of Living Survey, halfway between Vienna (always no. 1) and Paris in thirty-ninth place. Montreal ranked fifth among North American cities.
3. A recent Statistics Canada study on relative levels of satisfaction concludes that Quebecers, thus including Montrealers, are on average happier than other Canadians (Lu et al. 2016). Canada ranked fifth in 2016 on the World Happiness Index, with Quebecers, it seems, above other Canadians, which might make them the happiest people on the planet together with the Danes (Dubuc 2016).
4. Canada's population has historically hovered at about one-tenth that of the United States. Montreal's population (metro area) in 1950 was one-tenth that of New York.
5. Nader (1975, 218–219).
6. Cited in Roberts (1969, 341).
7. *Canadian Encyclopedia* (2016).
8. Vallières (1968).
9. Boulet (1978).
10. The project of which I was co-coordinator was called *Nouvel Aéroport de Montréal* (NAIM). The full report (six volumes) was submitted to the Quebec government in November 1970. Hard copies were available at INRS in Montreal (Lamonde and Polèse 1970).
11. Many African states boycotted the 1976 Olympics because of the presence of players who had taken part in sporting events in South Africa, which then was still under Apartheid rule.
12. Peritz (2009).
13. Drouin Paquin and Associates (1978).
14. The author's calculations, based on 1971 and 1991 census data.

15. The school boards were also divided by religion. That distinction was later abolished, keeping only school boards by language.

16. ISQ (2009).

17. A latent sense of existential insecurity will undoubtedly always be part of the Québécois identity, a cultural island of some seven million lost in a continent of over three hundred million English-speakers. As recently as 1989, a documentary was aired on public television entitled *Disapraite* (Disappearing), produced by a well-known nationalist author, presaging the inevitable disappearance of French in North America,

18. The only change to Bill 101 that the Supreme Court ruling introduced for schooling was the replacement of *in Quebec* by *in Canada*, meaning that Anglo-educated parents coming into Quebec from the rest of Canada retained the right to send their children to English schools.

19. Public signs, including the use of brand names (e.g., Starbucks, Winner), remain objects of controversy and legal challenges. The courts have generally upheld the right of Quebec to require French on public signs and advertising.

20. Higgins (1986, 152–153).

21. Picard (1986).

22. During those years, I acted on various occasions as consultant to the federal and provincial governments, informal advisor to the mayor, and sometime columnist for the Montreal Board of Trade.

23. Shearmur and Rantisi (2011).

24. Vaillancourt and Vaillancourt (2007).

25. The program was highly successful in its first years in fueling the creation and growth of Quebec-based firms, allowing the purchasers of stocks to claim generous tax credits.

26. I will not get into an argument on whether Quebec is a nation. Québécois have no qualms about thinking of themselves as a nation within Canada, no less than do the Welsh or Scots within Britain.

27. The assurance that employers could hold on to their (expensively) trained workers was cited to me on numerous occasions as a factor explaining the firm's location and growth in Montreal.

28. See also Séguin and Germain (2000) for an analysis of provincial policies aimed at maintaining social cohesion.

29. Source: https://www.livingin-canada.com/house-prices-canada.htm

30. Source: http://www.numbeo.com/cost-of-living/city_result.jsp?country=Canada&city=Montreal

31. The percentage of owner households spending over 30 percent of their income on housing was 16 percent in Montreal (Metro area), compared to 27 percent in Toronto. Comparable figures for tenants was 36 percent and 47 percent. Source: 2016 Canadian Census.

32. The father of public housing in Montreal was Guy Legault, the city's head of planning during the 1960s. Legault openly espoused the building of small-scale dispersed projects, in contrast to the concentrated high-rise project of Paris, Chicago, and

other cities. My thanks to Martin Wexler, head of the residential policy division at the city of Montreal, for his insights into the history of public housing in Montreal.

33. The classical measures of income distribution are the Gini and the Theil Indexes. On both indexes, Quebec systematically registers more equal distributions than the rest of Canada since 1975, with the gap increasing in recent years to the advantage of Quebec. Source: Crespo and Rheault (2014).

Chapter 7

1. The same holds for multinational economic unions, the European Union currently the principal example.
2. See https://en.m.wikipedia.org/wiki/Equalization_payments
3. Mill rates refer to the annual amount (per 1000 dollars or other monetary unit) of the assessed value of property to be paid as property tax.
4. Combined local and state taxes accounted, respectively, for 12.6, 12.5, and 12.1 percent of personal income (1972–2002 average) in greater Syracuse, Buffalo, and Rochester (Stansel 2012). Given the slight variance, we can safely assume that state taxes are the chief component. The equivalent percentage for Atlanta, located in a low tax state, was 9.6.
5. Tiebout (1956).
6. Stansel (2012).
7. TaxFound (2016). I have no separate data for Boston or San Francisco, but it is fairly safe to assume that their combined tax rates largely mirror those of their host states, respectively, Massachusetts and California.
8. Green et al. (2016). The figures are for the year 2016.
9. The *Régie du Logement* (Housing Board), created by the Quebec legislature in 1974, to arbitrate relations between tenants and landlords. The Board monitors the evolution of rental costs, publishing yearly guidelines for landlords and tenants. The tenants can go before the Board if they feel rent increases are unwarranted. In practice, few have done so.
10. For an excellent review of affordable housing policies in the United States, see Freeman and Schuetz (2017).
11. It is possible to argue convincingly both for and against cities in terms of their environmental impacts. For those interested in the subject, see Dodman (2009), Glaeser and Kahn (2010), and Meyer (2013).
12. For London, see *Economist* (2012a).
13. Florida (2017) makes very much the same argument.
14. *Economist* (2014).
15. Houston is not totally without urban planning regulations, but these are light compared to most other cities in the developed world; see Holeywell (2015).
16. California's fairly liberal pro-activist legislation continues to be a subject of heated debate. At the time of writing, possible repeal, or at least substantial amendment, of the CEQA was still before the California legislature.

17. Woo and Salviati (2017) and https://www.numbeo.com/cost-of-living/rankings.jsp. The data by neighborhood are from the former.

18. See Woo and Salviati (2017).

19. Krugman (1996).

20. A Pareto optimum in this case place implies that any move by a firm (or worker) to another location would reduce the national economic pie, making someone worse off.

21. The city has generally been able to keep its mill rate below one dollar per hundred dollars assessed property value. Most mill rates in the province vary between one and two dollars per hundred dollars.

22. *Société de développement économique de Drummondville*: http://www.sded.ca

23. Those opposed to the construction of the Erie Canal labeled it "DeWitt's Ditch" or "Clinton's Folly" in honor of then New York State Governor DeWitt Clinton, one of the chief promoters of the canal.

24. For an excellent history of the rise of Chicago, see William Cronon's masterful *Nature's Metropolis* (1992).

25. Glaab and Brown (1967).

26. Minneapolis-St. Paul, which we met earlier, is the other exception, but it is located outside what is generally considered the Rustbelt.

27. Source: Brodherson (2005).

28. Airlines can be ranked on several criteria including annual revenue, profits, passengers carried, and market capitalization. The rankings fluctuate yearly, but over the last two decades Delta Airlines has systematically come out first on several criteria. Other airlines in the same league are American and Lufthansa.

29. Atlanta's universities, notably Emory and Georgia Tech, were, however, among the best in the American South. But the South as a whole was still trailing behind the rest of the nation as a center of intellectual ferment.

30. Whitelegg (2000) provides an excellent history of the rise of Atlanta as a global air hub, from which I have unabashedly stolen many ideas. Other sources are Allen (1996) and Ambrose (2006).

31. Whitelegg (2000, 75).

32. Ibid. (76).

33. Ibid. (79).

34. Both have since been privatized.

35. Florida (2002).

36. Grant (2014) is a typical example.

37. Florida (2002a).

38. Hutton (2016) and Markusen and Schrock (2006) are two good examples of the literature on the arts and culture as drivers of urban growth and regeneration.

39. For a more detailed presentation of my thoughts on the arts as a development tool, see Polèse (2012). Phillips (2011) also provides an excellent critical overview of the literature.

40. I have discussed England's north–south divide elsewhere (Polèse, 2009, 9–11). Italy is another exception, its economic geography also shaped by a sharp north–south divide.

41. Canadas's six one-million-plus metro areas are in order: Toronto, Montreal, Vancouver, Ottawa, Calgary, and Edmonton.
42. A growing literature has accumulated on the migration of highly educated workers. See Betz et al. (2016) for a recent example, which also includes a good review of the literature.
43. Morretti (2013) convincingly documents the growing concentration of knowledge-rich jobs in the United States.
44. Florida (2017); see notably the Preface in which Florida describes how his thinking has evolved.
45. The author's calculations based on Maddison (2015) and World Bank data.
46. Source: https://en.m.wikipedia.org/wiki/Financial_centre#Rankings
47. Lee Kuan Yew was prime minister of Singapore before independence from 1959 to 1965 and continuously after independence until 1990, but remained the de facto power behind the throne until 2011 with honorific titles such as minister mentor and senior minister.
48. Source: http://www.worldairportawards.com/Awards/worlds_best_airport.html
49. Malay and Indonesian, both Malay languages, are closely related.
50. Two typical Lee Kuan Yew quotes: (1) "I have always thought that humanity was animal-like. The Confucian theory was man could be improved, but I'm not sure he can be. He can be trained; he can be disciplined." (2): "In the East, the main object is to have a well-ordered society so that everybody can have maximum enjoyment of his freedoms. This freedom can only exist in an ordered state and not in a natural state of contention and anarchy." Source: https://www.brainyquote.com/quotes/quotes/l/leekuanyew711033.html
51. The reader may, for example, wish to consult the Bloomberg Innovation Index or the Nestpick Best Start-up Cities Index.
52. Ethnic Chinese accounted for 75 percent of the population at the time of independence, a percentage that has varied only little since.

Chapter 8

1. My thanks to Jacques, Thisse, Professor Emeritus, University of Louvain-la-Neuve (Belgium), for his insights on Paris, which enriched this chapter considerably. All errors of interpretation are of course my own.
2. Aside from having lived in Paris, I was a member the *Conseil scientifique des économistes du Grand Paris* (Greater Paris Scientific Economic Consultative Council) from 2001 to 2017, mandated to oversee the Grand Paris Express automated light rail system, planned for completion in 2021.
3. The French geographer Bernard Marchand forcefully argues this point, maintaining that much of France's urban and regional policies since World War II have been driven by a "Hatred of the City" (my translation of his title), rooted in rural nostalgia,

which is also the subtext of the populist, nativist discourse on the rise in France as elsewhere in Europe (Marchand 2001)

4. For a more detailed analysis of the decline of Paris as an intellectual metropolis and business center, see Polèse (2014) and Polèse et al. (2014), both in French, from which much the material here is drawn.

5. Bellanger (2017). Two other examples of the genre are *Pars meurt-il?* (is Paris dying?: Burgel 2008) and *Paris s'endort* (Paris is falling asleep: Davezies 2008). The first was authored by a well-known geographer, and the second by a well-known economist.

6. The figures given here are for large urban zones defined by Eurostat.

7. According to the Shanghai academic ranking of world universities, only three French universities, all Paris-based, are in the top one hundred, compared to four Swiss universities (two in Zurich, one each in Geneva and Lausanne), three German universities (two in Munich and one in Heidelberg), and three Swedish universities (two in Stockholm and one in Uppsala). Source: http://www.shanghairanking.com/ARWU2016.html

8. TGV, *Train de Grande Vitesse* (High Speed Train).

9. *Ville lumière* in French, where *lumière* (light) also implies intellectual brilliance.

10. Source: European Commission (2012).

11. De Gaulle led the Free French (1940–1944) who refused to accept the defeat of France in June 1940. During this period, occupied France was ostensibly governed by the official government of France, recognized by the United States until Pearl Harbor and known as Vichy France after the city which became its temporary capital.

12. This is, of course, my personal reading of what went on in de Gaulle's mind. Having read almost all his work and closely followed his political career (including his press conferences and speeches), I feel confident that my reading is not far from the truth.

13. States such as Austria and Finland were bound to neutrality, while Soviet-controlled nations (Poland, Hungary, and Czechoslovakia), not to mention the three Baltic States, were bound to the Soviet sphere by force.

14. *Economist* (2003).

15. The Jacobins were the most radical group during the French Revolution, who advocated a strong central government to undo the privileges of provincial nobles and assemblies perceived as a threat to the Revolution and the unity of the nation.

16. This is not strictly true. Paris did have mayors before the advent of the Third Republic in 1871.

17. The total tax wedge (2014 fiscal year) as a share of labor costs was 48.4 percent in France compared to 31.1 percent for the UK (OECD 2015).

18. Sassen (2009).

19. My translation. The original is even more direct: "Delouvrier, mettez-moi de l'ordre dans ce bordel." Source: https://creditfoncier.com/paul-delouvrier-le-pere-des-villes-nouvelles-1914-1995/

20. Every Département is assigned a number, familiar to every Frenchman, and each figures prominently on license plates. This is an integral part of each Département's identity.

21. I recall a local mayor who recounted an occasion when police in his commune refused to enter a *cité* to intervene in a domestic feud for fear of being attacked by local residents, unless formally accompanied by the mayor in full regalia.

22. In France, the Republican principle of equality, dating back to the Revolution, states that all are French, preventing the census from including questions on race or religion.

23. Here, the reader might wish to compare the Montreal and Viennese experiences of public housing, which in both cases explicitly sought to disperse funded projects, also paying attention to design and quality of construction.

24. Relationships are further politicized by the French tradition of dual mandates in which elected officials can serve in several national and local offices, and thus be major, deputy, and cabinet minister at the same time.

25. Lefèvre (2012) provides an excellent English-language overview of the Paris region's administrative jungle; but it is already dated. For more recent work, see Enright (2016) and Scruggs (2016).

26. I'm indebted to Gérard-François Dumont, Professor of Geography at The Sorbonne, for this information.

27. Scruggs (2016).

28. For a map of Paris start-ups, see: http://www.presse-citron.net/une-cartographie-des-start-ups-parisiennes

29. Seth Pinsky, director of the New Economic Development Corporation, cited in *Economist* (2012).

30. I say this on the basis of meetings with mangers and planners involved in the Saclay project, as well as interviews on French television with the project's promoters. The reader may also wish to consult https://en.wikipedia.org/wiki/University_of_Paris-Saclay

31. The *Tour Montparnasse* (a large office tower) in central Paris is a notable exception. It is not an architectural success, sticking out like a sore thumb, and its unsightliness may have contributed to the continued Parisian aversion to higher buildings in the center.

32. Bellanger (2017, 39) makes very much the same point.

33. Its official name is *Centre national d'art et de culture Georges-Pompidou.*

Conclusion

1. H. L. Mencken was an American journalist and satirist (1880–1956). Source of quote: https://www.brainyquote.com/quotes/authors/h/h_l_mencken.html

2. The trend in recent years has been toward increased state and federal (nonproperty tax) funding of public education, a trend to be applauded with, again, major

variations across states. Chingos and Blagg (2017) provide a detailed study of recent trends in school funding in the United States. Only time will tell whether this (happy) trend survives the Trump presidency.

3. Thus, federal transfers have historically accounted for about a third of the revenues of the province of New Brunswick, one of Canada's poorer provinces.

4. *Mounties* is the popular name for Canada's federal police, the Royal Canadian Mounted Police.

5. The irony of a nation that so cherishes the freedom to move and also has the highest incarceration rate among advanced nations will undoubtedly not have escaped the reader.

6. Brazil is an evident exception, with an even more striking history of uneven development.

7. Florida (2017), Moretti (2012).

8. At the time of writing, a bill was before the U.S. Senate that would make federal grants for housing conditional on the withdrawal of locally adopted zoning ordinances or other restrictions on new housing construction. I do not know what happened to this legislation (Carlisle 2018).

9. Among the best current sites, often cited in this book, are CityLab newsletters@ citylab.com; City Observatory jcortright=cityobservatory.org@mail28.sea21.rsgsv. net; Citiscope newsletter@citiscope.org

10. Here, I differ with Richard Florida. One of his recommendations for fostering urbanism for all reads "Empower Cities and Communities" (Florida 2017, 211). I agree with many of his recommendations. However, most, like a land value tax or tax-increment local transfers (a form of revenue sharing to discourage NIMBYs) would require the prior approval of state legislatures. Florida notes America's Jeffersonian pastoralist anti-urban tradition and attachment to the principles of local autonomy (thus, the reluctance of suburban communities to share with the urban core); but he does not seem to see the contradiction with his call for community empowerment.

11. Two recent examples of gung-ho pro-city writings are Katz and Bradley (2013) and Katz and Nowak (2018), both of which are well documented and exhaustively argued, although I do not share their optimism.

12. For a detailed description of recent Department of Justice directives, see https://www.propublica.org/article/why-jeff-sessions-final-act-could-have-more-impact-than-expected. I also direct the reader to the Department's 2017 directive urging federal prosecutors to seek maximum penalties for first offenders with predictable consequences for the incarceration of African Americans.

Bibliography

Acs, G., R. Pendall, M. Treskon, and A. Khari. 2017. *The Cost of Segregation: National Trends and the Case of Chicago, 1990–2010*. Washington, DC: Urban Institute.

Allen, Frederic. 1996. *Atlanta Rising: The Invention of an International City 1946–1996*. New York: Taylor Trade Publishing, Rowman & Littlefield.

Ambrose, Andy. 2006. "Four Things You Should Know about Atlanta." American Historical Association, Supplement to the 121st Annual Meeting: https://www.historians.org/annual-meeting/supplement-to-the-121st-annual-meeting/four-things-you-should-know-about-atlanta

Amman, W., and A. Mundt. 2017. *The Austrian System of Social Housing Finance*. Vienna: Institute for Real Estate Construction and Housing. http://www.iut.nu/FindOutMore/Europe/Austria/Socialhousing_finance_Amman_Mundt.pdf

Barro, R. J., and X. Sala-i-Martin.1995. *Economic Growth*. New York: McGraw-Hill.

Bartimole, Roldo 2011. Cleveland's Decline from the 1960s. *Cool Cleveland*: http://coolcleveland.com/2011/04/roldo-clevelands-decline-from-the-1960s

Belfer, Lauren. 2000. *The City of Light*. New York: Island Books.

Bellanger, Aurélien. 2017. *Le Grand Paris*. Paris: Gallimard.

Bessen, James. 2015. *Learning by Doing: The Real Connection Between Innovation, Wages, and Wealth*. New Haven, CT: Yale University Press.

Bettencourt, L., Lobo, J., and Strumsky, D. 2007. "Invention in the City: Increasing Returns to Patenting as a Scaling Function of Metropolitan Size." *Research Policy* 36: 107–120.

Betz, M., M. Partridge, and B. Fallah. 2016. "Smart Cities and Attracting Knowledge Workers: Which Cities Attract Highly-educated Workers in the 21st Century?" *Papers in Regional Science* 95 (4): 829–842.

Biddulph, Matt. 2012. "How London's Silicon Roundabout Really Got Started." GIGAOM. https://gigaom.com/2012/12/11/how-londons-silicon-roundabout-really-got-started

Black, D., and V. Henderson.1999. "Spatial Evolution of Population and Industry in the United States." *American Economic Review* 89 (2): 321–327.

Boulet, Jac-André. 1978. "Évolution de la distribution des revenus de travail des groupes ethniques et linguistiques sur le marché montréalais de 1961 à 1971." In *Problèmes actuels de l'économie québécoise*, Luc-Normand Tellier (ed.). Montreal: Les éditions Quinze, 203–22.

Britannica. 1911. "Buffalo." *Encyclopedia Britannica*, Volume 4.5. Online. https://en.wikisource.org/wiki/1911_Encyclop%C3%A6dia_Britannica/Vol_4_BISH%C4%80R%C4%AAN_to_CALGARY

Britannica. 1960. "Buffalo." *Encyclopedia Britannica* 4: 341–343.

Britannica.1960a. "Louisiana." *Encyclopedia Britannica* 14: 424–430.

Brochu, P., M.-A. Deussing, K. Houme, and M. Chuy. 2013. "Measuring Up: Canadian Results of the OECD PISA Study." Toronto: Council of Ministers of Education. http://cmec.ca/Publications/Lists/Publications/Attachments/318/PISA2012_CanadianReport_EN_Web.pdf

Brodherson, David. 2005. "O'Hare Airport." *Encyclopedia of Chicago History.* http://www.encyclopedia.chicagohistory.org/pages/923.html

Brülhart, M., and F. Sbergami. 2009. "Agglomeration and Growth: Cross-country Evidence." *Journal of Urban Economics* 65: 48–63.

Buffalo Demographics. 2016. "Demographics of Buffalo, New York." https://en.wikipedia.org/wiki/Demographics_of_Buffalo,_New_York

Burgel, Guy. 2008. *Paris, meurt-il?* Paris: Perrin,

Burns, P., and M. Thomas. 2014. "Nothing's Easy in the Big Easy: Reforming and Governing New Orleans after Hurricane Katrina." Washington, DC: Paper, Annual Meeting of the American Political Science Association. August 2014.

Cabral, C., A. V. Mollick, and E. Saucedo. 2016. "Violence in Mexico and Its Effects on Labor Productivity." *Annals of Regional Science* 56: 317–339.

Camagni, R., R. Capello, and A. Caragliu. 2016. "Static vs. Dynamic Agglomeration Economies. Spatial Context and Structural Evolution Behind Urban Growth." *Papers in Regional Science* 5 (1): 133–159.

Campante, F., and E. Glaeser 2009. "Yet Another Tale of Two Cities: Buenos Aires and Chicago." *Working Paper 15104.* Cambridge, MA: National Bureau of Economic Research.

Canadian Encyclopedia. 2016. "Expo 67." *The Canadian Encyclopedia:* http://www.thecanadianencyclopedia.ca/en/article/expo-67

Carlisle, Madeleine. 2018. "Elizabeth Warren's Ambitious Fix for America's Housing Crisis. "*The Atlantic.* September 25, 2018: https://www.theatlantic.com/politics/archive/2018/09/elizabeth-warrens-fix-americas-housing-crisis/571210

Cheng, Boon Ong. 2017. "Tipping Points in Dutch Big City Neighbourhoods." *Urban Studies* 54 (4): 1016–1037.

Cheshire, P., and S. Magrini. 2009. "Urban Growth Drivers in a Europe of Sticky People and Implicit Boundaries." *Journal of Economic Geography* 9 (1): 85–115.

Chingos, M., and K. Blagg. 2017. *Making Sense of State School Funding Policy.* Washington, DC: Urban Institute. https://www.urban.org/research/publication/making-sense-state-school-funding-policy/view/full_report

Cortright, Joe. 2016 "The Triumph of the City and the Twilight of Nerdistans." City Commentary 28-7-2016: http://cityobservatory.org/the-triumph-of-the-city-and-the-twilight-of-nerdistans

Crandall, Robert W. 2002. "The Migration of U.S. Manufacturing and Its Impact on the Buffalo Metropolitan Area." Buffalo: Paper prepared for the Federal Reserve Bank of New York, Buffalo Branch.

Crespo, S., and S. Rheault. 2014. "L'inégalité du revenu disponible des ménages au Québec et dans le reste du Canada: bilan de 35 années." *Données sociodémographiques en bref*, Vol 19, No. 1. Quebec City: Institut de la statique du Québec.

Cronon, William. 1992. *Nature's Metropolis: Chicago and the Great West.* New York: W. W. Norton.

Davezies, Laurent. 2008. *Paris' sendort.* La vie des idées.fr: http://www.laviedesidees.fr/ Paris-s-endort.html

De Kosnik, Abigail. 2014. "Disrupting Technological Privilege. The 2013–14 San Francisco Google Bus Protests." *Performance Research* 18 (6): 99–107.

Denison, Edward. 1985. *Trends in American Growth 1929–1982.* Washington, DC: Brookings Institution.

Dillaway, Diana. 2006. *Power Failure: Politics, Patronage, and the Economic Future of Buffalo, New York.* Amherst, NY: Prometheus Press.

Dodman, David. 2009. "Blaming Cities for Climate Change? An Analysis of Urban Greenhouse Gas Emissions." *Environment and Urbanization* 21 (1): 185–201.

Drouin Paquin and Associates. 1978. *Analyse de l'industrie des sièges sociaux à Montréal, et stratégie d'intervention,* Montreal: Conseil du Patronat du Québec.

Dubé, J., and M. Polèse. 2015. "Resource Curse and Regional Development: Does Dutch Disease Apply to Local Economies? Evidence from Canada." *Growth and Change* 46 (1): 38–57.

Dubuc, Alain. 2016. "La satisfaction tranquille." Montreal: *La Presse,* July 5, 2016: http:// www.lapresse.ca/debats/chroniques/alain-dubuc/201607/04/01-4997810-la-satisfaction-tranquille.php

Duranton, G., and D. Puga. 2001. "Nursery Cities: Urban Diversity, Process Innovation, and the Life Cycle of Products." *American Economic Review* 91 (5): 1454–1477.

Duranton, G., and D. Puga. 2014. "The Growth of Cities." In *Handbook of Economic Growth,* P. Agnion and S. N. Durlauf (eds.), Vol. 2: 781–853. Amsterdam: Elsevier.

Duvivier, C., and M. Polèse. 2018 "The Great Urban Techno Shift: Are Central Neighborhoods the Next Silicon Valleys? Evidence from Three Canadian Metropolitan Areas." *Papers in Regional Science* 97 (4): 1083–1111.

Easterly, William. 2002. *The Elusive Quest for Growth.* Cambridge, MA: MIT Press.

Eckhart, C. Beck. 1979. "The Love Canal Tragedy." Washington, DC: EPA: United States Environmental Protection agency. http://www2.epa.gov/aboutepa/love-canal-tragedy

Economist. 2003. "The Galling Rise of English. The European Union Is Becoming an English-Speaking Zone." *The Economist,* February 27, 2003. http://www.economist. com/node/1606383

Economist. 2012. "Economic Diversification: Reimagining the Future." *The Economist,* January 7, 2012, 26–27.

Economist. 2012a. "High House Prices Make Life Difficult for Londoners and Threaten the City's Prosperity." *The Economist,* June 30, 2012. http://www.economist.com/ node/21557531

Economist. 2013. "Argentina's Wealth Gap. Barbarians at the Gate." *The Economist,* October 26, 20. http://www.economist.com/news/americas/21588416-capitals-exclusive-closed-neighbourhoods-face-heavy-new-tax-barbarians-gate?frsc=dg%7Cc

Economist. 2014. "Housing in Los Angeles: Why Homes Even in the Unfashionable Parts of LA Cost So Much." *The Economist,* August 23, 2014. http://www.economist.com/news/united-states/21613318-why-homes-even-unfashionable-parts-la-cost-so-much-la-storeys?frsc=dg%7Cc

Economist. 2015. "Cash in Argentina: A Government in Denial over Inflation." *The Economist,* April 11, 2015. http://en.wikipedia.org/wiki/Global_Financial_Centres_Index

Economist. 2016. "Cleveland Can Teach Valuable Lessons about the Rise and Fall of Economic Clusters." *The Economist,* July 23, 2016. http://www.economist.com/news/business-and-finance/21702387

Eeckhout, Jan. 2004. "Gibrat's Law for (All) Cities." *American Economic Review* 94: 1429–1451.

Ehrenhalt, Alan. 2012. *The Great Inversion and the Future of the American City.* New York: Knopf.

Einstein, K. L., M. Palmer, and D. Glick. 2018. "Who Participates in Local Government? Evidence from Meeting Minutes." *Perspectives on Politics* 17 (1): 28–46. https://www.dropbox.com/s/k4kzph3ynal3xai/ZoningParticipation_Perspectives_Final.pdf?dl=0

Eligon, J., Y. Alcindor, and A. Armendariz. 2017. "Program to Spur Low-Income Housing Is Keeping Cities Segregated." *The New York Times,* July 2, 2017. https://www.nytimes.com/2017/07/02/us/federal-housing-assistance-urban-racial-divides.html

Enright, Theresa. 2016. *The Making of Grand Paris—Metropolitan Urbanism in the Twenty-First Century.* Cambridge, MA: MIT Press.

Eurofound. 2009. *Housing and Segregation of Migrants—Case Study: Vienna.* Dublin: European Foundation for the Improvement of Living and Working Conditions. https://www.eurofound.europa.eu/

European Commission. 2012. "Europeans and Their Languages." *Special Eurobarometer* 386. http://ec.europa.eu/public_opinion/archives/ebs/ebs_386_en.pdf

Falk, Gerhard. 2006. *The History of Tel Aviv.* http://jbuff.com/c121202.htm

Fay, M., and C. Opal. 2000. "Urbanization without Growth: A Not So Uncommon Phenomenon." *Working Paper Series (WPS)* no. 2412. Washington, DC: The World Bank.

Fee, K., and D. Hartley. 2012. "The Relationship Between City Center Density and Urban Growth and Decline." *Working Paper,* 12–13. Federal Reserve Bank of Cleveland.

Florida, Richard. 2002. *The Rise of the Creative Class.* New York: Basic Books.

Florida, Richard. 2002a. "Bohemia and Economic Geography." *Journal of Economic Geography* 2: 55–71.

Florida, Richard. 2017. *The New Urban Crisis.* New York: Basic Books.

Foord, Jo. 2013. "The New Boomtown? Creative City to Tech City in East London." *Cities* 33: 51–60.

Freeman, L., and J. Schuetz. 2017. "Producing Affordable Housing in Rising Markets: What Works?" *Cityscape* 19 (1): 217–236.

Freire, M., and M. Polèse. 2003. *Connecting Cities with Macro-economic Concerns: The Missing Link.* Washington, DC: The World Bank.

Freire, M., M. Polèse, and P. Echeverria (Eds.). 2004. *Servicios públicos locales y competitividad urbana.* Puebla, Mexico: Puebla University Press.

Frisken, F., L. S. Bourne, G. Gad, and R. A. Murdie. 2000. "Governance and Social Sustainability: The Toronto Experience." In *The Social Sustainability of Cities,* M. Polèse, and R. Stren (eds.), 68–69. Toronto: Toronto University Press.

Fujita, M., and J. Thisse. 2013. *Economics of Agglomeration,* 2nd Edition. Cambridge, UK: Cambridge University Press.

Fukuyama, Francis. 1995. *Trust: The Social Virtues and the Creation of Prosperity.* New York: Free Press.

Fuller, Jaime. 2014. "Vance McAllister Is Part of a Long line of Scandalized Louisiana Politicians, A VERY Long Line." *The Washington Post* April 9, 2014. https://www.washingtonpost.com/news/the-fix/wp/2014/04/09/what-is-it-about-louisiana-and-political-scandals/?utm_term=.5ce56bf09f8e

Gabaix, Xavier. 1999. "Zipf's Law for Cities: An Explanation." *Quarterly Journal of Economics* 114: 739–767.

Galeano, Eduardo. 1971. *Open Veins of Latin America: Five Centuries of the Pillage of a Continent,* reedited in English in 1997. New York: Monthly Review Press.

Garreau, Joel. 1981. *The Nine Nations of North America.* Boston: Houghton Mifflin.

Girod-Boos, Claudine. 2017. "Mayors, Napoleons and Corruption: A Very French Curse." *Global Geneva* http://www.global-geneva.com/mayors-napoleons-and-corruption-a-very-french-curse

Glaab, C. N., and A. T. Brown. 1967. *A History of Urban America.* New York: Macmillan.

Glaeser, Edward. 2005. "Urban Colossus: Why Is New York America's Largest City?" *Economic Policy Review.* Federal Reserve Bank of New York, December, pp. 7–24. http://www.newyorkfed.org/research/epr/05v11n2/0512glae.pdf

Glaeser, Edward. 2005a. "Reinventing Boston 1630–2003." *Journal of Economic Geography* 5: 119–153.

Glaeser, Edward. 2007. "Can Buffalo Ever Come Back?" *City Journal.* Autumn 2007. http://www.city-journal.org/html/17_4_buffalo_ny.html

Glaeser, Edward (Ed.). 2010. *Agglomeration Economics.* Chicago: University of Chicago Press.

Glaeser, Edward. 2011. *The Triumph of the City: How Our Greatest Invention Makes Us Richer, Smarter, Greener, Healthier, and Happier.* New York: Penguin.

Glaeser, E., and J. Gottlieb. 2006. "Urban Resurgence and the Consumer City." *Urban Studies* 43 (8): 1275–1299.

Glaeser, E., and M. Kahn. 2010. "The Greenness of Cities: Carbon Dioxide Emissions and Urban Development." *Journal of Urban Economics* 67: 404–418.

Glaeser, E., and G. Ponzetto. 2010. "Did the Death of Distance Hurt Detroit and Help New York?" In *Agglomeration Economies,* E. Glaeser (ed.), 303–338. Chicago: University of Chicago Press.

Glaeser, E. L., Giacomo A. M. Ponzetto, and Kristina Tobio. 2014. "Cities, Skills, and Regional Change." *Regional Studies* 48 (1): 7–43.

Glaeser, E., M. Ressger, and K. Tobio. 2008. "Urban Inequality." *Working Paper 2008-10.* Cambridge, MA: Harvard Kennedy School, Taubman Center for State and Local Government.

Glaeser, E., and A. Saiz. 2004. "The Rise of the Skilled City." *Brookings-Wharton Papers on Urban Affairs* 5: 47–95.

Glaeser, E., J. Scheinkman, and A. Shleifer. 1995. "Economic Growth in a Cross-Section of Cities." *Journal of Monetary Economics* 36 (1): 117–143.

Goldman, Mark. 1984. *High Hopes: The Rise and Decline of Buffalo, New York.* Albany, NY: SUNY Press.

Goldman, Mark. 2007. *City on the Edge: Buffalo, New York, 1900–Present.* New York: Prometheus Press.

Goldstein, H., V. Peer, and S. Sedlacek. 2013. *Vienna as a Region of Knowledge: Increasing the Generation of University Spin-offs.* MODUL University-Vienna, Final Report to the Vienna Chamber of Commerce.

Grant, Jill (Ed.). 2014. *Seeking Talent for Creative Cities. The Social Dynamics of Innovation.* Toronto: University of Toronto Press.

Green, K., J. Filipowicz, S. Lafleur, and I. Herzog. 2016. *The Impact of Land-Use Regulations on Housing Supply in Canada.* Vancouver: Fraser Institute.

Gromov, Gregory. 2013. "From the Gold Mines of El Dorado to the 'Golden' Startups of Silicon Valley." *Internet History from NetValley.* http://silicon-valley-history.com

Grossmann, M. 2008. *Political Corruption in America: An Encyclopedia of Scandals, Power, and Greed,* 2nd Edition. Amenia, NY: Grey House.

Hackworth, Jason. 2016. "Why There Is No Detroit in Canada." *Urban Geography* 36 (2): 272–295.

Hall, Peter. 1999. *Cities in Civilization. Culture, Innovation, and Urban Order.* London: Phoenix Giant.

Hawaleshka, D., and J. Chidley. 2016. "Toronto's Struggle Against Amalgamation." *Canadian Encyclopedia.* http://www.thecanadianencyclopedia.ca/en/m/article/torontos-struggle-against-amalgamation

Henderson, Vernon. 1997. "Medium-sized Cities." *Regional Science and Urban Economics* 27: 583–612.

Henderson, Vernon. 2003. "Marshall's Scale Economies." *Journal of Urban Economics* 53: 1–28.

Higgins, Benjamin. 1986. *The Rise and Fall of Montreal?* Moncton, N.B.: Canadian Institute for Research on Regional Development.

Hirsch, A., and A. L. Levert. 2009. "The Katrina Conspiracies: The Problem of Trust in Rebuilding an American City." *Journal of Urban History* 35 (2): 207–219.

Holeywell, Ryan. 2015. "Forget What You've Heard, Houston Really Does Have Zoning (Sort of)." *The Urban Edge* September 9, 2015. Houston: Kinder Institute for Urban Research, Rice University. https://urbanedge.blogs.rice.edu/2015/ 09/08/forget-what-youve-heard-houston-really-does-have-zoning-sort-of/ #.WQd-goWcG71

Hutton, Thomas A. 2004. "The New Economy of the Inner City." *Cities* 21 (2): 89–108.

Hutton, Thomas A. 2016. *Cities and the Cultural Economy*. London: Routledge.

Indergaard, Michael. 2003. *Silicon Alley: The Rise and Fall of New York's New Media District*. New York: Routledge.

Indergaard, Michael. 2009. "What to Make of New York's New Economy? The Politics of the Creative Field." *Urban Studies* 46 (5–6): 1063–1093.

Indergaard, Michael. 2013. "Beyond the Bubbles: Creative New York in Boom, Bust and the Long Run." *Cities* 33: 43–50. www.stat.gouv.qc.ca/

Jackson, Kenneth. 2013. "The Dysfunctional City: Crime, Corruption, and the Social Elite in New Orleans." Paper, Annual Conference of the American Historical Association, New Orleans. https://aha.confex.com/aha/2013/webprogram/Paper11380.html

Jacobs, Jane. 1961. *The Death and Life of Great American Cities*. New York: Vintage Books

Jacobs, Jane. 1984. *Cities and the Wealth of Nations: Principles of Economic Life*. New York: Vintage Books.

Jaffe, Eric. 2013. "Be Careful How You Refer to the So-called 'Great American Streetcar Scandal.'" *Citylab*: https://www.citylab.com/transportation/2013/06/be-careful-how-you-refer-so-called-great-american-streetcar-scandal/5771

Kantor, P., C. Lefèvre, H. Saito, H. Savitch, and A. Thornley (Eds.). 2012. *Struggling Giants. City-Region Governance in London, New York, Paris, and Tokyo*. Minneapolis: University of Minnesota Press.

Katz, B., and J. Bradley. 2013. *The Metropolitan Revolution: How Cities and Metros Are Fixing Our Broken Politics and Fragile Economy*. Washington, DC: Brookings Institution Press.

Katz, B., and J. Nowak. 2018. *The New Localism: How Cities Can Thrive in the Age of Populism*. Washington, DC: Brookings Institution Press.

Katz, B., and J. Wagner. 2014. *The Rise of Innovation Districts: A New Geography of Innovation in America*. Washington, DC: Brookings Institution–Metropolitan Policy Program.

Kauder, Björn. 2015. "Spatial Administrative Structure and Intra-Metropolitan Tax Competition." *Journal of Regional Science* 55 (4): 626–643.

Ketterer, T., and A. Rodriguez-Pose. 2018. "Institutions vs. 'First-Nature' Geography: What Drives Economic Growth in Europe's Regions?" *Papers in Regional Science* 97 (1): 25–62.

Krugman, Paul. 1996. "Confronting the Mystery of Urban Hierarchy." *Journal of the Japanese and International Economies* 10: 399–418.

Kuznets, Simon. 1968. *Towards a Theory of Economic Growth*. New York: W. W. Norton.

Lamonde, P., and M. Polèse. 1970. *Rapport NAIM (Nouvel Aéroport de Montréal)*. Six studies on the economic impact of Montreal's new airport. Montreal: INRS-Urbanisation.

Lamoreaux, N., and M. Levenstein. 2008. "The Decline of an Innovative Region: Cleveland, Ohio, in the Twentieth Century." Paper, 2008 Annual Meeting of the Economic History Association. http://www.econ.ucla.edu/people/papers/Lamoreaux/Lamoreaux472.pdf

Landes, David.1998. *The Wealth and Poverty of Nations: Why Some Are So Rich and Some So Poor*. New York: W. W. Norton.

Lang, E. L., and K. A. Danielson. 2006. "Review Roundtable: Is New Orleans a Resilient City?" *Journal of the American Planning Association* 72 (2): 254–257.

Lefèvre, Christain. 2012. "Paris-Île-de-France: A Fragmented and Conflicting Territory." In Kantor et al., *op cit.*, 155–192.

Lu, C., G. Schellenbergm, F. Hou, and J. F. Helliwell. 2016. "How's Life in the City? Life Satisfaction Across Census Metropolitan Areas and Economic Regions in Canada." *Economic Insights No.46*. Statistics Canada, Ottawa. http://www.statcan.gc.ca/pub/11-626-x/11-626-x2015046-eng.htm

Macfarlane, Daniel. 2010. "Rapid Changes: Canada and the St. Lawrence Seaway and Power Project." Ottawa: Paper, Carleton University. http://powi.ca/wp-content/uploads/2012/12/Rapid-Changes-Canada-and-the-St.Lawrence-Seaway-and-Power-Project.pdf

MacPherson, Alan. 1997. "The Role of Producer Service Outsourcing in the Innovation Performance of New York State Manufacturing Firms." *Annals of the Association of American Geographers* 87 (1): 52–71.

Maddison, Angus. 2015. *Historical Statistics of the World Economy*. http://www.google.ca/url?sa=t&rct=j&q=&esrc=s&source=web&cd=3&cad=rja&uact=8&ved=0CCoQFjAC&url=http%3A%2F%2Fwww.ggdc.net%2FMADDISON%2FHistorical_Statistics%2Fhorizontal-file_02-2010.xls&ei=5FZsVckOsWogwTegYGwCQ&usg=AFQjCNF1Y6rvV8BTXpC-S5tsqbFlSZCevw&bvm=bv.94455598,d.aWw

Marchand, Bernard. 2001. "La haine de la ville: 'Paris et le désert français' de Jean-François Gravier." *L'information géographique* 65 (3): 234–253.

Markusen, A., and Schrock, G. 2006. "The Artistic Dividend: Urban Artistic Specialization and Economic Development Implications." *Urban Studies* 43 (10): 1661–1686.

Marshall, Alfred. 1890. *Principles of Economics*. London: Macmillan.

Mauro, Paolo. 1995. "Corruption and Growth." *Quarterly Journal of Economics* 110: 681–712.

Mayerhofer, P., O. Frtiz, and D. Pennerstorfer. 2010. *Dritter Bericht zur internationalen Wetbewerbsfähigkeit Wiens*. Vienna: WIFO (Austrian Institute for Economic Research).

Menes, Rebecca. 2003. "Corruption in Cities: Graft and Politics in American at the Turn of the Twentieth Century." *NBER Working Paper 9990*. Cambridge, MA: National Bureau of Economic Research.

Meyer, William. 2013. *The Environmental Advantages of Cities: Countering Commonsense Antiurbanisnm.* Cambridge, MA: MIT Press.

Mock, Brentin. 2017. "Why New Orleans Leads the U.S. in Wrongful Convictions." *Citylab.* https://www.citylab.com/crime/2017/06/why-new-orleans-leads-the-us-in-wrongful/529389/?utm_source=nl__link4_06091

Montagna, Joseph A. 1981. "The Industrial Revolution." Contents of Curriculum Unit: Yale-New Haven Teachers Institute: http://www.yale.edu/ynhti/curriculum/units/1981/2/81.02.06.x.html

Moretti, Enrico. 2012. *The New Geography of Jobs.* New York: Mariner Books.

Nader, George. 1975. *Cities of Canada—Volume One: Theoretical, Historical and Planning Perspectives.* Toronto: Macmillan of Canada.

NCES. 2013. *U.S. States in a Global Context: Results from the 2011 NAEP-TIMSS Linking Study.* Washington, DC: National Center for Educational Statistics. https://nces.ed.gov/nationsreportcard/subject/publications/studies/pdf/2013460.pdf

Nieva, Richard. 2014. "Vexed in the City: Silicon Valley's Invasion of San Francisco." *CNET.* August 22, 2014. https://www.cnet.com/news/vexed-in-the-city-silicon-valleys-invasion-of-san-francisco

OECD. 2015. *Taxing Wages 2015.* Paris: OECD. http://dx.doi.org/10.1787/tax_wages-2015-en

ONYSC. 2014. *2014 Fiscal Profile: City of Buffalo. Office of the New York State Comptroller.* https://www.osc.state.ny.us/localgov/pubs/fiscalprofiles/buffalo.pdf

Opillard, Florian. 2015. "Resisting the Politics of Displacement in the San Francisco Bay Area: Anti-gentrification Activism in the Tech Boom 2.0." *European Journal of American Studies* 10 (3): Document 1.8.

Peritz, Ingrid. 2009. "Montreal's Billion-Dollar 'Big Owe': What Went Wrong in '76?" *Toronto Globe and Mail,* April 10, 2009. http://www.theglobeandmail.com/news/british-columbia/montreals-billion-dollar-big-owe-what-went-wrong-in-76/article1152036/?service=mobile

Phillips, Ronnie J. 2011. "Arts Entrepreneurship and Economic Development: Can Every City Be 'Austintatious'?" *Foundations and Trends in Entrepreneurship* 6 (4): 239–313.

Picard, Laurent. 1986. *Rapport du Comité consultatif au Comité ministériel sur le développement de la région de Montréal.* Montreal: Ministère des Approvisionnements et Services Canada.

Polèse, Mario. 2005. "Cities and National Economic Growth: A Reappraisal." *Urban Studies* 42 (8): 1429–1451.

Polèse, Mario. 2009a. *The Wealth and Poverty of Regions; Why Cities Matter.* Chicago: University of Chicago Press.

Polèse, Mario. 2009b. "The Intrusive Rentier Syndrome." In Polèse 2009a, *op cit:* 18–23.

Polèse, Mario. 2012. "The Arts and Local Economic Development: Can a Strong Art Presence Uplift Local Economies? A Study of 135 Canadian Cities." *Urban Studies* 49 (8): 1811–1835.

Polèse, Mario. 2014. "Paris et le mal français: à propos de l'indissociabilité des économies urbaines et nationales." *Futuribles* No. 104: 41–52.

Polèse, Mario. 2017. "Montreal's Economy since 1930." In *Montreal: The History of a North American City*, D. Fougères and R. Macleod (eds.), 165–204. Montreal: McGill-Queens University Press.

Polèse, M., and R. Shearmur. 2006. "Why Some Regions Will Decline: A Canadian Case Study with Thoughts on Local Economic Development. " *Papers in Regional Science* 85 (1): 23–46.

Polèse, M., R. Shearmur, and L. Terral. 2014. *La France avantagée Paris et la nouvelle économie des régions*. Paris: Odile Jacob.

Polèse, M., and R. Stren (Eds.). 2000. *The Social Sustainability of Cities: Diversity and the Management of Change*. Toronto: Toronto University Press.

Porter, Michael. 1998. "Clusters and the New Economics of Competition." *Harvard Business Review* 76 (6): 77–90.

Relph, Edward. 2014. *Toronto: Transformations in a City and Its Region*. Philadelphia: University of Pennsylvania Press.

Renn, Aaaron. 2015. "Reinventing Buffalo: The Western New York City Should Focus on Getting Better Not Bigger." *City Journal*, Autumn: 110–117.

Roberts, Leslie. 1969. *Montreal: From Mission Colony to World Metropolis*. Montreal: Macmillan of Canada.

Rosenthal, S. R., and W. C. Strange. 2001. "The Determinants of Agglomeration." *Journal of Urban Economics* 50: 191–229.

Sassen, Saskia. 2009. "Cities in Today's Global Age." *SAIS Review of International Studies* 29 (1): 3–32.

Schrag, Zachary. 2017. "Urban Mass Transit in the United States." *E.H.* net, Economic History Association. https://eh.net/encyclopedia/urban-mass-transit-in-the-united-states

Schwartz. Harvey. 2010. "Toronto: Trouble in the Megacity, Facing a Financial Crisis in 2010." *Policy Options*, February 2010: 62–67. http://policyoptions.irpp.org/magazines/after-copenhagen/toronto-trouble-in-the-megacity-facing-a-financial-crisis-in-2010

Scruggs, Gregory. 2016. "The 'Grand Paris' Era Begins." *Citiscope* http://citiscope.org/story/2016/grand-paris-era-begins

Sedgley, N., and Elmslie, B. 2011. "Do We Still Need Cities? Evidence on Rates of Innovation from Count Data Models of Metropolitan Statistical Area Patents." *American Journal of Economics and Sociology* 70 (1): 86–108.

Séguin, A.-M, and A. Germain. 2000. "The Social Sustainability of Montreal: A Local or State Matter?" In M. Polèse and R. Stren, *op cit*, 39–67.

Shearmur, Richard. 2011a. "Are Cities the Font of Innovation? A Critical Review of the Literature on Cities and Innovation." *Cities* 29: 918.

Shearmur, Richard. 2011b. "Innovation, Regions and Proximity: From Neo-regionalism to Spatial Analysis." *Regional Studies* 45 (9): 1225–1244.

Shearmur, Richard. 2012. "Not Being There: Why Local Innovation Is Not (Always) Related to Local Factors." In *Foundations of the Knowledge Economy*, K. Westeren (ed.), 117–138. Cheltenham, UK: Edward Elgar.

Shearmur, R., and N. Bonnet. 2011. "Does Local Technological Innovation Lead to Local Development?" *Regional Science Policy and Practice* 3(3), 250–270.

Shearmur, R., and M. Polèse. 2007. "Do Local Factors Explain Local Employment Growth?" *Regional Studies* 41: 453–471.

Shearmur, R., and N. Rantisi. 2011. "Montreal: Rising Again from the Same Ashes." In *Canadian Urban Regions: Trajectories of Growth and Change*, L. S. Bourne, T. Hutton, R. Shearmur, and J. Simmons (eds.), 173–201. Oxford: Oxford University Press.

Simon, Curtis. J. 1998. "Human Capital and Metropolitan Employment Growth." *Journal of Urban Economics* 43 (2): 223–243.

Simon, C., and C. Nardinelli. 2002. "Human Capital and the Rise of American Cities: 1900–1990." *Regional Science and Urban Economics* 32 (1): 59–96.

Simpson, D. 2012. (Lead Author) "Chicago and Illinois Leading the Pack in Corruption." Antit-Corruption Report Number 5: https://web.archive.org/web/20140402153827/ http://www.uic.edu/depts/pols/ChicagoPolitics/leadingthepack.pdf

Slack, E., and R. Bird. 2013. "Merging Municipalities: Is Bigger Better?" Institute for Municipal Finance and Governance. Munk School of Global Affairs. University of Toronto.

Slack, E., and A. Côté. 2014. "Is Toronto Fiscally Health? A Check-up on the City's Finances." *Perspectives No.7/2014*. Institute for Municipal Finance and Governance, Munk School of Global Affairs. University of Toronto.

Stansel, Dean. 2012. "Why Some Cities Are Growing and Others Shrinking." *Cato Journal* 31 (2): 285–303.

Storper, Michael. 2013. *Keys to the City. How Economics, Institutions, Social Interaction, Politics Shape Development*. Princeton, NJ: Princeton University Press.

TaxFound. 2016. *State and Local Tax Burdens, 1972–2012*. Washington, DC: Tax Foundation. https://taxfoundation.org/state-and-local-tax-burdens-historic-data

Thomas, A. R., and P. J. Smith. 2009. *Upstate Down: Thinking about New York and Its discontents*. Langham, MD: University Press of America.

Thomas, G. Scott. 2014. "Turning Points # 1: Perfect Storm of Lethargy." *Buffalo Business First*, June 16, 2014 edition: http://www.bizjournals.com/buffalo/news/2014/06/16/ turning-points-1-perfect-storm-of-lethargy.html. Beginning June 2014, *Buffalo Business First* reprinted a series of ten articles, coordinated by G. S. Thomas, Project Editor, called "Turning Points" about post–World War II decisions that altered the course of Buffalo and the surrounding region. To save space, only the link to the first article is given here.

Thomas, G. Scott. 2014a. "Turning Points # 4: Behind the Curve." *Buffalo Business First*, June 19, 2014 edition: http://www.bizjournals.com/buffalo/news/2014/06/19/ turning-points-4-behind-the-curve.html

Tiebout, Charles. 1956. "A Pure Theory of Public Expenditures." *Journal of Political Economy* 64 (5): 416–424.

Tindal, C. R., and S. N. Tindal. 2000. *Local Government in Canada*. Scarborough, ON: Nelson Thomson Learning.

Tucker William. 2015. "How High Taxes and Regulation Are Killing One of the Most Prosperous States in the Nation." *Moneywise* April 10, 2015. http://national. deseretnews.com/article/4039/how-high-taxes-and-regulation-are-killing-one-of-the-most-prosperous-states-in-the-nation.html

U.S. Census Bureau. 2016. *Historical Census Statistics on Population Totals by Race, 1790 to 1990, and by Hispanic Origin, 1970 to 1990, for Large Cities and Other Urban Places In The United States.* http://www.webcitation.org/69hd5KAIE

Vaillancourt, F., and L. Vaillancourt. 2007. "La propriété des employeurs au Québec en 2003 selon le groupe d'appartenance linguistique." In *L'économie du Québec, mythes et réalités*, G. Bélanger (ed.). Quebec City: Éditions Varia, 207–301

Vallières, Pierre. 1968. *Nègres blancs d'Amérique.* Montreal: *Les* éditions Parti-pris.

Vogel, R. K., and D. Imbroscio. 2013. "Governing Metropolitan Regions in the United States." In *Governance and Finance of Metropolitan Areas in Federal Systems.* E. Slack and R. Chattepadhyay (eds.). Toronto: Oxford University Press, 290–323.

Wainright, Oliver. 2012. "Silicon Roundabout: Tech City to Pioneer a Radical New Public Space." *The Guardian*, December 13, 2012.

Weber, Max. 1930. *The Protestant Ethic and the Spirit of Capitalism.* New York: Charles Scribner's Sons.

Weinberg, Cory. 2015. "Why Startups Are Ditching Silicon Valley for San Francisco." *San Francisco Business Times*, April 3, 2015.

Whitelegg, Drew. 2000. "Keeping Their Eyes on the Skies: Jet Aviation, Delta Airlines and the Growth of Atlanta." *Journal of Transport History* 21 (1): 73–91.

Winsa, Patty. 2014. "Toronto Is 180 Years Old. Where's the Birthday Party?" *Toronto Star*, March 6, 2014. http://www.thestar.com/news/gta/2014/03/06/toronto_is_180_years_old_wheres_the_birthday_party.html

Wolf, Günther. 2013. "Affordable Housing Is Still Available for Most of Austria's Population." Report 3/2013, Bank Austria. https://www.bankaustria.at/files/Fokus_Wolf_03-13_e.pdf

Woo, A., and C. Salviati. 2017. *Apartment List National Reports* (for April 2017). Apartment List Inc. Rentonomics. https://www.apartmentlist.com/rentonomics/national-rent-data

Wortham, Jenna. 2010. "New York Isn't Silicon Valley. That's Why They Like It." *The New York Times*, March 6, 2010.

Index

Tables and figures are indicated by an italic *t* and *f*, respectively, following the page number.